SHERYL LINDSELL-ROBERTS

Strategic Business Letters
and E-mail

HOUGHTON MIFFLIN HARCOURT
Boston   New York

Visit our websites: hmhbooks.com *and* ahdictionary.com

ISBN-13: 978-0-618-44833-3
ISBN-10: 0-618-44833-0

Library of Congress Cataloging-in-Publication Data

Lindsell-Roberts, Sheryl.
    Strategic business letters and e-mail / Sheryl Lindsell-Roberts.
        p. cm.
    ISBN 0-618-44833-0
    1. Commercial correspondence. 2. Electronic mail messages. 3. Business commu-
nication. I. Title.
    HF5721.L545   2004
    651.7'5--dc22   2004014030

Manufactured in the United States of America

Book design by Catherine Hawkes, Cat & Mouse

10 11 12 13 14 - EB - 16 15 14 13

illustrations on page 244 are courtesy of Clips Ahoy! at www.clipartisland.com

To Brooke Lindsell, Brian Ferrick, and Jillian Ferrick.

My father always said that grandchildren are life's dividends that keep on giving. He was so right. Brooke, Brian, and Jillian bring to my life absolute joy and perspective!

Contents

Introduction   *ix*

PART ONE   **Making Your Mark in the Business World   1**

1   Catapulting Your Career   2
2   The A, B, Cs of Letters   8

PART TWO   **Crafting Your Own Letters   21**

3   Jump Start Your Writing Process   22
4   Fine-Tuning Your Message   38

PART THREE   **Writing Results-Oriented Letters   65**

5   Sales and Marketing with Pizzazz   66
6   Successful Job Search and Employment Issues   101
7   Customer Relations   137
8   Credit and Collections   160
9   You Are Cordially Invited   183
10   Placing and Acknowledging Orders   196
11   Personal Business Notes   204
12   Media Relations   218
13   Professional Potpourri   238

PART FOUR   **Applying E-mail and E-marketing Know-how   273**

14   E-mail Messages That Shout *Read Me!*   274
15   E-mail Etiquette   285
16   E-marketing for Results   293

Appendixes   319

A   Punctuation Made Easy   320
B   Grammar's Not Grueling   333
C   Commonly Confused Words   343
D   Abridged Abbreviations   350
E   Proper Forms of Address   357

Acknowledgments

I want to express my heartfelt thanks to my family (blood and extended) and my dear friends. Without their love and support, I wouldn't be the person I am today and wouldn't be realizing my dreams.

I also want to praise my friend (first and foremost) and agent, Mariangela Powley, and all the folks at Houghton Mifflin who made this book a reality. They are Marge Berube, Vice President, who asked me to write this book; Kevin McCarthy, Marge's assistant, who was always diligent and responsive; David Pritchard, my editor; and Diane Fredrick, my copyeditor.

And finally, a special thanks to my mother, Ethel Lorenz. All the years I was growing up, I remember family and friends coming to her with problems due to faulty products or poor service. She'd always write a letter on their behalf and shortly thereafter they'd receive an apology, a free sample, or some satisfactory action. A friend once said, "When Ethel writes a letter, the paper burns." She was my inspiration.

Introduction

Dear Colleague,

Several years ago I received a call from the editor of a leading business publication. He asked me if I knew the dollar amount that businesses are losing each year because of poor business writing. I told him that number doesn't exist and why.

When companies submit proposals and don't get the contract, they immediately think that the contract went to a lower bidder or to someone who knew someone on the inside. They never look at the quality of the writing and think that perhaps the writing missed the mark. When people write text for websites and the websites don't generate the traffic they expect, they blame it on all sorts of external factors and never look at the quality of the text.

With letters, memos, and e-mails accounting for about 90 percent of all written communications, businesses undoubtedly lose billions of dollars because of poor business writing, and they don't even realize it. That's how I developed the tag line for my business: *You make more dollars when you make more sense!*

About This Book

This book walks you through an extensive variety of letter-writing experiences. It abounds with letters for you to use verbatim or to tweak. Jump around to whatever topic interests you. Part Two is the only section I recommend that you read—and read sequentially.

To get the most out of Part Two, have in mind a letter, memo, or e-mail message you need to write. Apply the Six Step Process to the writing you select, and you will learn to write with confidence and competence. This book also has appendixes with simple and practical guidelines for punctuation, grammar, commonly confused words, abbreviations, and forms of address.

Six Steps to Energized Business Writing

The tremendous success of my business writing workshops is living proof that we continuously seek better ways to communicate in order to have a direct impact on our readers. The workshop teaches a unique Six Step Process that will cut writing time by 30 to 50 percent and get dramatically better results. It's all in this book.

CHAPTER 3	*Step 1:*	Getting Started
	Step 2:	Creating Headlines and Strategic Sequencing
	Step 3:	Writing the Draft
CHAPTER 4	*Step 4:*	Designing for Visual Impact
	Step 5:	Honing the Tone
	Step 6:	Proofreading

After you learn to use the Six Step Process, you'll become a skilled writer who gets results, prompts action, influences decisions, stimulates business, and maintains good will. You'll never again say, "I don't know where to start," "I can't get my point across skillfully," "I can't say 'no' tactfully," "I need to be more concise," "I don't get the results I want."

> ▶ Years ago I started to accumulate letters I received that had great impact. Many of those letters are featured in this book, along with successful letters I've written for clients. Start your own folder and save letters you send or receive that hit the mark. They can supplement the letters in this book. ◀

Empower Yourself to Write Strategically

After you go through the Six Step Process once or twice, you'll see how easy it is and what a difference it will make in your ability to get the results you want. It's my hope that this book will become your valued desktop companion to help you to write with competence and confidence.

Best wishes,

Sheryl Lindsell-Roberts, M.A.

P.S. I didn't know how to treat the *he/she* and *him/her* without getting wrapped around the axle. Therefore, you see *he* and *him* in the odd chapters and she and her in the even chapters. I didn't arbitrarily decide that men are odd; I flipped a coin.

PART ONE

Making Your Mark in the Business World

A business letter—and this includes faxes, memos, and e-mail messages—is often the first impression your reader has of you. It says as much about you as a solid handshake. Make your message strong and impressive.

Writing good letters—communicating on the deeper level of thought, feelings, and ideas rather than on the shallow, superficial level of events—affects your ability to think, to reason accurately, and to be understood effectively.

—STEPHEN R. COVEY
The 7 Habits of Highly Effective People

CHAPTER 1

Catapulting Your Career

As a reader, have you ever felt that your brain was fried from all the paper-based and electronic materials on your computer and your desk? Do you often think that the writer thought about himself, and not you? Have you ever read a message and wondered, Where's the beef (the key point)? Or have you looked at a screen of incoming e-mail messages that have meaningless subject lines giving you no clue as to what the message is about?

> **WHAT'S IN THIS CHAPTER**
>
> - *Gaining the business advantage*
> - *Ten reasons letters fail*
> - *Seeing is believing*

As a writer, do you plan what you need to say? Do you have trouble getting started? Do you organize your thoughts to have the most impact on your reader? Do you write clearly and concisely? Does your message have visual impact? Is your tone right for your reader?

Exceptional writing is the hallmark of exceptional professionals. According to the National Center on the Evaluation of Quality in the Workplace, employers list communications skills as the second most critical job skill. (Attitude is first.) A well-written message can catapult your career by landing your dream job, bolstering your reputation, influencing decisions, providing leadership, delighting clients and customers, earning profits for your company, and much more.

Letter writing is of noble ancestry (going back at least 3500 years) and has been a key part of communicating for eons. The ancient kings of Egypt wrote letters to their vassal-princes. The kings inscribed letters on moist clay tablets, baked the tablets, and sent the messages on their way. If the king's writing wasn't concise, the messengers would collapse under the weight of the tablets and the messages wouldn't be delivered.

Of course, methods have changed drastically from the demise of the clay tablet, the quill pen, and the manual typewriter to the advent of Bill Gates, e-mail, and the Internet. But one thing hasn't changed — the need to get your point across clearly and concisely.

Gaining the Business Advantage

In an era where slipshod compromise is much too common, your well-crafted letter will make you stand out. Because you often write to people you haven't met, a business letter is somewhat like a first meeting — it becomes the reader's impression of who you are. (Yes, even your e-mail messages.) Don't make your first impression your last.

> ▶ Throughout this book, I use the generic term *business letters* to refer to letters, faxes, e-mail messages, and memos. ◀

When you feel that brief moment of panic as you're ready to write, relax! You're in good company. Most people don't like to put thoughts in writing; they procrastinate and procrastinate. Have you ever mumbled these words to yourself?

- I don't know where to start, so I'll wait 'til later. (Later never comes.)

- I've written the letter and realize that it's to-o-o long and so-o-o boring.

- I can't seem to get my point across clearly and concisely.

- How can I say *no* tactfully?

- I hate to send dunning letters to my customers. I'm afraid of losing their business.

- I saw a wonderful job advertised in the newspaper. How can I write a letter that stands out from the hundreds of letters the company will get?

▶ If you're intimidated by movie depictions of divinely inspired writers who've written the Great American Novel while you struggle with the muse of business writing to create the Great American Letter, you're not alone. Business people at all levels of the business spectrum—from the neophyte professional to the articulate CEO—experience moments of self-doubt when it comes to writing. The good news is that everyone can be taught to write successfully and strategically. ◀

Ten Reasons Letters Fail

Here are ten reasons why letters fail. You can avoid all of these pitfalls by reading chapters 3 and 4 and using the Six Step Process before you start to write.

1. **Where's the beef?** The message is so poorly written and the visual impact is so poor that the message is lost in a sea of gobbledygook.

2. **Insensitive salutation.** The salutation is so impersonal that it's equivalent to yelling "Hey you" when you enter a room. For example, "To whom this may concern" isn't an appropriate salutation.

3. **I've been framed.** People often try to squeeze too much onto a single page, forsaking margins on the top, bottom, and sides. Your margins should create an imaginary frame around your words.

4. **Your "John Hancock" please.** It's amazing how many people forget to sign their names on letters or include salutations on e-mail messages.

5. **Spelling "errers."** Spelling errors pop out like zits.

6. **Grammatical goofs.** Grammatical faux pas make you sound illiterate.

7. **All about "Me."** The letter is focused on the writer, not the reader. You need to remember the reader doesn't care about you.

8. **Kid in a candy store.** The writer overwhelms the reader with too many font styles and colors.

9. **Tinny tone.** The tone is stuffy (taxidermy), not conversational. Can you actually imagine someone saying, "Pursuant to the aforementioned conversation"?

10. **The 500-word paragraph.** The paragraphs are so long that the reader tends to skip over them. This is especially true in e-mail messages.

Seeing Is Believing

Well-written letters are easy to read and understand. On the following pages are two memos, Examples 1-1 and 1-2. Please don't look at either—just yet. Follow these simple instructions:

1. Quickly scan (don't read, scan) Example 1-1. See if you can find answers to these questions instantly.

   - What's the date of the meeting?

   - How many agenda items are there?

   - Who's the new EEO coordinator?

2. Look at Example 1-2 to see how quickly and easily you can find answers to the same questions. (*I can almost see light bulbs turning on.*)

These two examples make it obvious that when writing is clear, concise, and well formatted it delivers key information at a glance. And that's the purpose of all business writing.

When you take a moment to compare the two examples, you realize what makes Example 1-2 a well-written and well-formatted document.

- The subject line tells the story and mentions the key word *meeting*.

- There's plenty of white space that provides a resting place for your eyes.

- Paragraphs are short and readable.

- Sentences are short, simple, and easy to read.

- Key information pops out without your having to read the entire message.

- Headlines direct your eye to key pieces of information.

- Critical information is numbered for easy reading.

MEMORANDUM

Date: November 1, 20—
To: All Employees
From: Pat Dallas, Human Relations Director
Re: Reaffirm Equal Employment Opportunity Policy

As you know, it is illegal to discriminate against any employee or applicant for employment because of race, color, religion, sex, national origin, handicap, or veteran status. I've scheduled a meeting because we need to discuss these critical issues. The meeting will be held in the cafeteria on November 12, from 10:30 to 11:30, and everyone is expected to attend. There are several questionable issues that have come to my attention, and we need to reaffirm our company's policy.

Here are some of the issues we need to discuss: We must ensure opportunities for all employees and applicants for employment in accordance with all applicable Equal Employment Opportunity/Affirmative Action laws, directives, and regulations of federal, state, and local governing bodies or agencies. Promotion decisions must be in accord with the principles of equal employment opportunity. And we must ensure that all personnel actions such as compensation, benefits, transfers, layoffs, return from layoff, company-sponsored training, education, tuition assistance, and social and recreational programs will be administered fairly.

Because we've added so many members to our staff in recent months, I've hired Barbara Chang as a new assistant. She will be responsible for equal employment opportunity issues. I'll be introducing Barbara to you at the meeting. Employees with suggestions, problems, or complaints with regard to equal employment opportunities should report their claims to their managers. If this is not comfortable for any reason, see Ms. Chang. She will monitor the program and be responsible for making quarterly reports to us on the effectiveness of the program.

Example 1-1: Boring three-paragraph memo that's all too commonplace

MEMORANDUM

Date: November 1, 20—
To: All Employees
From: Pat Dallas, Human Relations Director
Re: Meeting to Reaffirm Equal Employment Opportunity Policy

There are several issues regarding possible EEO violations that have come to my attention. I've scheduled a meeting for the entire staff. Attendance is mandatory.

Date: November 12
Time: 10:30 to 11:30
Place: Cafeteria

Agenda Issues

1. We must ensure <u>opportunities</u> for all employees and applicants in accordance with all applicable Equal Employment Opportunity/Affirmative Action laws, directives, and regulations of federal, state, and local governing bodies or agencies.

2. <u>Promotion decisions</u> must be in accord with the principles of equal employment opportunity.

3. We must ensure that all <u>personnel actions</u> such as compensation, benefits, transfers, layoffs, return from layoff, company-sponsored training, education, tuition assistance, and social and recreational programs will be administered fairly.

Barbara Chang: new EEO coordinator

I'll be introducing Barbara at the meeting. Employees with suggestions, problems, or complaints with regard to equal employment opportunities should report their claims to their managers first. If this is not comfortable for any reason, see Barbara. She will monitor the program and be responsible for making quarterly reports to us on the effectiveness of the program.

Example 1-2: Key information is easy to find

*All things began in order, so shall they end, and
so shall they begin again ...*

—SIR THOMAS BROWNE
On Dreams

CHAPTER 2

The A, B, Cs of Letters

From the time we're born, we learn the natural order of things. We crawl before we walk. We wash our hands before we eat. We eat our entree before dessert. And we learn our A, B, Cs before we read or write. And so it was that we made Grandma and Grandpa beam with delight as we recited the little ditty: "a, b, c, d, e, f, g, ... l-o, men-o, p ...." Yes, we learn the natural order of things.

WHAT'S IN THIS CHAPTER

- *Where the parts go*
- *Popular letter styles*
- *Multiple-page letter heading*
- *Memo format*

Business letters also have a natural order. There's everything that comes before the body, the body, and everything that comes after the body. In this chapter you learn the natural order of letters.

Where the Parts Go

This section identifies all the parts that can be included in a letter and the order in which they appear. At the end of this section, Example 2-1 (p. 13) shows a letter with all the parts. It's doubtful that you'd use every part in any one letter, so this is to illustrate placement only.

Date line: Open every letter with a date. The horizontal position of the date depends on the letter style you use. (Learn more about letter styles later in this chapter.) Write the current date with arabic numerals and no abbreviations.

> June 1, 20—
>
> 6 June 20— (military or European usage)

Mailing or in-house notations: Place mailing notations (special delivery, certified mail, registered mail, air mail, by messenger) or in-house notations (personal, confidential) two lines below the date. Type them in all capital letters.

> PERSONAL
>
> CERTIFIED MAIL

Inside address: Start the inside address four lines below the date line. (If you use a mailing or in-house notation, start the inside address two lines below the notation.) The inside address contains everything you need to deliver the letter: name, job title, street address or post office box number, suite or room number, city, state, and ZIP code. (Check out Appendix D for two-letter state abbreviations.)

> Dick Eaton, Founder
> Leapfrog Innovations
> 25 Washington Avenue
> Natick, MA 01760

Whether the person's title appears on the same line as the name or on the following line is determined by the length. Try to square the address as much as possible. If the title appears on the same line, place a comma between the name and title. If it appears on the next line, dispense with the comma.

> Dick Eaton, Founder
> *- or -*
> Dick Eaton
> Founder

► The postal carrier delivers mail to the address element on the line above the city, state, and ZIP. Therefore, if you want the letter delivered to a post office box, place the post office box number underneath (or instead of) the street address. The post office requests that you use the 9-digit ZIP code. If you know it, use it.

> 607 Arboretum Boulevard
> P. O. Box 7344
> Austin, TX 78959-7344 ◄

Use an attention line when you write directly to a company and want the letter directed to a particular person and/or department. An attention line indicates that the letter should be handled by someone else if the addressee isn't available. If you know the name of the recipient, locate the name above the company instead of on an attention line. Following are two styles for an attention line:

Acme Construction Company
34 Madison Avenue
Galata, MT 59444
(double space)
Attention: Jerry Jones

Acme Construction Company
ATTENTION JERRY JONES
34 Madison Avenue
Galata, MT 59444

Salutation: Place the salutation two lines below the address. The salutation should correspond directly to the first line of the inside address. Check out Appendix E for proper forms of address for health care providers, attorneys, academics, and military, government, and religious leaders.

INSIDE ADDRESS	SALUTATION (FORMAL)	SALUTATION (INFORMAL)
Mr. John Smith	Dear Mr. Smith:	Dear John,
Ms. Ann Coffou	Dear Ms. Coffou:	Dear Ann,
Mr. and Mrs. John Smith	Dear Mr. and Mrs. Smith:	Dear John and Joan,
Messrs. Max and Harry Lorenz	Dear Messrs. Lorenz:	Dear Max and Harry,
Mmes. Ethel and Marilyn Lorenz	Dear Mmes. Lorenz:	Dear Ethel and Marilyn,
Messrs. James Taylor and Bob Grant	Dear Messrs. Taylor and Grant:	Dear James and Bob,
Mmes. Sally Jones and Jan Fox	Dear Mmes. Jones and Fox:	Dear Sally and Jan,
Dr. James Smith and Dr. Alice Smith (husband and wife)	Dear Doctors Smith:	Dear Jim and Alice,
Robert Kleinman, Esq. (attorney)	Dear Mr. Kleinman:	Dear Robert,
Bates & Bates, Esqs. (two men)	Dear Messrs. Bates:	Dear Sam and George,
Bigelow & Mason, Esqs. (one man and one woman)	Dear Mr. Bigelow and Ms. Mason:	Dear Dean and Christine,

Subject line: Place the subject line two lines below the salutation; it's part of the body, not the heading. The subject line describes the purpose of the letter. You can mix and match any of the following styles:

SUBJECT: ACCOUNT NO. 2261-B

Re: Special Rebate

Subject: Yes, we can honor your request

Body (message): The body supports the theme of the message. You may expect this section to take up more space than the others because the body is the longest part of a letter. The body, however, differs greatly from one letter to another, so this is just to show you where it fits into the natural order of a letter.

Single-space the body of the letter, and double-space between paragraphs. Double-space the body only when the message is just a few sentences.

Complimentary closing: Place the complimentary closing two lines below the last line of the body. Capitalize only the first word, and place a comma after the last word.

Formal	Yours truly, Very truly yours, Yours very truly, Respectfully, Respectfully yours,
Less formal	Sincerely, Sincerely yours, Cordially, Cordially yours,
Personal	Best wishes, As always, Regards, Kindest regards,

Signature line: Place the signature line under the complimentary closing, leaving enough room to sign your name.

Very truly yours,

Harry Pape

Harry Pape

Very truly yours,

Harry Pape

Harry Pape, Process Manager

Very truly yours,

ALVERS, INC.

Harry Pape

Harry Pape, Process Manager

Very truly yours,

Harry Pape

Harry Pape

Process Manager

> ▶ The date, complimentary closing, and signature must align. When writing a full-block letter, place them at the left margin. When writing a modified-block or semiblock letter, place them slightly to the right of center. (Learn more about alignment later in this chapter.) ◀

Reference initials: Use reference initials to identify the author of the letter and/or the typist. Type them at the left margin, two lines below the signature line. *When you write your own letter, don't use initials.* You can use any of the following styles:

HLorenz/lz   HL/LZ

HL:lz   lz

> ▶ Never use reference initials in e-mail messages ◀

Enclosure notation: When you enclose anything in the envelope besides the letter, place an enclosure notation on the line directly below the reference initials. When something is attached rather than enclosed, some offices use the word *Attachment* in place of *Enclosure.* You can use any of the following styles:

Enclosure   1 Enc.

Enc.   Attachments: 2

Encls.   Enc. (2)

l Attachment   Enclosure:
                      1. Purchase Order No. 3434
                      2. Check No. 567

Copy notation: When you send a copy of the letter to a third person, place a notation to that effect directly below the enclosure notation or reference initials. The *cc* notation is a holdover from the days of carbon copies. Many offices are now using *pc* (for photocopy).

PC: Margot Rutledge   cc: Margot Rutledge

CC: Margot Rutledge   Copy to: Margot Rutledge

> ▶ If you don't want the addressee to know that a copy is being forwarded to a third party, use *bc* for blind copy. This notation appears on the office copy and third-party copy only, *not on the original.* ◀

Brian & Jill, Incorporated
11737 Ferrick Lane, Lakewood, NJ 08701-2344
(908) 234-5654

December 27, 20—*<Date>*

PERSONAL *<In-house notation>*

<Inside address>
Ms. Dawne Roberts
Columbia Housing Association
One Cradlerock Way
Spring Valley, NY 10977

Dear Ms. Roberts: *<Salutation>*

Subject: Letter of recommendation for Eric Laurence *<Subject line>*

<Body>
It's with great pleasure that I write this letter on behalf of Eric Laurence. He was employed by me as a Contracts Manager for five years and left to pursue his Master's degree full time. We told Eric that the position would be waiting for him when he finished, but he now wants to pursue opportunities with a larger company.

I'm enclosing a copy of an award Eric received while he was with us. Eric is a person of the highest integrity, who works efficiently and tirelessly to get the job done. He's creative and delightful to work with. You'd be most fortunate to have him join your staff.

Sincerely, *<Complimentary closing>*

Anna Katherine Boucher *<Signature line>*

AKB/stl *<Reference initials>*
Enclosure *<Enclosure notation>*
cc: Eric Laurence *<Copy notation>*

P.S. Please send Eric my warmest regards. *<Postscript>*

Example 2-1: Basic letter parts and where they go

Postscript: Studies show that postscripts are one of the first things people read and one of the things they remember, especially when the postscripts are hand-written. This is especially valuable in sales letters.

Use postscripts sparingly because they can appear as afterthoughts, indicating a lack of organization. When you do use a postscript notation, place it two lines below your last notation. It isn't strictly necessary to include the letters *P.S.*

Popular Letter Styles

Following are three popular letter styles with the characteristics of each:

LETTER STYLE	CHARACTERISTICS AND COMMENTS
Full-block *(Example 2-2)*	• Everything starts at the left margin; there's no need to indent. • Efficient, businesslike, and very popular.
Block (or Modified-block) *(Example 2-3)*	• The date, complimentary closing, and signature blocks are slightly to the right of center. • Everything else starts at the left margin. • Very traditional and very popular.
Semiblock *(Example 2-4)*	• Identical to modified-block, except the first line of each paragraph is indented. • This isn't as popular as it once was.

Multiple-Page Letter Heading

Never try to squeeze everything on a single page if it means forsaking margins, formatting, and white space. When typing a multiple-page letter, use letterhead for the first page and matching plain paper for the ensuing pages. Following are two styles to consider for multiple-page letters:

Ms. Katherine Wertalik   Page 2   October 2, 20—

Ms. Katherine Wertalik
Page 2
October 2, 20—

LETTERHEAD

Date

Addressee
Street Address
City, State ZIP

Salutation:

Subject: Full-Block Letter Style

Characteristics
The full-block letter is quickly becoming the style of choice in the modern office. Everything starts at the left margin, so there's no need to set tabs or wonder where to put the date and complimentary closing. The full-block letter style is efficient, businesslike, and very popular.

Benefits
We live in a fast-paced society and people are constantly trying to simplify their cluttered lives. The full-block letter style will—over time—increase the flow of paperwork and save time.

Complimentary closing,

Justin Case

P.S. Some critics feel that the full-block style looks somewhat crowded.

Example 2-2: Full-block letter style

LETTERHEAD

Date

Addressee
Street Address
City, State ZIP

Salutation:

Subject: Block (or Modified-Block) Letter Style

Characteristics
The block style is quite similar to the full-block style. The key difference is that the block style's date and complimentary closing are slightly to the right of center, so you have to tab over. Everything else is flush with the left margin. The block style is very traditional and quite popular.

Benefits
The block letter style has traditionally been the most commonly used of all letter styles. Therefore, it's the one most people are comfortable with.

Complimentary closing,

Justin Case

Example 2-3: Block (or modified-block) letter style

LETTERHEAD

Date

Addressee
Street Address
City, State ZIP

Salutation:

Subject: Semiblock Letter Style

Characteristics

The semiblock style is quite similar to the block style. The key difference is that the semiblock style's paragraphs are indented one tab stop. Therefore, you need to use two tabs: one for the indented paragraphs and one for the date, complimentary closing, and signature line.

Benefits

The semiblock style also looks more familiar and people are comfortable with it. It is, however, playing second fiddle to the full-block or block styles. Many people consider the semiblock style somewhat of a dated look.

Complimentary closing,

Justin Case

P.S. This letter style is a throwback to the days when June Cleaver was the standard-bearer of domestic righteousness.

Example 2-4: Semiblock letter style

> ► When you divide a paragraph between pages, leave at least two lines on the first page and carry over at least two lines. If the paragraph is only three lines, don't split it. ◄

Memo Format

The office memorandum, universally known as a *memo,* is sent between employees in a company to transmit ideas, decisions, announcements, or suggestions. Although e-mails have replaced many of the memos that used to float around offices, memos are still used for interoffice correspondence. They are more private than e-mails and can become part of a permanent archive of an individual, department, or company.

Memo Header

Unlike a letter, a memo doesn't have an inside address, salutation, complimentary closing, or formal signature. It has a heading instead. If your organization uses memos frequently, it probably has established forms. If not, here are a few to consider:

Date:
To:
From:
Subject:

Date:

To:
From:
Subject:

TO:
FROM:
DATE:
SUBJECT:

Memo Body

The body of a memo is very much like the body of a letter; however, you don't have to center the text vertically. The tone you use depends on the relationship between you and the reader. For example, it's appropriate to use jargon and technical terms when you and the reader have the same frame of reference.

> ▶ Although memos generally don't have a place to put your signature, you may consider writing your name either next to the heading, as you see in Example 2-5, or at the end of the memo. ◀

Date: December 15, 20—

To: All Managers

From: Lois Lawrence

Re: Capping salary increases for employees

Starting January 1, we will institute our new policy of capping salary increases at 3.5% for all employees. This is due to the economic downturn in our industry and our need to curtail expenses in an effort to avoid further layoffs.

To help you prepare to answer any questions members of your department may have, I've called a meeting which you all must attend.

Date: December 20
Time: 10:30 to noon
Place: Conference Room 200

We want this to remain <u>confidential</u> until we make the announcement to everyone. That announcement will follow the meeting. If you have any questions in the meantime, please give me a call.

Example 2-5: Sample memo

The Six Step Process

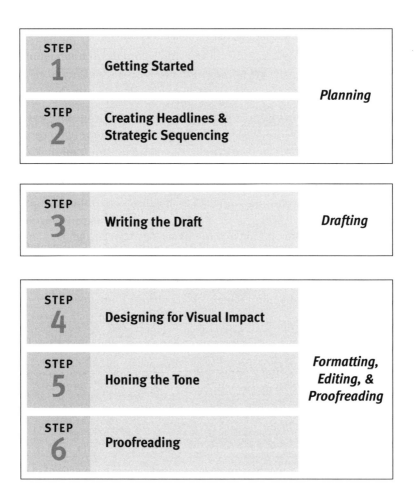

| STEP 1 | Getting Started | |
| STEP 2 | Creating Headlines & Strategic Sequencing | *Planning* |

| STEP 3 | Writing the Draft | *Drafting* |

STEP 4	Designing for Visual Impact	
STEP 5	Honing the Tone	*Formatting, Editing, & Proofreading*
STEP 6	Proofreading	

PART TWO

Crafting Your Own Letters

You no longer have to rack your brain trying to compose a letter. The Six Step Process walks you through the tried-and-tested writing process I developed that thousands of people use to write persuasive letters that get results. The Six Steps include:

Step 1: *Getting started*

Step 2: *Creating headlines and strategic sequencing*

Step 3: *Writing the draft*

Step 4: *Designing for visual impact*

Step 5: *Honing the tone*

Step 6: *Proofreading*

Success is not a doorway; it's a stairway.

—DOTTIE WALTERS
Speaker, Agent, and Writer

CHAPTER 3

Jump Start Your Writing Process

When I conduct business writing workshops for companies throughout the United States, I often ask participants to estimate the amount of time they spend planning, writing the draft, and editing and proofreading. This is a typical response:

WHAT'S IN THIS CHAPTER

- **Step 1:** *Getting started*
- **Step 2:** *Creating headlines and strategic sequencing*
- **Step 3:** *Writing the draft*

Planning	10% (if at all)
Drafting	80%
Editing and proofreading	10%

After they complete the workshop, I ask them how they expect to allocate their time for future writing. This is a typical response:

Planning	50%
Drafting	20%
Editing and proofreading	30%

The first set of percentages shows how much frustration people connect with writing because they fail to plan. Masterful letter writers aren't born, they're developed. Like anything else, writing is a process—it's approached one step at a time. After you learn the Six Step Process outlined in Part II, you'll *write strategically and get better results!*

> ▶ In order to get the most from chapters 3 and 4, think of a letter, memo, or e-mail you need to send and follow the Six Step Process. You'll be amazed at how quick and easy writing can be. The Six Step Process gives you a strategy to write messages that get attention . . . messages that drive action . . . and messages that help you have the impact you want to have in the marketplace. ◄

✔ **The ✔ is used throughout chapters 3 and 4 as a reminder to apply the step it specifies to your own message. You can apply this process to any writing challenge you have, from letters, memos, and e-mail messages to proposals, presentations, reports, and more.**

Step 1: Getting Started

The Start Up Sheet in Example 3-1 walks you through the process of determining three crucial elements for strategic writing—your audience, your purpose, and the key issue. It also gives you food for thought about delivery. For each letter, e-mail, or memo you write, fill out the Start Up Sheet. After the first time, filling it out takes only a few minutes, and you'll wonder how you ever lived without it. Keep it handy for all your correspondence. You get more out of the Start Up Sheet if you relate it to a particular document you need to write. Here's how to proceed:

1. Look at Example 3-1 to understand the Start Up Sheet.

2. Read through the portion of this chapter that describes the Start Up Sheet. (Don't attempt to answer any of the questions yet.)

3. Think of a letter, memo, or e-mail you need to write, and fill out each section as it relates to your document.

Using the Start Up Sheet to Write Reader-Focused Messages

The first time you go through this process, it may take you a little while because it's new and different. After that, it'll take you only a few minutes and will save you

START UP SHEET

Audience

1. Who is my primary reader? Do I have multiple levels of readers?

2. What does my reader *need to know* about the subject?

3. What's in it for my reader?

4. Does my writing need a special angle or point of view?

5. What's my reader's attitude toward the message?

Purpose

6. My purpose is to _____, so that my reader will
   _____.

Key Issue

7. What's the one key point I want my reader to remember?

Delivery

8. Who should receive a copy of this message?

9. What's the best way to deliver this message? Hard copy? E-mail? Fax? Phone? In person?

10. When is the best time to deliver the message? When is it too early? When is it too late?

Example 3-1: Start Up Sheet

hours. Answer the questions honestly. Remember that your reader will never see these answers; however, the answers help you to create a plan so you can get the results you want.

When you send a document to someone, you create a relationship between yourself and the reader. In order for this relationship to work, you must know precisely what you want to say and how the reader will process the information. The Start Up Sheet is a way for you to understand your audience, purpose, and the key issues. The following explains how you can make the Start Up Sheet work for you.

Audience: Your goal is to write reader-focused messages, not writer-focused messages. The following section will help you understand your reader so you can do just that.

1. Who is my primary reader? Do I have multiple levels of readers?

You must see your target so you know where to aim. Identify your reader and the relationship (if any) that you have with him. If the message is to someone you don't know, try to imagine what he looks like. In that way you're not writing to a faceless humanoid.

When you write to multiple readers, rank them on the basis of who will take action or in their order of importance. If you're writing a long message to a mixed audience of managers, technical people, and salespeople, you may deal with each audience separately in clearly identified sections of your message. Consider the following:

- Write an opening summary of high points for those at the managerial level.
- Attach technical materials for technical people.
- Highlight the benefits for salespeople.

2. What does my reader *need to know* about the subject?

Think of what your reader needs to know, not what he already knows. You don't want to give too much or too little information. Consider these questions:

- What's the reader's level of knowledge about the subject?
- Does he have any preconceived notions?
- Are there barriers to his understanding your message?

3. What's in it for my reader?

When you receive a message, you mentally ask, "What's in it for me?" Your reader asks the same question. After you write what's in it for your reader, take the "So what?" test. For example, if you wrote that what's in it for your reader is "being more efficient," ask "So what?" From the reader's point of view, efficiency in itself may not be critical, but making more money because of efficiency may be. Perhaps what's in it for your reader is a chance to make his job easier, to help him look good to his superiors, to be healthier, or to make more money. Understand what's in it for him!

4. Does my writing need a special angle or point of view?

People at different levels need different information. For example, managers are big-picture people; they need the bottom line. Technical people need the details. Salespeople need the benefits. What does your reader need? This relates directly back to No. 3.

5. What's my reader's attitude toward the message?

You may not always tell your reader what he *wants* to hear, but you must tell him what he *needs* to hear. When you understand your reader's reaction, you can sequence the message for greater impact. (You learn more about sequencing in Step 2, later in this chapter.) Following are the three reactions your reader may have:

Reaction	Example
Responsive	You're sending a congratulatory note.
Neutral	You're asking the reader to renew a subscription.
Unresponsive	You're disputing existing data.

Purpose: Fill in the blanks:

6. My purpose is to _____, so that my reader will _____.

Whether you think your purpose is to communicate, to inform, to sell, or whatever, chances are you're trying to persuade someone to do something. For example, if you're writing to inform your customer of a new product offering, you're trying to *persuade* him to make a purchase. If you're writing to let your manager know of an idea that could save the company big bucks, you're trying to *persuade* him that you're worth listening to. Once you realize that most of the writing you do is to persuade, you'll start to write *strategically,* rather than generically.

When your reader knows exactly what action you want him to take, he can digest your message more intelligently and act on your request. Do you want your reader to call you, write to you, send a check, discontinue testing, make a purchase, do nothing?

> ▶ When thinking about what you want your reader to do, *be specific.* For example, if you want the reader to send you something, do you want it sent via e-mail or snail mail? If you're asking him to send something that's important, should he send it via Federal Express or certified mail? Following are other examples of being specific:
>
> • Replace *most of* with the actual percentage.
>
> • Replace *change* with "increase" or "decrease."
>
> • Replace *personnel* with "faculty," "managers," "administrators." ◀

Key Issue: Your key issue must be clear in your own mind so you can send a clear message to your reader.

7. What's the one key point I want my reader to remember?

Billboard advertisers, ad people, and designers know that reading is done on the fly. Kids know this too. Have you ever found (or left) a note on the table saying, "Don't forget to leave me $5—I'll explain later"? Business readers want the key issue clear so they can get to the point immediately. Put on your advertising hat.

If your reader forgets just about everything in your message, what's the one key point you want him to remember? It's only after you distill the message into a single sentence that you're ready to write.

Delivery: Following are several things to think about before you deliver your message.

8. Who should receive a copy of this message?

You don't get points for contributing to information overload, so send messages only to the people who need to read them. This is especially important when you send an e-mail message to a distribution list. Send a message to the entire distribution list *only* when everyone needs to read the message.

9. What's the best way to deliver this message? Hard copy? E-mail? Fax? Phone? In person?

Always decide on the most appropriate way to deliver your message. You don't want to be like the insensitive doctor (true story) who sent a letter to his patient stating, "I have reviewed your skin biopsy and found it to show cancer. Please call me if you have any questions." Following are several situations and the most appropriate delivery methods:

SITUATION	DELIVERY
You're letting your department know about a staff meeting you scheduled for next week.	E-mail
It's noon, and you just learned that a 2:30 meeting that day must be moved up to 2:00.	In person or by telephone
You want to apologize to Mary for a condescending remark you made.	In person, by phone, or by handwritten note
You want to thank a potential employer for an interview.	Letter

▶ Following are tips on leaving a useful telephone message. I know this book is about writing and not telephoning, but I'd feel remiss if I didn't throw in these little tidbits:

- Say your name slowly at the beginning and end of the message. If your name is unusual or difficult to understand, spell it.

- Clearly leave your phone number, even if the person knows it. The person may be in Outer Mongolia and not have your number handy.

- Have everything ready that you need to make the call, and get to the point immediately. Don't ramble on, search for files, or look for missing information. ◀

10. When is the best time to deliver the message? When is it too early? When is it too late?

Timing is everything! For example, if you're sending an announcement about a Christmas special, you must know that one of the biggest shopping days is the day after Thanksgiving. Your message should reach your reader a few days before Thanksgiving.

Also, don't take it for granted your letter will have your reader's full attention the moment it arrives. He may be away from the office, have an emergency at the office, or just be preoccupied. Additionally, he may have to take action on your message—consult with his accountant or attorney, get additional information, or send the letter to others. Although this letter may be vital to your business, it may not be vital to your reader's business. Give him enough time to respond.

✔ **Fill out the Start Up Sheet for the message you're writing.**

Questioning Technique

This is somewhat like putting on your reporter's hat. By filling out the Start Up Sheet, you took the first step toward writing your document. Now, think of the questions your reader will have. Then answer them. Be specific, not vague. For example, don't say, "I'll be in Washington next week." Be specific as to Washington, DC, or the state of Washington. Following are examples of possible questions and their specific answers:

	READER'S QUESTIONS	YOUR SPECIFIC ANSWERS
Who?	Whom should I call?	Call James McKinney, the sales manager.
What?	What should I do next?	Please send me your response by e-mail.
Where?	Where is the meeting?	The meeting is in Washington, DC.
Why?	Why should I care?	This will help you to further your career.
When?*	When do you need the information?	I need the information no later than May 1, 20—.
How?	How much is the software?	The software costs $49.95.

* Never use "as soon as possible" (ASAP). It isn't a date. When you need something by a certain date, give the date.

✔ **Make a list of the questions your reader will have and answer them.**

▶ Another getting-started exercise you may try is free writing, which is a warm-up exercise for the brain. If you jog, you warm up beforehand; if you do aerobics, you warm up beforehand. Your brain is an organ, and it too needs to warm up beforehand. Also, if you have something on your mind that prevents you from concentrating on the message at hand, free writing is a great way to put those thoughts behind you.

Just start writing—anything. It can be a shopping list, an e-mail message, or anything that comes to mind. Once you transfer the ideas from your head to your computer, you calm your mind for your message. Don't worry about spelling, grammar, or punctuation—just keep writing. Thoughts about the subject at hand will pop into your head and out your fingers. ◀

Step 2: Creating Headlines and Strategic Sequencing

Headlines are powerful. Notice how newspapers and magazines use headlines to tell a story and direct the reader's eye to what's important. Here's a perfect example: Hal Prince, the noted Broadway producer, was interviewed on television. The commentator asked how Mr. Prince knew when a show was a flop or a success. Mr. Prince answered something like this: "The morning after the show opens, I open the newspaper and read the headlines. The headlines make or break the show." The headlines are that powerful!

Companies should apply the power of dynamic headlines to their business documents so that readers can scan the document and find key information quickly and easily. You can apply the power of headlines to all your messages. Here's what headlines do:

- Give directions

- Offer results

- Make recommendations

- Extend invitations

- Offer conclusions

Headlines also provide inferences from which people draw conclusions. For example, a newspaper carried an inaccurate article with a very damaging headline about a criminal investigation into a pharmaceuticals company. That same day— on the basis of the headline—the company's stock plummeted by 50 percent.

As a *writer,* your headlines direct your reader's attention to what's important and guide the flow of information. As a *reader,* you can get the gist of the message and find key information quickly.

Following are some headlines that you can use in your documents to bring focus to key parts of your message. You can highlight them with underscoring, bold, italic, or another font. You can even use a color.

Action requested	**Meeting information**
Next step	**When:**
Deadline: [date]	**Where:**
Effective date: [date]	**Any questions?**

> ▶ I don't delude myself into thinking that you're going to read every pearly word I write in this book. That's why I wrote headlines for you to scan to get the gist of the contents of each section. ◀

Writing Headlines That Give Critical Information

You can apply the power of newspaper headlines to all your documents. As a writer, you direct your reader's attention to what's important. As a reader, you get the gist of the message and find key information quickly. Check out Examples 3-2 and 3-3 on the following pages.

- Example 3-2 is the typical multiple-paragraph message; nothing jumps out.

- Example 3-3 calls out the key information at a glance and has an informative subject line.

✔ **Before you write headlines for your document, circle all the answers from the questioning technique that could be headlines and circle every word or phrase in the free writing that could be a headline. Now write compelling headlines for your document.**

▶ Perhaps you're not accustomed to seeing headlines used in letters, memos, and e-mail messages other than on the subject line. However, I've started to look carefully at the mail I receive, and I notice that more and more companies are including headlines in their letters. These are the companies that write strategically for results. ◀

NAME THE HEADLINE

Can you translate the following headlines into the names of commonly known stories or fairy tales? In the book of life, there are no answers. In this book, there are. They are printed upside down at the bottom.

1. Youngster Vanishes in Freak Storm
2. Couple Suffering from Dietary Allergies Reaches Agreement
3. Poor Bargain Brings Ultimate Wealth
4. Remote Country Home Vandalized by Blond
5. Friendless Waif Adopted by Group of Miners

1. The Wizard of Oz
2. Jack Sprat
3. Jack and the Beanstalk
4. Goldilocks and the Three Bears
5. Snow White

LETTERHEAD

Date: December 1, 20—

To: All staff members

Subject: About the merger

You've all been hearing rumors that we may be merging with Marric Company. Yes, it's been a long road, but the merger is complete. We start the new year as a wholly owned subsidiary of Marric Company. We've worked very hard for this and know it will come as good news to all of you. Here are some of the advantages for us: We'll have added strength in terms of public acceptance and operating capital. We'll be able to serve our customers more promptly, efficiently, and thoroughly.

We'll be sponsoring a company-wide luncheon at noon on December 13, 20—, at the Wayside Inn, Wayside Inn Road, Sudbury, MA, so you can meet the Marric group. Please make every effort to be there. Principals from Marric will be on hand to answer your questions and let you know of their sincere intentions to let us operate this division on an autonomous basis. Please call Aline Barbera at extension 212 by December 11 to let her know what you'd like for lunch. The choices are chicken, fish, or vegetarian.

Example 3-2: Ho-hum memo where nothing stands out

L E T T E R H E A D

Date: December 1, 20—

To: All staff members

Subject: **Merger with Marric Company effective January 1, 20—**

Yes, it's been a long road, but the merger is complete. The good news is that we start the new year as a wholly owned subsidiary of Marric Company. We've worked very hard for this and know it will come as good news to all of you.

Advantages: Increased capital and enhanced customer services

Here are some of the advantages for us:

- We'll have added strength in terms of public acceptance and operating capital.
- We'll be able to serve our customers more promptly, efficiently, and thoroughly.

Information luncheon on December 13, 20—

We'll be sponsoring a company-wide luncheon so you can meet the Marric group. Please make every effort to be there. Principals from Marric will be on hand to answer your questions and let you know of their sincere intentions to let us operate this division on an autonomous basis.

Date: December 13, 20—
Time: Noon
Place: Wayside Inn, Wayside Inn Road, Sudbury, MA

Call Aline to select your lunch choice

Please call Aline Barbera at extension 212 by December 11 to let her know what you'd like for lunch. The choices are chicken, fish, or vegetarian.

Example 3-3: Attention-getting memo where the headlines tell the story

Sequencing Your Message for the Greatest Impact

We all learned to write when we were in school. We filled our document with a lot of information, yet the reader didn't read the key information until he reached the end of the document. Our school experiences taught us to babble at the beginning of the document—write a lot of information before getting to the key issue, which was generally in the last paragraph. Business people don't have time for babble. They want the key issue at the beginning of the document or in the subject line of an e-mail.

In the Start Up Sheet you identified the reaction your reader will have. You have a strong impact on your reader when you sequence the message properly, even if you deliver bad news. Here are some guidelines to carve in granite:

☺**Responsive or neutral readers:** Put your key issue at the beginning of your message.

☹**Unresponsive readers:** Cushion the key message between a positive opening and a friendly closing.

Putting good news up front: When the reader will have a responsive or neutral attitude to your message, the message is easy to write because everyone likes to be the bearer of good news. Consider delivering the key issue in the subject line, as you see below.

> Yes, we can meet your deadline of 12/5/—
>
> Sales expected to increase 5% in Q2

After you craft the main headline, proceed with the supporting headlines. Use the direct approach and good judgment in deciding what to include and where. For example, do you need to include background information or is the reader familiar with the subject?

Giving special attention to an unresponsive reader: There are times you must send distressing information, say no, or deliver information the reader doesn't want to hear. When you must disappoint the reader, you need special planning. Remember that your intention is to maintain goodwill. If you must disappoint the reader, try the following:

Offer options	A friend received a letter from a major university denying her daughter the financial aid she had requested. The letter started, "We're sorry to inform you that we can't...." When my friend

called the university, she found out that there were other financial aid options she could pursue.

Instead of saying no, the university might have said, "Although we can't grant you the financial aid you asked for, we'd like to let you know of other opportunities you may pursue." That creates goodwill.

Give an explanation Don't tell someone "It's company policy." Readers don't care about your policies; however, they understand logical reasoning. Following is a letter I wrote for an insurance company explaining why the company couldn't pay for cosmetic surgery.

"Thank you for choosing <company> as your insurance provider. We know you have choices, and are delighted that you've chosen us. We'd love to say yes to everyone who *wants* an elective procedure. But if we did, we wouldn't have the funds to say yes to everyone who *needs* a procedure. We are confident that you'll understand and will be assured that if you ever need a procedure, we'll be right there for you. Once again, thanks for selecting <company> as your insurance provider."

Change the order Don't start with the bad news. Open with a buffer that's upbeat, and close on a friendly note. Put the bad news in the middle and try to soft-pedal it as much as possible. You may even consider using a neutral subject line (such as Policy No. 3445) or no subject line at all.

Get creative I received a letter from my financial planner showing a graph of how the stock market rebounded after the last two severe downturns. That was a very creative way to show people that they shouldn't panic, because things do get better.

✔ **Refer to No. 5, "What's my reader's attitude toward the message?" on your Start Up Sheet. Then sequence your headlines for the greatest impact on your reader.**

Step 3: Writing the Draft

You may have heard the story of the aspiring novelist who kept rewriting the opening sentence. He never got beyond the first sentence, because he didn't have a structure. You have now used strategies for getting started and have written headlines to provide that much-needed structure.

Up to now you haven't written your document—you've only planned it. Now it's time to write the draft. Using your headlines as guides, put meat on the bones. Remember that this isn't a finished document—it's a first pass. At this point, *don't get it right—get it written.* That means you shouldn't worry about spelling, grammar, or punctuation. That's editing, not writing. Here are a few tips for writing the draft:

- **Create a comfortable environment.** If you work better with music, try headphones. If you like to snack, have some munchies nearby.

- **Gather all your material.** Have all your supplies and reference material handy. When you stop to look for things, you break your concentration.

- **Set realistic time limits.** Decide how much time you want to spend at each writing session. Your goal may be either to write for 15 to 20 minutes or to expand one or two headlines. Write continually until you meet your goal, no matter how good or bad the writing seems to be. The point is to keep writing. When you reach your goal, you may either stop writing or continue if you're on a roll.

- **Develop one headline at a time.** *Don't be concerned about starting at the beginning. You reader will never know where you started.* Start with the headline that's easiest to write. Then go to the second easiest, and so on.

> ▶ Here's why you shouldn't worry about spelling, grammar, or punctuation now. In 1981, Dr. Roger Sperry won the Nobel Prize in Physiology or Medicine for his research on the theory that the brain is divided into two hemispheres, each performing a different function.
>
> - The right side deals with nonverbal, intuitive, spatial, and creative thinking.
> - The left side deals with verbal, logical, and analytical thinking. ◀

If you try to use both sides of your brain at the same time, you may cause a cranial traffic jam. You'll deal with these issues in chapter 4, where you'll see the next three steps in the Six Step Process.

✔ **Put meat on the bones of your headlines and write the draft.**

Getting Some Distance

When you finish the writing session, get some distance. In a perfect world, you could put your draft aside and revisit it in a day or two. But this isn't a perfect world, and time is a rare luxury. Nonetheless, try to get some distance. Get a cup of coffee, go for a short walk, make a quick telephone call, pat yourself on the back.

Revisiting the Draft

After you've gotten some distance, you can revisit the draft with a more critical eye. You're not editing or proofreading yet, you're just revisiting.

- Check to see if your headlines are action packed.
- Determine whether you explained the problem or situation clearly.
- See if you need to change the sequencing.
- Notice if you provided closure.

✔ **Revisit your draft and see if you need to address any of these issues.**

▶ By now, you undoubtedly realize that you saved a great deal of time by planning your message. You didn't just sit at your computer and wait for pearls of wisdom to materialize. You had a strategy and a process. But you're not finished yet. Turn to chapter 4 to complete the final three steps of the Six Step Process. That's where the rubber truly meets the road. ◀

The difference between the almost right word and the right word is really a large matter— 'tis the difference between the lightning-bug and the lightning.

—MARK TWAIN
The Art of Authorship

Fine-Tuning Your Message

Now that you have completed chapter 3 (at least I hope you have), you're ready to complete your letter, e-mail message, or memo. Here's a quick recap of the first three steps:

WHAT'S IN THIS CHAPTER

- **Step 4:** *Designing for visual impact*
- **Step 5:** *Honing the tone*
- **Step 6:** *Proofreading*

Step 1: You filled out the Start Up Sheet and answered the questions you expect your reader to have.

Step 2: You wrote an attention-getting subject line followed by headlines that tell your story. Then you sequenced them to elicit the desired reaction from your reader.

Step 3: You wrote the draft.

You're already in high gear; now you need to format, edit, and proofread. Your letter, memo, or e-mail message must have visual impact with a tone that "talks" to your reader. It must also be free of errors.

Step 4: Designing for Visual Impact

Creating a strong visual impact isn't a luxury, it's a necessity. The effectiveness of your words depends on the way your message looks. From the early wall drawings of cave dwellers to manuscripts during the Renaissance to today's daily newspapers, history is rich with examples of the importance that presentation has in communications. Here's why a strong visual impact adds pizzazz to your message:

- **Visual impact organizes information.** A good design breaks information into manageable, bite-sized chunks, making it easy for the reader to find the key pieces of information. It lets the reader concentrate on one idea at a time.

- **Visual impact emphasizes what's important.** You can create a hierarchy of information so your reader can separate the major points from the minor points. In today's harried world where people are pulling their hair out because of tight schedules, your reader will appreciate your logical presentation of ideas.

A picture *is* worth a thousand words. This is true of every document you'll ever read or write. People's eyes automatically go to something visual, whether it's white space, a headline, a bulleted or numbered list, a chart, or anything that breaks up the text. Yet writers often overlook the importance of including visual elements in their writing, especially in letters, memos, and e-mails.

> ▶ You don't need a degree in graphic design to generate a good-looking document that will have impact on your readers. This chapter gives you the nitty-gritty of how to prepare documents so you look like a pro. ◀

Using White Space Appropriately

White space includes all areas on the paper or screen where there's no text or graphics. White space makes the document inviting and approachable, it provides a resting place for the reader's eyes, and it makes the message easy to read. Here are some ways to create white space:

- On a paper document, use 1- to 1^1/$_2$-inch margins on the top, bottom, and sides. It's better to write a two-page letter or memo than it is to cram lots of information onto a single page. (See chapter 2 for writing a multiple-page letter.)

- On a computer screen, use the default margins.

- Double-space between paragraphs, leaving a blank line between each paragraph.

- Use lots of headlines, lists, chart, and tables (when appropriate).

> ▶ White space doesn't have to be white. If your paper is tan, ivory, or whatever, the background color is called *white space.* ◀

Knowing Appropriate Paragraph and Sentence Lengths

Limit paragraphs to 7 to 8 lines of text. When paragraphs are too long and dense, the reader may skip over them. When they're too short and choppy, the reader doesn't see the connection between your thoughts. Vary the length of your sentences to make for interesting reading. As a general rule, use long sentences for detailed explanations and short sentences for emphatic statements. Limit sentences to 20 to 25 words.

Paragraph too dense

The Belmont Hotel offers four distinct services: dining, accommodations, conferences, and special events. Each of these services can be promoted individually or in packages. It's important to craft the best strategy and positioning for each service prior to the "National Outreach" launch. This launch will be geared primarily toward the business traveler. With this assumption, we crafted specific tactics to generate visibility and brand recognition for the hotel. In addition, we recommend that the Belmont Hotel focus on specific industries, such as the biotech industry, which has strong roots in Scarsborough, as well as the high-tech industry, with its well-established foundation along the Routes 495/9 corridors. This focus will open up new avenues for brand awareness campaigns, as we'll then target trade publications in these industries. We plan to partner with the Scarsborough Development Council's national campaign to promote the Belmont Hotel as the premier place to stay when visiting the city of Scarsborough. Following the first …

Paragraphs too choppy

> Your career isn't just about money, is it?
>
> Probably not. It's about something more meaningful.
>
> Something so central to your core that you can't imagine living without it.
>
> Your career is about leadership. It's about making things happen. It's about having your say.
>
> For more than 100 years our publication has stood out from the crowd and has influenced leaders around the globe.

✔ **Check your draft to make sure you have ample white space and the recommended paragraph and sentence lengths.**

Understanding When to Use Bulleted and Numbered Lists

Bulleted and numbered lists help the reader focus on important information by vertically listing key items. When you overuse lists, however, you take away from the importance of each list. Save lists for information you want to have jump out. Bullets or numbers? Following are three sentences that present the same information; however, the visual message differs.

Sentence form: When you present a list in sentence form, you treat the sentence the same as other text. You don't call attention to any of the items.

> You can use his advice when selecting a vendor, agreeing on a price, issuing the order, and paying the invoice.

Bulleted list: When you present a bulleted list, you call attention to the items, but none of them takes priority. If you list people's names or something sensitive and don't want to offend anyone, consider using alphabetical order.

> You can use his advice when
>
> - selecting a vendor
> - agreeing on a price
> - issuing the order
> - paying the invoice.

Numbered list: When you present a numbered list, you assign priority to the items on the list or show steps in a process. Your visual message to the reader is that No. 1 is the most important; No. 2, the second most important; and so forth down the line.

You can use his advice when

1. selecting a vendor
2. agreeing on a price
3. issuing the order
4. paying the invoice.

> ▶ Notice that I put a period at the end of the sentence even when the sentence is a list. You put a period after each component when the components of your list complete full sentences. For more information on punctuation, check out Appendix A. ◀

Considering Sidelines as an Alternative to Bullets and Numbers

Often when you need to break out information, neither bulleted nor numbered lists are appropriate. Following is a section from a letter proposal I wrote for an agency that was relating its experience in the banking industry in order to attract a new banking customer. Although the bullets in *Before* call out this experience, *After* uses sidelines to show at a glance the names of the banks.

Before

- The agency developed service and product names for the 401(k) offerings of the Bank of Riches. The work involved marketing strategy and a complete naming architecture.

- The agency provides direct marketing and advertising programs to Nickel Bank, enabling it to reach consumers and businesses outside New York City.

- The agency developed the brand name and the agent-channel identification system for Quarter Savings Bank as part of its restructuring of the bank's business. This project involved considerable research with agents and consumers to validate the positioning and image of the new brand.

Bank of Riches	The agency developed service and product names for the 401(k) offerings of the Bank of Riches. The work involved marketing strategy and a complete naming architecture.
Nickel Bank	The agency provides direct marketing and advertising programs to Nickel Bank, enabling it to reach consumers and businesses outside New York City.
Quarter Savings Bank	The agency developed the brand name and the agent-channel identification system for Quarter Savings Bank as part of its restructuring of the bank's business. This project involved considerable research with agents and consumers to validate the positioning and image of the new brand.

✔ Check your draft to see if there are opportunities to create a bulleted list, numbered list, or sidelines.

Incorporating Tables and Charts

If a visual element such as a chart or table will enhance your message, include it. After all, why use a thousand words when a picture will do? The *Before* example that follows uses bullets excessively. The *After* example takes the same information and turns it into a readable chart that highlights the differences.

Before

Injection Molding	Blow Molding	Extrusion
• Increases MFI/reduces resin viscosity	• Increases MFI/reduces resin viscosity	• Increases MFI/ reduces resin viscosity
• Provides for quicker cycles	• Provides for quicker cycles	• Uses less energy
• Uses less energy	• Uses less energy	• Allows easy mold/die release
• Allows easy mold/die release	• Allows easy mold/die release	• Improves dispersion of color and filler
• Allows for easy cavity fill	• Improves dispersion of color and filler	• Eliminates stress and flow marks
• Eliminates stress and flow marks	• Eliminates stress and flow marks	• Improves cosmetic surfaces

Benefit	Injection Molding	Blow Molding	Extrusion
Increases MFI/reduces resin viscosity	✔	✔	✔
Provides for quicker cycles	✔	✔	
Allows easy mold/die release	✔	✔	✔
Improves dispersion of color and filler	✔	✔	✔
Allows for easy cavity fill	✔	✔	
Eliminates stress and flow marks	✔	✔	✔
Improves cosmetic surfaces	✔	✔	✔
Reduces sink marks	✔	✔	✔
Reduces coefficient of friction	✔	✔	✔
Provides clean parts, ready for finishing	✔	✔	✔
Cleans continuous extrusion		✔	✔
Eliminates residue from barrel and screw	✔	✔	✔
Uses less energy	✔	✔	✔

✔ **Check your draft to see if there are opportunities to use a chart or table.**

Using Color

Color interprets the meaning of what we see. It adds visual impact so we can separate the ripe from the unripe, match our clothes, enjoy flowers, etc. Color can be used to create a mood and give a real-world look to the written word. And, yes, you can use color in your letters, memos, and e-mail messages. Think of the power of including a headline in color. You can select a color from your logo or select one that has the visual impact you want to create. The following chart shows you the visual impact of a wide range of colors.

COLOR	ASSOCIATIONS EVOKED
White	Sanitary, pure, clean, honest
Black	Serious, heavy, death, elegant
Red	Stop, danger, excitement, hot
Dark Blue	Calming, stable, trustworthy, mature

Light Blue	Masculine, youthful, cool
Green	Growth, organic, go, positive
Gray	Neutral, cool, mature, integrity
Brown	Organic, wholesome, unpretentious
Yellow	Positive, cautious, emotional
Gold	Elegant, stable, rich, conservative
Orange	Emotional, organic, positive
Purple	Contemporary, youthful
Pink	Feminine, warm, youthful, calming
Pastels	Sensitive, feminine, soft
Metallic	Wealthy, elegant, lasting

Step 5: Honing the Tone

Some people say that business writing was developed during the Victorian era. Perhaps it was. Think about how styles have changed over time. In the 1940s and 1950s women in the work force held low-paying and often menial jobs (if they were employed in an office). They showed up to work donned in a hat, white gloves, and nylon stockings with seams. Men with professional jobs always dressed in three-piece suits, not the casual attire you see now.

Today, people are less formal in all aspects of their lives. Times have changed, and writing has followed suit—pardon the pun. This is apparent in the more conversational tone people use in business writing.

Tone is the key factor in writing. It's how you "sound" to the reader. Through your choice of words, you can sound personable, enthusiastic, positive, or active. Or you can sound stuffy, skeptical, hostile, or passive. It's all in the words you select.

Letting Your Personality Shine

People often tell me that when they read my books, they feel as if I'm talking with them. I take that as a great compliment. For people who don't know me, they can get a sense of who I am through my "paper" voice. For people who do know me, my letter substitutes for my dulcet tones. Laurence Sterne, the British novelist, once said, "Writing, when properly managed, is but a different name for conversation."

Are you *formal, chatty,* or *personable?* Chances are that you're personable. Formal can be stuffy and stilted, and chatty can be too casual, even in an e-mail message. Try to make your style personable, so you sound as if you're talking to the reader. Take a look at the following examples:

Formal   I am writing in reference to your kind invitation to address the New York chapter of the American Technology Association. I appreciate your regard for my expertise. However, it is with deep regret that I must decline your kind invitation.

(Thank goodness this Neanderthal declined the speaking invitation. Can you imagine listening to that bore drone on for an hour or more?)

Chatty   Many thanks for the invite to chat with the American Technology Association. Sorry—can't make it. Have to be on the West Coast then.

(This is so chatty that it's completely unprofessional.)

Personable   Thank you for asking me to speak at the New York chapter of the American Technology Association. I would very much like to accept the invitation, but I must be on the West Coast that week.

(You can actually "hear" someone saying this.)

Keeping It Short and Simple (KISS)

Keeping your writing simple is the essence of honing the tone. Choosing simple yet specific words that convey your message helps you to write in a tone appropriate for your reader. Remember that the less you say, the more you say—and this isn't a contradiction. As an example, when Victor Hugo sent a letter to his publisher in 1802 asking how they liked his manuscript *Les Miserables,* the publisher sent this reply:

Here's another letter that was KISS-ed. I don't know the context, but the words are brief and powerful.

Gentlemen:

You have undertaken to cheat me. I won't sue you for the law is too slow. I'll ruin you.

Yours very truly,

Cornelius Vanderbilt

▶ It's interesting to note that publications such as *The Wall Street Journal*, *Time*, and *Newsweek* are written at high-school reading level. Classic novels such as *The Catcher in the Rye* and *Moby-Dick* are written at eighth-grade level. And Hemingway rarely used words of more than two syllables. *Keep it short and simple!* ◀

In 1998, President Clinton signed the Plain Language Law. It states, "Shorter is better than long... Active is better than passive... Clarity helps advance understanding. By using plain language, we send a clear message about what the government is doing, what it requires, and what services it offers. Plain language saves the government and private sector time, effort, and money."

Too bad plain language mandates weren't in effect when Franklin D. Roosevelt issued the following blackout order in 1942: "Such preparations shall be made as will completely obscure all Federal buildings and non-Federal buildings occupied by the government during an air raid for any period of time from visibility by reason of internal or external illumination." Instead of using 37 words of gobbledygook, FDR might have used the following 15 words: "Tell them to cover the windows in buildings where they have to keep work going." Even Homer Simpson would understand that.

Eliminate every word that doesn't add value: Many expressions that were considered "trendy" years ago are nothing more than gobbledygook today. Following are phrases to use and to avoid:

Use	Avoid
adjust	make an adjustment
allows	allows the opportunity
although	in spite of the fact that
appeared	put in an appearance
as you asked	pursuant to your request
as you requested	pursuant to your request
as soon as	at the earliest possible date
aware	cognizant of
because	due to the fact that, inasmuch as
because of	in view of the fact that
before	prior to
concluded	arrived at the conclusion
consider	take into consideration
costs	costs the sum of
delay	hold in abeyance
distribute	send around
do	take appropriate measures
early	ahead of schedule
enclosed is	enclosed herewith please find
each	each and every
except	with the exception of
finally	in the final analysis
find out	ascertain
grouped	grouped together
have	are in receipt of
help	be of assistance
if	in the event of
in March	during the month of March
in the future	at a future time
investigate	conduct an investigation
know	are fully cognizant
met	held a meeting
named	by the name of
now	at the present time

payment	remuneration
postpone	hold in abeyance
regardless	irregardless (not a word)
regularly	on a regular basis
remain	continue to remain
return	arrange to return
satisfactorily	in a satisfactory manner
separately	under separate cover
show you	draw your attention to
soon	in the near future
study (read)	peruse
thank you	I wish to take this opportunity to thank you
then	after that has been done
to provide	for the purpose of providing
try	endeavor
twice	on two occasions
undoubtedly	there is no doubt
until you can	until such time as you are able to

Get to the heart of the matter: The essence of good business writing is to strip the message down to the bare essentials. Try to imagine that every word you use costs $100. Cut to the quick. When you keep your sentences simple and get to the heart of the matter, your reader will understand your message. Notice the differences in what follows:

Original version

I wish to take this opportunity to thank you for taking the time to send us your recent inquiry. As you no doubt are aware, your membership entitles you to all the rights and privileges afforded to current members. Also, you will be receiving on a monthly basis a copy of our newsletter, which we hope you will find to be of value. Please feel free to share this newsletter with any of your colleagues who you feel might also find it worthwhile.

We do look forward to seeing you at the various meetings and events during the upcoming year. Listings of these events will appear in the calendar section of the newsletter each month.

If you have any further questions or concerns, please do not hesitate to call me.

(130 words)

Edited version

~~I wish to take this opportunity to~~ Thank you for ~~taking the time to send us~~ your recent inquiry. ~~As you no doubt are aware,~~ Your membership entitles you to all the ~~rights and~~ privileges ~~afforded to~~ of current members. Also, you will ~~be~~ receiv~~eing~~ ~~on~~ a monthly ~~basis a copy of our~~ newsletter which we hope you will find to be of value. Please ~~feel free to~~ share this newsletter with ~~any of your~~ colleagues who ~~you feel~~ might also find it worthwhile.

We ~~do~~ look forward to seeing you at ~~the various meetings and~~ events during the ~~upcoming~~ year. Listings of these events ~~will~~ appear in the calendar section of the newsletter ~~each month~~.

If you have any ~~further~~ questions ~~or concerns~~, please ~~do not hesitate to~~ call me.

Final version

Thank you for your recent inquiry. Your membership entitles you to all the privileges of current members. Also, you will receive a monthly newsletter which we hope you will find to be of value. Please share this newsletter with colleagues who might also find it worthwhile.

We look forward to seeing you at events during the year. Listings of these events appear in the calendar section of the newsletter.

If you have any questions, please call me.

(77 words)

BRAIN DRAIN

Can you simplify the following sentences into commonly known expressions that would be clear to your reader? You'll find the answers upside down at the bottom.

1. Scintillate, scintillate asteroid minified.

2. Similar sire, similar scion.

3. Every article that is coruscated is not fashioned from aureate metal.

4. Members of an avian species of identical plumage congregate.

5. Pulchritude possesses solely cutaneous profundity.

1. Twinkle, twinkle little star.
2. Like father, like son.
3. All that glitters is not gold.
4. Birds of a feather flock together.
5. Beauty is only skin deep.

✔ **Check your draft to see where you may save $100 a word by keeping the message short and simple.**

Using Positive Words

Your glass should be half full, not half empty. This is a winning strategy that will help you to have greater impact on your reader. Following are just a few of the words that communicate a positive message:

bonus	congratulations	convenient	delighted
excellent	friend	generous	glad
honest	immediately	I will	of course
pleasant	pleasing	pleasure	qualified
right	safe	sale	satisfactory
thank you	vacation	value	yes

These communicate a negative message:

apology	broken	cannot	carelessly
complaint	damaged	delay	difficulty
disappoint	discomfort	failure	guilty
impossible	inconvenient	loss	mistake
problem	regret	sorry	suspicion
trouble	unable	you claim	you neglected

Create positive thoughts: To create positive thoughts, say something in a positive way, rather than a negative way. Sometimes it's merely a matter of saying what you can do, rather than what you can't do.

Negative	We can't charge orders under $20.
Positive	We can charge orders over $20.

Negative	This product is no more harmful than a hair dryer.
Positive	This product is as safe as a hair dryer.

Negative	Participation for the month of January hasn't increased. It remained at 45%.
Positive	Participation for the month of January remained steady at 45%.

Negative	Please don't send me any bad news.
Positive	I look forward to your sending me good news.

Think about small words: Often small words change the meaning of a sentence. For example, "but" is a small word with a large influence. Notice the difference in the two sentences when you change "but" to "and."

Negative	Angelo was new to consulting but outperformed expectations. *(Sounds as if that was a surprise.)*
Positive	Angelo was new to consulting and outperformed expectations. *(Sounds as if that was the expectation.)*

▶ Check out the section "Sequencing your message for the greatest impact on your reader" in chapter 3 for other suggestions for making a negative message more positive. ◀

Applying the Active Voice

When you use the active voice, you focus the sentence on the doer (or the actor). Using the active voice is a major factor in projecting a tone that's alive and interesting. To understand the difference between the active and passive voices, picture the following:

You're on a Caribbean vacation with your loved one sailing aboard a 100-foot yacht. You're sitting on the deck and the fiery crimson sun is slowly sinking into the distant horizon. The waves are gently rolling over the craggy shore, while you sip a glass of your favorite wine. The special someone you're with leans over and whispers tenderly in your ear the words you've been longing to hear: *I love you.*

Doesn't that make you feel warm and fuzzy? *I love you* is probably the most wonderful example of the active voice. It's animated and alive! Now imagine that same scenario, and that special someone leans over and whispers in your ear, *You are loved by me.* That's phony and stilted.

In most situations, you should use the active voice because it makes the sentence lively and interesting; it starts with a doer.

Passive	Activities should be approved by your supervisor.
Active	Have your supervisor approve all activities. *("You" is understood.)*

| Passive | The circuit boards were inspected by Jim. |
| Active | Jim inspected the circuit boards. |

| Passive | The printer is shared by Bob and Sally. |
| Active | Bob and Sally share the printer. |

▶ Active sentences don't always start with a person. In some cases the doer is some*thing*, rather than some*one*.

| Active | The future holds promise. |
| Passive | There is much to look forward to in the future. |

| Active | Removing the soil plug allows additional pile penetration. |
| Passive | Additional penetration may be obtained by removing the soil plug. ◀ |

Using the Passive Voice

There are instances when you might want to use the passive voice. However, do so strategically. When you use the passive voice, your subject plays a passive role or none at all. For example, in "The law firm was established in 1900," it's not important who started the law firm; it's the date that's important. Following are some examples of when the passive voice is appropriate:

- **You want to place the focus on the object of the action, not the doer.** For example, "Dennis was cited for his outstanding contribution." (The accent is on Dennis, not on the person who cited him.)

- **You want to hide something.** Perhaps you remember this famous line that came out of President Nixon's Watergate scandal: "The tapes were erased." (The passive voice was used deliberately, so that no one would take the rap for that $18\frac{1}{2}$-minute gap.)

- **You want to take the focus off yourself.** Instead of saying, "I will be hiring a new accountant for your department," you may say, "Your department is getting a new accountant." (This takes the focus off the person who is doing the hiring.)

One way to tell if your sentence is passive is to look for a form of the verb *to be*. That includes *is, was, were, will be, has been, should have been,* and so on. These words don't always indicate the passive voice, but they give you pause to take a second look.

✔ **Check your draft and turn passive sentences into active sentences where appropriate.**

Applying the "You" Approach

Have you ever noticed that advertisers talk directly to customers? That's a deliberate attempt to draw "you" into the message. You can draw your readers into the message by incorporating *you* and *your,* instead of *me* and *my,* into the message. This is the essence of a reader-focused message.

You may have to use the passive voice to do this, but you would be doing it strategically. In the following examples, notice how seven references to the writer change to four references to the reader.

Writer-focused	**We** want you to know that **we** appreciate having you as one of **Mason's** catalog customers. **We** have decided that **we** can make catalog shopping a lot easier by issuing you one of **our** credit cards. With this card, **we** can take your orders by phone.
Reader-focused	As one of Mason's valued catalog customers, **you** will receive a convenient credit card. **You** can phone in **your** orders and merely give us **your** account number.

✔ **Check your draft and remove references to yourself, where appropriate. Replace them with references to the reader.**

Thinking about Translations

We adapt our tones for different people and situations. We use one tone for our friends and family, another for peers, another for managers, and yet another for people whose primary language isn't English. With e-mail allowing you to send messages instantly to people or groups in most parts of the world, global savvy is a must. Here are a few examples:

Geographic expressions	Be attuned to geographic references. If you write "I'll be visiting the West Coast next week," someone outside the United States may not understand your frame of reference.

	You can state your message clearly by saying, "I'll be visiting the West Coast of the United States next week," or more specifically, "I'll be visiting California next week."
Dates	It's good business practice to write out the month, date, and year because you never know who may read your message. People in other parts of the world abbreviate dates differently from the way we do. For example, April 5, 2000, to Europeans is 5/4/00. To the Japanese, it's 00/4/5.
Metric measurements	We're one of the few countries in the galaxy that doesn't use the metric system. Therefore, it's wise to write metric measurements with American equivalents in parentheses. (Check out Appendix D for commonly used metric measurements.)
Common terms	Someone whose first language isn't English may know the meaning of both "hot" and "dog," but she may not understand the meaning of a "hot dog."

Using Repetition

Many people go out of their way to avoid repeating words. Repeating a key word or thought is often the bond that gives a thought its cohesion. Repetition can produce a nicely balanced flow and give added impact to key points. Consider the impact of the following familiar expressions:

Cohesive	We have nothing to fear but fear itself.
Unglued	We have nothing to fear but dread itself.

Repetition can add strength: Use repetition when you want to emphasize or strengthen a thought. See how this is done strategically:

Strong	Keep it short. Keep it simple. Keep it flowing.
Weak	Keep it short, simple, and flowing.

Repetition can add consistency: When you're not consistent, you may confuse the reader. For example, if you refer to a document as a "brochure," then a "flier," then a "pamphlet," the reader may think you're talking about three different documents.

Using Gender-Neutral Terms

Sexism is a hot topic these days. The English language, as rich as it is, has no clear-cut solution. Without getting into absurdities (such as changing *man*hole cover to *person*hole cover), the key is to be aware of hidden meanings and be sensitive to your reader. This section talks about ways to bridge the gender gap.

Avoid gender judgments in job titles: When you speak of someone's job title, don't make a gender judgment. Judges aren't always males, and nurses aren't always females. Someone who's employed in a stockroom isn't a stockboy, but a stockclerk. The following is a sampling of gender-neutral terms:

Instead of ...	Try
anchorman	newscaster, anchor
cameraman	cinematographer
chairman	chairperson, chair, moderator
clergyman	member of the clergy
councilman	councilor, council member
delivery boy	delivery person, messenger
fireman	firefighter
forefather	ancestor
insurance man	insurance agent
layman	nonprofessional
mailman	mail (*or* letter) carrier
man-made	synthetic
mankind	humanity, human race
manpower	work force, personnel
newsman	reporter, journalist
policeman	police officer
repairman	service technician
salesman	sales representative
spokesman	spokesperson
stewardess	flight attendant
stockboy	stockclerk
waitress	waiter, waitperson
weatherman	meteorologist
workman	worker

Reword the sentence: Gender neutrality is often a matter of rewording the sentence. The examples that follow show a number of ways to say the same thing:

Sexist	Each person did his work quietly.
Awkward	Each person did his/her work quietly.
Grammatically incorrect	Each person did their work quietly.
Acceptable	Each person did the work quietly.
Acceptable	Each person worked quietly.
Acceptable	Everyone worked quietly.

Use plurals: In some cases you can make a sentence plural to avoid the awkward he/she or his/her situations.

Singular	A doctor is trained to heal his/her patients.
Plural	Doctors are trained to heal their patients.
Singular	Each candidate for the human resources position must file his/her application no later than June 5. He/she should include his/her educational background.
Plural	All candidates for the human resources position must file their applications no later than June 5. They should include their educational backgrounds.

▶ Notice how I address this delicate issue in this book. I explain early in the book that I use the male gender in the odd chapters; the female gender in the even chapters. (I didn't determine that men are odd; my penny did that.) ◀

Honing Other Tones

There are a few other areas where you may hone the tone.

Euphemisms	Euphemisms are word substitutions that shade meaning. Tone plays a part in the unspoken meanings that both words and expressions evoke. For example, notice the difference in tone of the following word choices:
	problem and *opportunity*
	subordinate and *direct report*
	boss and *supervisor*

Humor	Will Rogers once said, "Humor is funny as long as it is happening to somebody else." Humor is a sensitive area. Using humor in letters, memos, or e-mails may be appropriate on rare occasions; however, you must be sensitive to the way your reader will perceive what you say. If in doubt, leave it out.
Clichés	Clichés are worn-out expressions that have little, if any, meaning. If you've heard the cliché "crazy as a bedbug," have you ever wondered why bedbugs are crazier than tsetse flies? Avoid clichés like the plague.
Jargon	Jargon is specialized "shop talk" whose use is generally restricted to people within a particular industry. Avoid jargon when you write to people outside the industry. Your tone may become bogged down in obscure and unfamiliar words that the reader may view as exclusionary. Don't confuse jargon with street slang. Stay away from expressions such as *cool, dude, awesome,* and the like.

▶ Contractions don't belong only in the labor room. It is often perfectly appropriate to use contractions in your writing. After all, that's the way you speak. The apostrophe in a contraction also offers a visual clue that the thought is negative. For example, the reader's eyes may skip over the word not in "do not," but they can't miss the apostrophe in "don't." ◀

✔ **Check your draft to see if you used euphemisms, inappropriate humor, clichés, inappropriate jargon, or sexist language.**

Step 6: Proofreading

Imagine this scenario: The new CEO of a major corporation walks into his first board of directors' meeting. He really wants to dazzle the board. He's wearing a $2,500 pin-striped suit, silk shirt, power tie, and $500 black leather shoes. He sits down, crosses his legs, and (Oops!) you notice that he's wearing one black sock and one blue sock. What does that do to his dazzling image? Blows it, right? Every time you think of Mr. CEO, you're going to snicker and think of his mismatched socks.

Well, imagine yourself spending hours or days preparing a document you're proud of. If you send it with even one error—that's your mismatched socks. A colleague of mine who works at Emory College received a proposal for a very large contract. On the cover, the sender typed *Emery* instead of *Emory*. My colleague tossed the proposal into the garbage without ever looking beyond the cover.

▶ The following sentences are taken from actual letters. The writers might have avoided these lulus by reviewing their texts carefully.

Written by doctors
- James has chest pain if he lies on his side for over a year.
- Prior to the patient's birth, she was told that her pregnancy was a normal one.
- On the first day his knee was better and on the third day it had completely disappeared.
- Margaret Smith was given a genealogical exam at the hospital.
- The patient's leg became numb at times and he walked it off.

Written on insurance claims
- The pedestrian had no idea which direction to go, so I ran over him.
- Coming home, I drove into the wrong house and collided with a tree I didn't have.
- The accident happened when the right front door of a car came around the corner without giving a signal.
- The telephone pole was approaching fast. I was attempting to swerve out of its path when it struck my front end.
- I was on the way to the doctor's with rear end trouble when my universal joint gave way causing me to have an accident.
- The guy was all over the road. I had to swerve a couple of times before I hit him. ◀

Proofreading isn't an innate talent; it's a learned skill. You must proofread until your eyeballs hurt so you aren't mortified like the woman in the following scenario. This is a true story, but I changed the name to protect the guilty.

Ann was the public relations director of a major corporation. She was sending a very sensitive e-mail message to thousands of employees in the United States,

Europe, and Asia. This message was so sensitive that Ann had it checked by the CEO, the legal department, and just about everyone who mattered. Ann concluded by signing the message: *Regards, Ann Onymous, Pubic Relations Director.* (She left the *l* out of *public.*)

Putting Out Fires Before They Start

Proofreading is a skill that you can learn quite easily. It's a matter of following a few simple guidelines.

- **Check all names, including middle initials, titles, and company distinctions.** Are you spelling *Glenn* with two *n*'s instead of one? Are you writing *Corp.* instead of *Co.*?

- **Double-check numbers.** Are you telling the reader she'll receive a check for $15,750.00, and the check reads $15,570.00?

- **Keep an eye out for misused or misspelled homophones (words that sound the same but are spelled differently).** Are you writing *affect* instead of *effect?*

- **Watch out for repetitive words.** Perhaps you wrote, "Please let me me know if I can be of further help." (Your word processing program may pick this up; your e-mail probably won't.)

- **Be on the alert for small words that are repeated or misspelled.** Perhaps you typed *it* instead of *at* and didn't notice the error. (You tend to read what you expect to be there.)

- **Make sure you're consistent with labels.** For example, do you typically do business with dealers, distributors, or manufacturers? Do you have customers, clients, or accounts? Are you sending a contract or an agreement?

- **Check dates against those on the calendar.** When you type Monday, September 15, be sure September 15 is a Monday.

- **Check for omissions.** Perhaps you left off a ZIP code, policy number, or other critical piece of information.

- **Check spelling, grammar, and punctuation.** Check out the appendixes for nifty tips on spelling, grammar, and punctuation.

- **Print out the letter and reread the hard copy.** Don't take the letter from the printer and put it directly in an envelope. Reread it first. Face it, despite the hours you spend in front of your computer, you're still more accustomed to reading hard copy. Therefore, you tend to see errors on hard copy that you may miss on the screen.

- **Read the letter aloud.** Can you read the letter just once and thoroughly understand it? If not, rewrite whatever parts may be confusing.

- **Read from bottom to top and/or from right to left.** This lets you view each word as a separate entity and helps you find errors.

- **Scan the letter to see that the formatting is correct.** Are there 1- to $1\frac{1}{2}$-inch margins all around? Are the sentences limited to 25 words or less and the paragraphs to 5 to 7 lines or less? Did you mix letter formats (full-block and modified-block, for example)?

▶ Although the computer is a wonderful way to check spelling and grammar, don't turn on your computer and turn off your brain. For example, the computer won't detect an error if you write, *I will not allow that,* instead of *I will now allow that.* That one typographical error sends the opposite message. ◀

Also, before you send an important e-mail message, print out the document and read the hard copy. Your eyes are more accustomed to reading paper copy.

Striving to Be Letter-Perfect

Take a look at Example 4-1 and see what oversights you notice. Then look at Example 4-2 for the answers. If you found all the goofs, rip the proofreading section out of the book and give it to a deserving colleague. (You know—one of the ones who send letters with errors that are as obvious as ketchup stains running down a bridal gown.)

Then go through the Checklist you see in Example 4-3 so you don't wind up with egg on your face as did Ann, the public relations director.

Febuary 30, 20—

Mr. and Mrs. Harry Lorenz
14 Ivy Lane
Atlanta, Georgia 30303

Welcome to Atlanta!

Dear Mr. and Mrs. Lorenz

It's a pleasure to welcome you and your family to Atlanta—the Peachtree State. To help you get to know this wonderful area, we've enclosed a map of the recreational and cultural facilities in and around the city. Here are some of the highlights.

1. Georgia State Capital
2. Peachtree Center
3. Tullie Smith House
4. Martin Luther King, Jr., Historic District

And while you're getting to now the city, stop by the Georgia State Bank so I may welcome you personally and share many of the wonderful experiences you can have banking with us. Georgia State Bank is celebrating their 15th anniversary and is sending you as a $10 gift certificate to start a savings account to help us celebrate.

Sincerely Yours,

Leah Zimmerman,
Branch Manager

Looking forward to seeing you!

Example 4-1: What's wrong with this picture?

February 28, 20—   <February *was misspelled and has 28 days, other than in leap years.*>

Mr. and Mrs. Harry Lorenz
14 Ivy Lane
Atlanta, GA 30303   <*Use the two-letter state abbreviation.*>

Dear Mr. and Mrs. Lorenz: <*Use a colon after a formal salutation.*>

Welcome to Atlanta!   <*Subject line should follow salutation.*>

It's a pleasure to welcome you and your family to Atlanta—the capital of the Peachtree State. <*Atlanta isn't a state.*> To help you get to know this wonderful area, we've enclosed a map of the recreational and cultural facilities in and around the city. Here are some of the highlights:
<*Colon after a sentence introducing a list.*>

    1. Georgia State Capitol   <*Capitol is a building.*>
    2. Peachtree Center
    3. Tullie Smith House
    4. Martin Luther King, Jr., Historic District

And while you're getting to know <*not "now"*> the city, stop by the Georgia State Bank so I may welcome you personally and share many of the wonderful experiences you can have banking with us. Georgia State Bank is celebrating its <*not "their"*> 15th anniversary and is sending you <*removed "as"*> a $10 gift certificate to start a savings account to help us celebrate.

Sincerely yours,   <*The date and complimentary closing should be aligned. "Yours" shouldn't be capitalized.*>

Leah Zimmerman   <*No comma when job title is on a line below the name.*>
Branch Manager

Looking forward to seeing you!

Example 4-2: What's right with this picture?

CHECKLIST

❏ My subject line and headlines are informative and will spark my reader's interest.

❏ My headlines include key words.

❏ My message tells the story.

❏ My message has visual impact including

  ❏ ample white space

  ❏ bulleted and numbered lists, where appropriate

  ❏ paragraphs limited to 7 to 8 lines of text

  ❏ sentences limited to no more than 25 words.

❏ My message is clear, well organized, and properly formatted.

❏ The message is sequenced to keep the reader interested and moving forward.

❏ The tone reflects my personality on paper and includes the active voice and "you" approach.

❏ The spelling, grammar, and punctuation are correct.

❏ There are no coffee stains on the page.

Example 4-3: Check before you send

PART THREE

Writing Results-Oriented Letters

Is this you? You stare out the window, glance at your clock, then look back at your blank computer screen. "I just don't know where to begin," you muse. So you start typing, I am writing this letter to let you know that... *"No," you say to yourself, "that sounds as if I just had Novocain injected into my brain."*

If this is you, help comes in the form of this part. It's chock-full of letters for all occasions to use verbatim or tweak for your unique needs.

In our factory we make lipstick. In our advertising, we sell hope.

—CHARLES REVSON
former Chairman of Revlon, Inc.

CHAPTER 5

Sales and Marketing with Pizzazz

At one time, most of us were part of a highly targeted and elite group of people (which Dave Barry describes as "people with phones") who were earmarked for dreaded telemarketing calls at the exact moment we sat down for dinner. Many industries relied on telemarketing to sell their products and services. However, when people signed up in droves for the national Do Not Call Registry, these same industries had to rely on other means of getting on the radar screens of potential and existing customers.

WHAT'S IN THIS CHAPTER

- *Hallmarks of sales letters with pizzazz*
- *Choosing the right words*
- *Sales letter taboos*
- *Miscellaneous sales letters*
- *Sources for mailing lists*
- *Tricks of trade shows*

Sales letters, postcards, and e-marketing (more about e-marketing in chapter 16) are just a few avenues that continue to explode. Your ability to write a clear and concise message can mean the difference between your success and failure. When you make your points more clearly, more noticeably, and more persuasively than your competitors, you'll be more successful.

If you've ever questioned whether marketing is the conduit for sales, count the number of sales letters, postcards, press releases, e-marketing communications, and more that you receive. They work. They get results. They also cost much less than media coverage and can be targeted to specific audiences. Sales and marketing are the lifeblood of most companies.

> ▶ • Save the paper and electronic sales materials you commonly toss out or delete because you consider them to be junk mail or spam. They have many good ideas that you can use.
>
> • Remember the rule of three—send a series of three mailings. The first mailing introduces you to the reader. The second generates recognition. The third may prompt a call.
>
> • Consider mixing up the series of three with a letter, postcard, or e-marketing.
>
> • Remember that everything your company does and sends out has the potential to influence your customers and can either increase or hurt sales. Use sales and marketing writing as an opportunity to touch your customers. Well-written messages persuade customers that your products or services are second to none. Once you get the hang of writing dynamite sales materials, you'll get noticed, get read, and be remembered. ◀

Hallmarks of Sales Letters with Pizzazz

A sales letter is a written sales call. When you make a sales call, however, you've already gotten the prospect's attention. When you send a sales letter, getting your reader's attention is your first task. Here are some suggestions:

- Learn all you can about your products and services.
- Know your customer base.
- Understand what motivates people and gets them to respond.

> ▶ How long should a sales letter be? Many people have the misconception that you should limit a sales letter to one page. That's not always true. The best length is whatever it takes to deliver your message clearly and concisely. When you write a compelling multiple-page letter, the reader will read it. (Check out chapter 2 to see how to format the second page of a multiple-page letter.) ◀

Planning Your Sales Campaign

Remember to fill out the Start Up Sheet you used in chapter 3. It's critical that you understand your audience, purpose, and key issue. When you understand your customers and know your products and services inside and out, you're ready to start a sales campaign.

- **Generate a list of prospects with common characteristics.** For example, if you're promoting a golfing magazine, you must know that your prospects are golfers. If you write to members of a chamber of commerce, you know they're all business owners.

- **Understand the demographics.** Know the sex, age, occupation, geographic location, and financial situation of your target audience. You wouldn't get too far trying to sell snowblowers to urban apartment dwellers.

- **View your product or service from the eyes of your reader.** In sales, emotions often spur buyers, not logic. Use No. 3 on your Start Up Sheet, "What's in it for my reader?" to appeal to your reader's emotions. Some people buy a new car every two years, not because they need reliable transportation, but because they want the status of having a late-model car. Understand what your reader is buying—comfort, prestige, enjoyment, convenience, health, loyalty.

- **Determine the key selling point.** The key selling point may be ease of use, appearance, durability, price, comfort, education, or anything else. Then put yourself in the reader's shoes. Being in poor health. Living on a small income. Living in a crowded apartment. Using antiquated hardware and software. Paying inflated prices.

- **Plan the sales spiel.** When you write your sales letter, think of AIDA. (This has nothing to do with Verdi's famous opera.)

  Attention: Get the reader's attention.

  Interest: Pique his interest.

  Desire: Create the desire.

  Action: Then call for action.

- **Remember that timing is everything.** When should you send the letter? When would it be too early? When would it be too late? If you're announcing a 25-percent discount on all Christmas merchandise, remember that the day after Thanksgiving is considered to be the heaviest shopping day of the year.

Capturing the Reader's Attention

When people receive unsolicited mail, it takes them about eight seconds to decide if they'll read it, set it aside to read later, or throw it away. Don't let your message drown in the sea of similarity. The "grabber" is the written equivalent to a salesman's friendly smile and sincere handshake.

- **Arrange the first sentence of the letter as a compelling headline or question.** You see compelling openings in Examples 5-1 and 5-2. Novelists call them hooks, journalists call them leads, and business writers call them opening lines. Here are a few:

Headlines

Success starts with <...>.
Taste the difference!
For those special people in your life.
The <...> that never quits.
Everything you've always wanted in a <...>.
As good as money in the bank.
Innovation is a tradition at <...>.
<...> doesn't have to cost an arm and a leg.
<...> with a twist.
The best kept secret in <...>.
Your one-in-all <...>.
I'm inviting you to join a distinctive group.
You come highly recommended to us.
We extend this invitation to very few.

Questions

How much money are you spending on <...>?
What's the most profitable <...>?
Enjoy meeting new people? Going new places?
Can you recall the first time you <...>?
Can you recall the last time you <...>?
Are you secretly afraid of <...>?
Are you drowning in a sea of <...>?
Are you looking for just the right <...>?
Are your frustrated by <...>?
Why sacrifice <...> for <...>?
What's the safest <...>?

Sheryl Lindsell-Roberts & Associates   117 Sudbury Street, Marlborough, MA 01752
508-229-8209 • sheryl@sherylwrites.com
www.sherylwrites.com

- **Are you troubled by lost revenue due to inconsistent marketing messages?**
- **Do you get frustrated because people don't flock to your trade show booth?**
- **Does your company's marketing plan enhance its goals?**

If any of these questions resonate with you, your bottom line is dramatically impacted. Let the marketing team—with more than 80 years of combined experience—help you to create a rich marketing experience that will quantify and communicate the value of your products or services.

In an ongoing effort to provide greater services to my clients, I have partnered with several marketing experts to bring you a full-service marketing team that can supplement your current marketing group or be your outsourced Marketing Department. Let me introduce the marketing team.

Award-Winning Graphic Designer Mike Jewell is an award-winning graphic designer and web developer. He combines the power of information technology with the human touch of creative design. Benefits of working with Mike include increased market share, time-to-market savings, and cost reductions. If you have critical issues with corporate identity, employee productivity, or business-to-business commerce, Mike has a strategy.

Strategic Marketing Guru Brigitte Casemyr is the critical link to establishing a strong position for your products and services. She has the talent, credentials, and track record to help you prosper through the ups and downs in the economy. Brigitte has initiated innovative marketing campaigns that have helped national and global companies to prosper by providing corporate positioning, marketing strategies, lead generation, and much more.

Trade Show Exhibitor Mike Fiorelli can help you to provide a unique experience for all your trade shows, expos, and special events. His common sense, ingenuity, willpower, and drive create a potent mix that will satisfy the most demanding of corporate appetites.

Next Step Call us today to learn why you should rely on Sheryl Lindsell-Roberts & Associates to get the job done right, on time, and with pizzazz. Marketing is our business!

Sincerely,

Sheryl Lindsell-Roberts

Example 5-1: Opens with thought-provoking questions

LETTERHEAD

Thinking about moving?
Cleaning out your attic or basement?
Getting rid of debris or rubbish?

If so, what will you do with all the stuff? The answer is simple. Call <company> and rent one of our dumpsters. They come in a variety of sizes and will be delivered and removed in a timely manner. We have radio-dispatched trucks so we can generally accommodate you on short notice.

One of the things that sets us apart from the competition—in addition to our reliability and the presentable appearance of our dumpsters—is that we put wooden skids under the dumpsters to help prevent damage to your property. *Our dumpsters leave an impression on you, not on your property.*

If you don't have room for a dumpster or you don't have enough debris to warrant one, call our crew. We'll send in a team to clean up the debris and take it away.

SPECIAL OFFER

$25 off the rental of a dumpster
10% off the price of a pickup

This offer expires on _____,
so call now and mention this special rate.

<Company> is a family-owned and operated business that has been serving the community since 1989. Our key to success is making each customer our No. 1 priority. To learn more about <company>, our rate schedule, and the areas around Boston that we serve, visit our website or phone us and speak with a "real person" who's anxious to help you.

<Phone>
<Web>

Example 5-2: Sales letter announcing a limited-time offer opens with questions

- **Start with a relevant, interesting quote.**

  In skating over thin ice, our safety is our speed.

  —RALPH WALDO EMERSON

  Do not dishonor the earth lest you dishonor the spirit of man.

  —HENRY BESTON, *The Outermost House*

- **Start with an anecdote, a fable, or a parable.**

  The door closed slowly as Jon entered the president's office and sank slowly into the dark leather chair in the far corner. Jon had been there many times but knew by the tone of the president's telephone conversation that she'd had another one of her "brainstorms."

- **Include a teaser on the envelope that will compel the reader to open it.** Check out Examples 5-3a and 5-3b to see a teaser that got an overwhelming response. Following are other teasers to consider:

  VALUABLE DOCUMENT ENCLOSED

  $$-MAKING OPPORTUNITY

  CLAIM YOUR FREE <...>

  STARTLING NEWS ABOUT <...>

  BE THE FIRST TO <...>

> ▶ Your first line of defense is the envelope. If you don't want your envelope to shout "junk mail," use a postage stamp rather than a postage meter. Even consider hiring a minimum-wage earner with decent handwriting to handwrite each reader's name and address. That makes the mailing look personalized. ◀

Holding the Reader's Attention and Creating Desire

Now that you've captured the reader's attention, the following suggestions will hold the reader's interest and create a desire:

- Address the letter to a specific person—never "To whom this may concern."

- Explain how the products or services will be a direct benefit to the reader.

- Keep the message brief, interesting, and informative.

Dear Friend and Valued Customer,

We'll take care of whatever is bugging you
One of the first things ants look for after a long winter is a tall glass of water. That's why they make tracks for your sink and bath areas. Before you know it, the "scout" ants will be leading the entire ant colony into your home to find water.

Eliminate these bugs as they come out of dormancy
In March, we'll apply a thorough treatment on all your basement sills and outdoor foundation. We'll return in September to treat your outdoor foundation once again. This two-step treatment ensures that no carpenter ants enter at the critical time that they're looking for nesting areas in your home.

> ## Save $25
>
> All of our preferred customers who call by
>
> _____
>
> for a March appointment will save $25
> on the spring inspection and treatment.

Get our 12-month guarantee
As always, we guarantee our pest-control treatment for a full year. And don't forget that our service includes an inspection of your home for pest damage.

Sincerely,

Nat Stinger

Example 5-3a: Letter with a compelling teaser

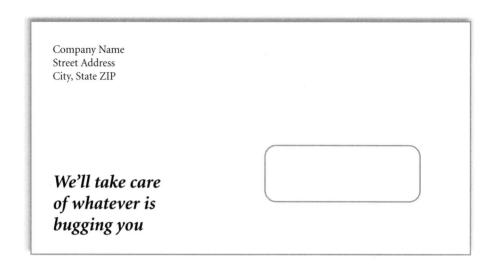

Company Name
Street Address
City, State ZIP

We'll take care
of whatever is
bugging you

Example 5-3b: Envelope with a compelling teaser

- Be certain your information is accurate and honest.

- Don't apply high-pressure tactics or knock competitive products.

> ▶ Whether you introduce the price is truly a judgment call. If your key selling point is the price, introduce it early. If not, focus on the advantages and consider not mentioning the price. If you entice the reader, he'll call for the price. ◀

Calling for Action

Always conclude by letting the reader know what to do. You may want the reader to fill out an order form, make a phone call, wait for a phone call, attend a seminar, or do something else. See Example 5-4 for a subtle call to action and Example 5-5 for a strong call to action. Following are some calls to action you may consider:

- *Order now, while there's still time.*

- *Please fill in the order form that's enclosed and return it in the postage-paid envelope.*

- *Write us for your free <…>.*

- *Stop by the dealer nearest you.*

sound MInds and sound Bodies make sound Profits

Did you know that there's a direct link between the health of your employees and the health of your profits? During these tough economic times, perhaps you're looking for benefits to offer your employees that benefit both you and them.

The benefits of healthier employees include lower health care costs, fewer medical claims, improved productivity, better morale, reduced absenteeism, and more. Here's how you can help your employees to have sound bodies that will improve your company's profits:

- Provide them with World Fitness health club discounts.
- Bring our aerobics, massage, weight loss, and educational programs onsite.
- Have us manage your onsite fitness center.

After a prevention and early intervention [health] program was implemented, loss claims for L.L. Bean dropped by approximately 40%.
                              —*Business Insurance* magazine

Call World Fitness now to learn how you can add to the health of your employees and your bottom line.

508-852-8209   www.worldfitness.com

The Surgeon General has determined that lack of physical activity is detrimental to your [physical and fiscal] health. ™

Example 5-4: Postcard with a subtle call to action

If you're a new or growing company, managing your financial decisions may be akin to looking through a kaleidoscope, with each turn creating an ever-changing picture. Let <company> bring you financial clarity. Sound financial decisions are the backbone of your business.

Call us now. We'll come to your place of business and provide a complimentary one-hour assessment of the state of your finances.

<phone number>
<website>

Example 5-5: Postcard with a call to action in a call-out box

- *Check out our website at <…>.*
- *Call us this week to set up an appointment to see <…>.*
- *<…> will call you to set up a mutually convenient appointment.*
- *If this isn't for you, please pass it on to a friend or colleague.*
- *In a hurry? Call <…>.*
- *Please send this information by registered mail.*
- *To reserve your place, <…>.*
- *For even faster service, <…>.*
- *We'll be delighted to start your service as soon as you call us.*

Including a Postscript

A postscript is a very effective way to call attention to a sentence or two. You can put the postscript in script or in a different font or color. Example 5-6 shows a mailer sent from a real estate agent. Every month this agent sends mailings of interest to her readers that have nothing to do with real estate. Notice how she uses the postscript effectively to bring the focus back to her business. Here are a few postscripts worth considering:

- *Remember that the deadline for ordering is <…>.*
- *For the fastest possible service, <…>.*
- *If you have a friend or relative who may benefit from this offer, please pass it along.*
- *Please let me emphasize <….>.*
- *Don't send any money now, <…>.*
- *If you're looking for a convincing argument to help you make up your mind, please look at the enclosed literature.*

Choosing the Right Words

It's critical to understand what your customers are buying, not what you are selling. You want to entice them with the right words. For example, when people buy light bulbs, they aren't buying glass or filaments. And they aren't buying bulbs. They're buying *light*. Light so they don't go bump in the dark. Women who buy cosmetics aren't buying blush or eyeliner—they're buying *beauty*.

LETTERHEAD

IS TIME ON YOUR SIDE?

Dear Friend:

I hope you enjoy this month's time tip. It's about time that we started to pay more attention to those two hands on the clock and try to make the most effective and efficient use of the 86,400 seconds in each 24-hour day.

This month, I'd like to offer you some effective time-management tips that I have found to be very useful. However you try to manage time, set attainable goals and deadlines. Do any of these resonate with you?

- Don't do work that you can delegate to others.
- Make a weekly "to do" list and highlight priorities for the following week.
- Carry an idea book with you.
- Discourage random visitors.
- Group similar activities together.
- Don't procrastinate.
- Learn to say no.

Remember that people who manage time skillfully are both effective and efficient.

Sincerely,

Name

Whenever you come across people who are thinking of buying or selling a home and would appreciate the level of service I provide, please refer them to me. Thank you.

Example 5-6: Effectively used postscript

The following are some phrases that may be helpful in finding just the right words for what your customers are buying:

WHAT ARE YOUR CUSTOMERS BUYING?	DESCRIPTIVES
Authenticity	*Frequently imitated, but never duplicated.*
	<...> has withstood the test of time.
	Unadulterated.
	There's simply no substitute for the real thing!
	We're one of the originators.
	<...> is an old family recipe.
	We pioneered <...>.
	The one and only!
Beauty	*Breathtakingly beautiful.*
	Timeless beauty.
	Slim and sultry.
	Roguish good looks.
	A page out of Vogue.
	Impeccably rendered.
	Cloud-capped mountains.
	Shimmering moonlight.
	Like a field of daisies.
	A peaches 'n' cream complexion.
	Richly textured.
Color	Instead of *red,* use
	Raspberry, Claret, Poppy, Cardinal
	Instead of *orange,* use
	Sunset, Tangerine, Pumpkin, Peach
	Instead of *yellow,* use
	Flaxen, Lemonade, Sunflower, Mustard
	Instead of *green,* use
	Seafoam, Lime, Spruce, Jade
	Instead of *blue,* use
	Aquamarine, Cobalt, Wedgwood, Ultramarine
	Instead of *purple,* use
	Lavender, Plum, Boysenberry, Wisteria
	Instead of *brown,* use
	Cocoa, Taupe, Palomino, Camel
	Instead of *white,* use
	Alabaster, Pearl, Oatmeal, Bone

Instead of *black*, use
Raven, Blackberry, Jot, Onyx

Comfort	*All the comforts of home.*
	As cool as a summer breeze.
	As warm as the glow of embers.
	Just the way you like it.
	The ultimate in comfort.
	<...>, for unsurpassed warmth.
	Cool and comfy.
	Tranquil.
	For the moments in your life when you <...>.
	Bathes you in <...>.
Convenience	*Keep <...> accessible.*
	Push-button convenience.
	Portable enough to <...>.
	No more endless searching.
	The ideal traveling companion.
	Fold away when not in use.
	Direct from the manufacturer.
	Stackable! Expandable! Pliable!
	Requires little or no maintenance.
	Never needs replacing.
Ease	*No complex commands to remember.*
	So advanced, yet so simple.
	It takes no time at all.
	Maintenance-free.
	Takes the stress out of <...>.
	Automates your office.
	At a glance.
	Easy to follow and easy to use.
	Great for beginners!
	A streamlined approach.
Elegance	*Aristocratic.*
	Continental.
	Stunning.
	Like a penthouse high above the city.
	Fifth Avenue.
	High style.
	With grace and splendor.
	Stately.
	Regal.
	Classically proportioned.

Experience	*America's leading <…>.*
	We beat the competition hands down.
	Leaders in the industry.
	Craftsmanship.
	There's simply no substitute for experience.
	Five-star quality.
	Our reputation for excellence.
	<…> is our strong suit.
	Expertly engineered.
	We pioneered <…>.
	Virtuoso.
Flavor	*Savory.*
	A flavorful extravaganza.
	Plump and juicy.
	Mouthwatering.
	A taste of the Orient.
	Bursting with <…>.
	Fit for a king.
	Just like mama used to make.
	Sinfully rich.
	Delicately seasoned.
Fragrance	*As fragrant as a summer garden.*
	The exquisite aroma of <…>.
	Intoxicating.
	The fragrance of springtime.
	Like a gentle sea breeze.
	The incense of burning autumn leaves.
	Heavenly scent.
	Takes you back to your childhood.
	Mysterious aromas.
Honesty	*The buck stops here.*
	We explode the myths about <…>.
	The astonishing truth.
	The unequivocal truth about <…>.
	A reputation for honesty.
	Honest-to-goodness.
	We don't pull any punches.
	Forthright.
Improvement	*A metamorphosis in the making!*
	Rejuvenated.
	Better than ever.
	<…>, based on a new, startling discovery.
	We must all change with the times.

A renaissance.
We've changed the rules.

Information	*Keeps you ahead of the pack.*
	A plethora of information.
	Keep pace with the latest developments.
	<...> takes the mystery out of <...>.
	Separate fact from fiction.
	Illuminating.
	You find all the answers in <...>.
	Get a new perspective on <...>.
Luxury	*Built by master craftsmen.*
	The Rolls Royce of <...>.
	Old Masters.
	We've spared no cost.
	Nothing is too good for our guests.
	An affordable extravagance.
	Pamper yourself.
	Becomes more precious with time.
	Museum quality.
Naturalness	*Like Grandma used to make.*
	Good for the soul.
	Honest-to-goodness <...>.
	A trackless expanse of wilderness.
	Cascading streams.
	Pristine.
	Untouched by man.
	We've been making it the same way for years.
	Homegrown.
	Unspoiled.
Money-making or money-saving opportunities	*Multiplies your investment.*
	Watch your profits soar!
	As good as gold.
	Pays off.
	Unheard-of low prices.
	Save on <...>.
	No middleman.
	Packed with value.
Peace of mind	*Lets you forget about <...>.*
	Don't lose another night's sleep.
	You're in total control.
	Your defense against <...>.
	Built-in safety.

No more guesswork.
Shelters you from <...>.
Don't be caught shorthanded.
Full protection.
You can always count on <...>.

Performance	*The proof is in the <...>.*
	Outperforms the competition.
	Say goodbye to <...>.
	An immediate and dramatic effect.
	Watch it work!
	Boosts <...>.
	Whisks away <...>.
Power	*Knocks your socks off.*
	Commanding.
	Extraordinary capabilities.
	Running on all cylinders.
	Hurricane force.
	Vitality.
	No-holds-barred.
	Turbo.
	Sweeping you along.
	Energetic.
Rarity	*Unlike any other <...>.*
	Nothing even comes close.
	There's simply nothing quite like <...>.
	Dramatically different.
	Incomparable.
	There are only a few times in your life when <...>.
	Custom designed.
	Exceptional.
	Nobody else gives you <...>.
	In a class by itself.
Romance	*Creates an aura of <...>.*
	Deserted beaches.
	Enter a timeless realm of <...>.
	As memorable as your first kiss.
	The mystery and intrigue of <...>.
	Whispered intimacies.
	Exchanged glances.
	A storybook world.
	Captivating.
Self-improvement	*Tap the resources of <...>.*

	Stretch your mind.
	You will learn by doing.
	Broaden your experiences.
	Pick up a vital new skill.
	Live life more confidently.
	Self-mastery.
Sex appeal	*Silky smooth.*
	Long, tumbling tresses.
	A garden of earthly delights.
	Sizzling.
	A moonlit frolic.
	Softly feminine.
	Naughty!
	Shamelessly <…>.
	Rapturous.
Size	*A treasure trove of <…>.*
	Of epic proportions.
	A sweeping variety of <…>.
	Voluminous.
	Gargantuan.
	Olympian.
	A multitude of <…>.
	Space aplenty.
	Pocket-sized <…>.
	A little giant.
	Cozy.
	Remarkably compact.
Status	*A symbol of <…>.*
	Underscore your authority.
	The Harvard of <…>.
	You join a distinguished <…>.
	Among the most select <…>.
	Connects you with <…>.
	Recognized by cultured people everywhere.
	Highest ranking.
	VIP treatment.
	A discerning few.

▶ Be wary of overused words and expressions that have lost their meaning. For example, years ago every user manual was *user-friendly*. Today, every company is a *solutions provider* and offers something that's *unique*. ◀

Sales Letter Taboos

The preceding section talks about things that add pizzazz to your sales letters. Following are some taboos that make sales letters pizzazz-less:

- **Being too chummy with the reader.** He'll get irritated and think you're insincere. You must always maintain a professional tone.

- **Being too cutesy.** It's inappropriate in most industries to be anything but professional. Cutesy demeans both you and your message.

- **Making idle statements.** Comments such as "You'll be sorry if you miss this opportunity" don't tell the reader anything.

- **Making too many points in one letter.** Concentrate on your strongest selling point—the key feature. You want to appeal to the reader's emotions.

- **Badmouthing the competition or making unwarranted claims.** Let your product or service sell itself. If you have to put down the competition, "The man protest-eth too much."

- **Making exaggerated claims.** Claims using words such as "revolutionary," "incredible," or "astounding" sound bogus.

Miscellaneous Sales Letters

Following are a variety of sales letters you can use verbatim or tweak for your needs. (Of course, that holds true for all the letters in this book.)

Welcoming a New Family to the Community

One way to drum up continued business is to send a welcome letter to newcomers to your area, as you see in Example 5-7.

- Explain who you are and the service you provide.

- If appropriate, offer an incentive such as a gift certificate.

Following Up on a Sales Call

Whenever you make a sales call, always send a thank-you note, such as the one you see in Example 5-8. As you learned at your mother's knee, *please* and *thank you* go a long way.

February 13, 20—

Mr. and Mrs. Joe Newcomer
123 Maple Lane
Eadytown, SC 29468

Dear Mr. and Mrs. Newcomer:

Subject: Congratulations on the purchase of your new home

We congratulate you on the purchase of your new home and welcome you to the Eadytown community. We hope you'll spend many wonderful years here.

The Eadytown Restaurant has been serving patrons in the community at its downtown Main Street location for more than 50 years. We vary our menu each month, and patrons always enjoy a wide selection, large portions, high quality, and friendly service.

Stop by the Eadytown Restaurant and apply this gift certificate to your first meal. Please ask for Jim, so I can welcome you personally.

Sincerely,

Jim Collins

Enclosure

Example 5-7: Welcoming a new family to the area

September 12, 20—

Mr. Tom Collins, President
Collins & Collins, Inc.
345 Speen Street
Narragansett, RI 02882

Dear Mr. Collins:

It was a pleasure meeting with you this morning. I'm delighted that you gave me the opportunity to offer you and your family the protection you need.

Next step
I'll call you early next week to see if you have any questions and thank you for your confidence in me.

Sincerely,

Ray Burrows

Example 5-8: Following up on a sales call

- Send the note as soon after the sales call as possible.

- Thank the person for taking the time to meet with you.

- Establish a time for the next contact.

Soliciting Business from a Former Customer

Repeat business is the backbone of a company. If you haven't gotten business from a customer in a while, make contact. See Example 5-9.

- Highlight improvements (if any) since the customer last did business with you.

- Find out why they went elsewhere.

- Let them know you want them to return.

Generating Seasonal Business

Seasonal businesses have special challenges because they appear on people's radar screens on an occasional basis. As you learned in chapter 3, timing is key. Example 5-10 advertises a spring spruce-up, and Example 5-11 offers a discount on a seasonal rate.

- Explain your services and typical pricing, if appropriate.

- Call for action.

- Distribute widely to a targeted audience.

Asking Colleagues for Help

When you launch a new business, colleagues can be a wonderful source of referrals. Example 5-12 is an appeal to colleagues to help spread the word about a new business.

Spreading the Word for a New Business

Example 5-13 promotes a food drive to announce the opening of a chiropractic office, and Example 5-14 announces the opening of a health and healing center.

Collaborating as Service Providers

When I started to partner with a marketing strategist, we initiated a joint direct mail campaign. Because we're in marketing, we needed to be creative. We came

LETTERHEAD

June 12, 20—

Ms. Pat Long
545 Castle Hill
White Castle, PA 15478

Dear Ms. Long:

Subject: How can we get you to return?

We are disappointed to see that you didn't renew your contract for oil delivery this year. If you had a problem, please give us a chance to remedy it.

[ ] Were you dissatisfied with our service?
[ ] Did you have a problem with our drivers?
[ ] Were you dissatisfied with payment terms?
[ ] Other _____

What will it take to get your business back?
I'll call you next week to answer any questions you may have.

Sincerely,

Morgan Short

P.S. Please note that we have expanded our hours of service and are now on call 24 hours a day.

Example 5-9: Soliciting business from a former customer

LETTERHEAD

March 22, 20—

Mr. and Mrs. Robin Spring
One Maple Drive
Zutphen, MI 49426

Dear Mr. and Mrs. Spring:

Subject: Spring Spruce-up Time

This winter will go down in the record books as one of the worst ever. Lots of wind, subzero temperatures, and the deepest snowfall ever recorded in this region. With spring just around the corner, the temperatures will rise and the snow will disappear.

- Does your driveway have cracks or need sealing?
- Does your lawn need to be raked, seeded, or fertilized?
- Can your house use a fresh coat of paint?
- Did ice dams cause roof damage?

For quick and reliable service, please call Jim or Pete at <phone number>. One of us will be delighted to come by, assess your needs, and give you a price you can't afford to pass up. We are fully insured and have a long list of satisfied customers.

Sincerely,

GRADY LANDSCAPING SERVICES

James Grady, Owner

Example 5-10: Spring cleanup

LETTERHEAD

April 2, 20—

Mr. Pat Yachtsman
34 Catalina Drive
Miami Beach, FL 33139

Dear Mr. Yachtsman:

<u>Subject: Your genoa</u>

We looked at the genoa you left with us last Saturday and can make the repair for $100. You can have it within one week.

The sail is badly worn
We notice that the sail is badly worn. There are black marks along the luff tape that are caused by pollution and dirt that's wicking to the luff tape at the extrusion joints. This is usually a sign that the extrusion joints are loose.

It may be time to consider a new sail
Your current genoa is 150%, and you may want to consider one that's 135%. We've listed our prices below with a special fall discount. Yes, it's slightly smaller, but the difference in speed is very slight. Here are the advantages of a 135% genoa:

- Better visibility behind the leech
- Easier to sheet in because of its smaller area

150% Genoa, 300 sq. ft., 6.5 oz. Dacron	Regular price..................$1995
	Fall discount price............$1755
135% Genoa, 270 sq. ft., 6.5 oz. Dacron	Regular price.................. $1875
	Fall discount price……........ $1650

Next step
Please feel free to give us a call at 800-123-3334 if you have any questions. If we don't hear from you, we'll have your genoa ready on <date>.

Sincerely,

Grace Docker
Manager

Example 5-11: Opportunity to make a "sail"

Dear Friend and Colleague,

FLATLANDS

I'm asking for your help as my new business venture moves into its next phase. Along with several other principals who have successful track records in launching businesses, we have started Flatland Systems, Inc.

About the Company

Flatland Systems (Flatlands) is developing an Internet-based software service that will allow companies to integrate and share information with their business partners without installing additional software systems, hardware, or integration platforms. Flatland Systems provides a significant reduction in complexity, effort, and cost (more than 80% less than current solutions) for businesses, making information sharing affordable to small- to mid-sized companies.

> *You can cut 100,000 medical errors and save lives by sharing data. That's huge. Without this information, pharmacists cannot be sure whether they are filling prescriptions that could be dangerous if used in combination with other drugs.*
> —John Bentivoglio, Former Chief Privacy Officer at the Department of Justice

About the Principals

The team consists of several partners with a wealth of successful entrepreneurial experience—including executive operations, legal and intellectual property management, software product development, enterprise-level deployments to Fortune 500 companies, and much more. We have been successful individually and together in past start-up environments. Together we form a team that will make its mark on the industry.

How You Can Help

Please share this letter and attached invitation with anyone in the health care, manufacturing, pharmaceutical, law enforcement, homeland defense, financial, or insurance arenas that may be willing to:
- Talk with me to review the Flatlands service and the potential benefits that information sharing and integration may provide to his/her industry,
- Consider using this technology as a test site to derive its benefits,
- Entertain the idea of becoming a development partner to help finance this exciting venture, or
- Pass this on to someone else who may know of such people.

Please contact me if you know of someone to whom this may be helpful—and thank you so much for your help.

Sincerely,

David Femia, President

Flatland Systems, Inc. • 172 Wintergreen Drive, Groton, MA 01450 • 978-448-0354

Example 5-12: Asking colleagues to spread the word

You're Invited
to a Food Drive

To Celebrate the Grand Opening of
ESSENTIAL FAMILY CHIROPRACTIC
July 17, 20—

Dr. Eric Lindsell is eager to meet and welcome you to Columbia's premier center for health care. Essential Family Chiropractic is located in Owen Brown, across from Lake Elkhorn. We are dedicated to providing you and your family EXTRA-ordinary care with affordable fees.

Help Us Help Others

On Saturday, July 17, 20— Dr. Lindsell will be hosting a food drive to benefit FISH of Howard County. FISH is a nonprofit organization helping folks in Howard County with food and other special needs. We will accept your nonperishable food items between the hours of 11:00 A.M. and 3:00 P.M.

What's In It For You?

In exchange for your kind donation, you will receive a complimentary computerized spinal analysis designed to detect any underlying spinal condition that can interfere with your health and vitality.

If you need directions or have any questions, call Essential Family Chiropractic at (410) 312-7790.

"Optimal Health Through Chiropractic"

Example 5-13: Sponsoring a food drive to announce a business opening

Choices
Wellness Community Center, Inc.

Life is all about choices

Dear Friend,   May 15, 20—

Life is all about choices. We made the choice to bring a center to the greater-Marlborough community that advances a *wholistic* approach to health and healing. We opened our doors in February 20— and would like to share with you some of the exciting community projects Choices sponsors:

Earth Day Events
Choices sponsors events in honor of Earth Day to help increase the awareness of the interrelationship between a healthy natural environment and healthy people. Earth Day events involve organizing a community cleanup campaign, a nature walk, an open house with demonstrations and educational material, and a coffee-house with live nature-themed music.

MetroWest Network for Integrative Health
This initiative seeks to advance the best of traditional and alternative practices within a wholistic paradigm. It brings together practitioners and friends to enhance understanding, communication, and collaboration to promote health and well-being.

Day-to-Day Choices
Choices sponsors support groups for bereavement and health-related issues, educational workshops, and a variety of individual health care services that include Acupuncture, Addiction Counseling & Psychotherapy, Alcarrest™, Chiropractic, Coaching, Holistic Counseling, Osteopathic Manipulative Treatment, Personal Training, Polarity, Reflexology, Reiki, Rolfing/Structural Integration, and Spiritual Counseling. To increase access to these services, discounts and waivers are available for seniors and persons with low income. There is also a wellness lending library with books, tapes, and videos available to the community.

Please help us to continue to advance a wholistic approach to health & healing
Choices is a nonprofit organization, and we need your help to continue offering healthy choices, such as the ones mentioned above and more, to individuals and the larger community. We invite you to put your tax-deductible gift in the mail today and be part of the friends who are dedicated to advancing a wholistic approach to health, healing, and living. Your gift will help further the many health-promoting efforts in our community. Thank you for your friendship and your generosity.

To your health,

Beverly Wedda, MD   Denise Frizell, MPA
Cofounder & Director of Integrative   Cofounder & Executive
& Complementary Health Services   Director

340 Maple Street, Suite 300
Marlboro, MA 01752
774-463-0001
www.choiceswellness.org

Example 5-14: Announcing a new health and healing center

up with a cooking theme. Examples 5-15a and 5-15b are the front and back of a postcard mailer.

Announcing a New Principal or Employee

Use every opportunity you can to get your name in front of your colleagues. Example 5-16 shows a postcard sent to announce a new principal in an accounting firm. (Check out chapter 12 to learn how to supplement such an announcement with a press release.)

Announcing a New Location

When you move or expand, it's another opportunity to get your name in front of your customers. Example 5-17 announces a move.

Sources for Mailing Lists

Your list may be compiled from existing clients and/or customers, permission-based rental lists, or list brokers. You can also get lists from the following:

- City and state directories and licensing bureaus
- Clubs and professional organizations
- Commercial agencies that specialize in selling mailing lists
- Conventions and conferences
- Educational and mercantile directories
- Newspapers (columns or special articles)
- *Standard and Poor's Register of Corporations*
- *Thomas Register of American Manufacturers*
- Trade directories or publications.

Tricks of Trade Shows

Trade shows and conferences are opportunities to increase your contact base, get information on the latest products and services, check out the competition, and just have fun. After all, where else would you find so many people from a single industry assembled under one roof?

Example 5-15a: Front side of marketing postcard

Marketing Ingredients:
1. Take two seasoned marketing professionals
2. Add a ripe understanding of marketing strategies, tactics, and communications
3. Mix with your corporate objectives
4. Blend in a huge helping of innovation and originality (in stock)
5. Let rise and grow until fully successful

Marketing Chefs:

Sheryl Lindsell-Roberts is an award-winning business writer and the author of 18 books. She's written brochures, proposals, and text for websites that have helped clients to close multi-million dollar contracts.
www.sherylwrites.com
508-229-8209

Brigitte Casemyr is a marketing strategist. She has helped organizations grow by initiating influential marketing strategies on national and global scales since the early 80's, through the ups and downs of the economy.
www.turfbuildermarketing.com
508-366-9212

Serve immediately on a regional, national, or global scale.
Bon Appetit!

Example 5-15b: Back side of marketing postcard

ADELMAN KATZ & MOND LLP

Takes Pleasure in Announcing

that

WARREN M. BERGSTEIN, CPA

Has Become a

Principal in the Firm

as of July 17, 2003

ADELMAN KATZ & MOND LLP (AKM), founded in 1962, is a full service accounting, financial planning and business management firm, which provides accounting, auditing, tax, personal financial planning, computer consulting, and management advisory services to businesses and individuals. We are large enough to solve the most complex business and personal financial problems, yet small enough to provide the close personal attention our clients need and deserve.

ADELMAN KATZ & MOND LLP

CERTIFIED PUBLIC ACCOUNTANTS

230 WEST 41ST STREET
15TH FLOOR
NEW YORK NY 10036•7207

www.akmcpa.com

Example 5-16: Card announcing a new principal

LETTERHEAD

Dear Valued Patron:

We want to thank you for your continued support and confidence in us. Our No. 1 priority is to provide you with impeccable service, and we always do our best to make working with us a pleasurable and rewarding experience.

The Same Service You Depend on Has a New Location
In an effort to serve you even better, we've expanded our services and have moved into larger quarters. As you can see by our new letterhead, we're now located at 300 Main Street, only one block from where we were before. Here's what else is new at Montana Café & Catering:

- New equipment.
- New ideas to assist you in every aspect of your event planning.
- New policy to have all of our drivers carry cell phones so they can cater to your needs more efficiently.

As Much as Things Change, They Stay the Same
Montana Café & Catering continues to offer quality you can count on for all your corporate meetings, cocktail receptions, outdoor events, and formal dinners. That's why the *Butte Business Journal* rated us in the top 15 catering companies in the state.

- You continue to see the friendly faces and enjoy the high-quality, flexible service you've come to appreciate.
- You continue to get same-day service.
- When you call during normal business hours, someone answers the phone. Our voice mail operates after hours.

Once again, thank you for your continued confidence in us. We look forward to partnering with you for all your catering needs.

Bon appétit,

Gleason Biggers
President

Example 5-17: Letter to customers announcing new location

Marketing the Trade Show

Several weeks before the show, send letters out to your current clients, potential clients, and anyone who may be interested. Check out Example 5-18. Here's what to include in the letter:

- Stress the products you'll have on display.
- Mention where to find your booth. (Include a site map if you have one.)
- Mention the location of vendors with whom you have a relationship.

Following Up

You must follow up on all the hot leads. At trade shows, companies generally have depositories where people can leave business cards. The savvy company sends letters to everyone who leaves a card and follows up with a phone call or e-mail. Example 5-19 shows a follow-up letter.

> ▶ Sales don't stop with the sale. Companies spend enormous amounts of money trying to woo new customers, yet they often lose sight of continuing to delight existing customers. Check out chapter 7 for creative ways to foster customer relations. ◀

October 12, 20—

Mr. Samuel Walker
Walker & Sons
100 Main Street
Suite 303
Suffern, NY 10901

Dear Sam,

Subject: Be our guest at the East Coast BioTech Convention

Please be our guest at the East Coast BioTech Convention. I've enclosed two complimentary passes.

> **Date:** October 23 and 24, 20—
> **Place:** Holiday Inn
> **Hours:** 9 a.m. to 5 p.m.

Our product specialists will be on hand to answer any of your questions at booth number 234 on the second floor. While you're at the show, be sure to stop by the booths of vendors with whom we do business:

> ABC Company at Booth 267
> LMN Company at Booth 268
> XYZ Company at Booth 251

We look forward to seeing you there.

Regards,

Beth Hogan
Vice President, Sales

Example 5-18: Trade show announcement and invitation

LETTERHEAD

October 25, 20—

Mr. Sander Client
Sander & Sander, Inc.
345 North Hampton Road
Spring Valley, NY 10977

Dear Mr. Client:

Thank you for visiting our booth at the recent East Coast BioTech Convention in Suffern. We hope you enjoyed it as much as we did. Many who visited our booth commented on the latest benefits of <product or service>.

* <benefit>
* <benefit>
* <benefit>
* <benefit>

Next step
I've enclosed a brochure that describes <product or service> in greater detail. If you're interested in learning more about <product or service>, please call us toll-free at <number> and ask for <name>. Also, please check out our website at **www.company.com**.

Sincerely,

<name>
<title>

Example 5-19: Follow-up to trade show

The only place where "success" comes before "work" is in the dictionary.

—VIDAL SASSOON

CHAPTER 6

Successful Job Search and Employment Issues

Employment letters run the gamut—from cover letters that accompany resumes to announcements of leaving a job for a new opportunity. If your dream job appeared in the classified ads or on the Internet tomorrow, would you be ready? Perhaps the following isn't your dream job, but sooner or later you'll see one that is. Make sure you're the "mane" candidate.

WANTED: LION TAMER

No experience needed. Must be able to use a whip and run fast, and must love cats. Great medical coverage, but no death benefits. (The premiums would kill *us*.)

If interested, call Leo Lyons at 800-555-LION.

Gone are the days of the cradle-to-grave mentality where a worker stayed with a company

---

WHAT'S IN THIS CHAPTER

- *Starting your job search*
- *Writing a cover letter and resume*
- *Composing a broadcast letter*
- *Crafting a networking letter*
- *Sending a thank-you letter*
- *Writing a letter of resignation*
- *Acknowledging receipt of a resume*
- *Denying a request for an interview*
- *Extending a formal job offer*
- *Sending a letter of recommendation*
- *Introducing a new hire*

101

for a lifetime. That was the generation of our parents or grandparents, when a postage stamp cost four cents and the Dow Jones was looking good at 700. Statistics show that Americans today typically have two or three careers within a lifetime and change jobs periodically. Therefore, you should have an assortment of cover letters and resumes as part of your repertoire. This chapter contains employment letters from both the job seeker and the employer.

Starting Your Job Search

Before you can write a dynamic cover letter or resume, you must gather the raw material that will interest a potential employer. Here's some information to include at the gathering phase of your job search:

- **Key employable skills**
  - Work-content skills you used to perform certain aspects of a specific job
  - Functional skills you can transfer from one position to another
- **Job experience for each company where you were employed**
  - Title and responsibilities
  - Major accomplishments
  - Benefits to each employer with as many dollar amounts and percentages as can be included, to add sizzle to your qualifications
- **Education**
  - Degrees and certifications
  - Special honors
  - Relevant courses, if you're a recent graduate
- **Foreign languages that will benefit you in the position**
- **Volunteer work, if you're a recent graduate**
  - Organizations
  - Responsibilities
  - Skills acquired
  - Quotable remarks

Writing a Cover Letter and Resume

A cover letter (also known as an application letter) should be part of your arsenal because you must fire one off with each resume—paper or electronic. Although you can reuse a lot of the same wording from one letter to another, customizing the letter gives you a much better chance of getting a positive response.

Your well-written cover letter can launch an interview and determine the course of your career. It takes a lot of thought and planning to write a dynamite cover letter, but the time you invest is well worth the effort. Following are some helpful hints for writing a cover letter:

- **Direct your letter to an individual by name and title whenever possible.** There are many resources to help you find this information. The Internet or the company's receptionist are good places to start.

- **Keep the letter short.** Generally, three paragraphs is ideal.

- **Select the highlights and qualifications that best "sell you."** Don't reiterate all the information in your resume.

- **Make the letter results oriented.**

- **Emphasize the contribution you can make to the company.**

- **Mention that your resume is enclosed or attached.**

Some advisers suggest that your letter gets more attention if you mail it the week after a listing appears. In that way you avoid the initial flood of replies. In a thin job market, however, you may consider responding quickly.

Writing an Opening Paragraph

Create an interesting opening paragraph that identifies how you found out about the job listing or company. This paragraph must get the reader's attention, because you have a very short time in which to make an initial impression.

- When you answer an ad that uses key words such as *reliable, creative, professional,* and the like, describe yourself in those exact terms somewhere in the letter.

- When you're not answering an ad, mention an experience or colleague you may have in common with the intended reader.

Newspaper, magazine, or Internet advertisement

Your advertisement for a <position > posted in <publication> (or on <website>) is of great interest to me. I have a <degree> from <college or university> and would like to continue my career in the <field>.

Sparked by your need for a <position> with <special experience>, as appeared in <publication> (or on <website>) on <date>, I feel confident I can save you the stress of having to interview a lot of candidates.

My broad experiences in <field> are an excellent match for the needs you describe in <publication> (or on <website>) on <date>.

<Aspect of profession, such as pediatric nursing> is my first love. That's why I was delighted when <person> informed me that you'll soon be needing a <aspect of profession>. Please consider this my letter of application.

Referral

<Name>, of your <department>, brought to my attention your need for a top-quality <position you want to fill>. She is confident that my background and experience will enable me to meet all your requirements.

After speaking with <name> of your <department>, I'm excited to learn that there's a strong match between your needs and my skills.

Direct solicitation

During my visit to <company> last fall, I had the pleasure of hearing you speak on <topic>.

I'm a recent graduate of <college or university> and am very interested in starting my career with <company>.

<Name> of <company> suggested that I contact you regarding changes in your organization. She indicated that you're expanding and may be in need of a <profession>.

A very wise man once said, "Never miss an opportunity to solve a problem." My father was that wise man, and that's what prompted me to become a world-class problem solver, which has helped me to be a successful <profession>.

Writing a Convincing Middle Paragraph

Elaborate on your qualifications and explain how they can serve the company. Try to point out how you can do a better job for the company because of lessons you learned at previous jobs or in school (if you're a recent graduate).

My background includes 16 years of experience in manufacturing and engineering. I am experienced in the construction of production machinery and plant engineering requirements. Former supervisors have praised me for my ability to direct and motivate others and meet very tight deadlines.

For five years I was the manager of marketing communications at Sterling Corporation. I managed a $3.6 million budget, against which I saved $760,000 in one year. My responsibilities included a broad range of assignments for international audiences, including sales and customer training, *newsletters, product brochures, advertising, news releases, user documentation, and video productions.*

My employment with A & B Life Insurance Company and Delta Mutual Insurance Company taught me a great deal about human relations and the finer techniques of selling. As a result of this experience, I am convinced that I can build sales and goodwill for <their company name>.

Writing a Closing Paragraph

Request an interview, and include a telephone number where you can be reached. It's not necessary to repeat your phone number if it appears on your letterhead. (More about letterhead later in this chapter.)

I would welcome the opportunity to meet with you so that you can evaluate the creative contributions I can make to <company name>. You can reach me at <phone number> any afternoon after two o'clock.

Enclosed is a copy of my resume. As you will see, my background closely matches your job description. Please call me at <phone number> so we can arrange for a personal interview.

I'm willing to travel and would be more than willing to relocate. Please call me at the number above so that we can discuss how my qualifications can be of benefit to <company name>.

Once we've established a mutual interest, I would be delighted to meet with you personally.

My experience in <field> is at your disposal. I'm confident that when we meet to discuss my qualifications and your company's goals, we will find many areas of commonality.

I'll call you next week to set up a time that we can discuss these opportunities further.

▶ Let your personality shine, and write a letter in your own style. Don't use someone else's cover letter, no matter how wonderful and successful it may have been. Wouldn't an employer be disappointed to meet you and find out that you're an entirely different person from the one who wrote the letter? ◀

Dealing with Salary Requirements

Try to avoid addressing salary requirements in your cover letter; this weakens your bargaining power. If you mention too low a salary, you devalue your abilities. If you mention too high a salary, you may appear too expensive for the company.

Unless you're responding to an ad that requires you to name your salary needs, save that discussion for the interview. If you are required to give a salary, how blunt should you be? Ignore it completely, mention the range, give your current salary, or state that you expect a salary commensurate with your experience? The experts vary in their opinions, so go with the option that makes you most comfortable (or least uncomfortable). Here are some lines for dodging the issue of salary:

> *If your compensation package is based on performance, I'm sure that we'll reach a salary agreement once you see the contribution I will make.*
>
> *Assuming that the position offers market-value compensation, I'm sure we'll be able to agree on a figure.*
>
> *I'd be happy to discuss my salary requirements after you've had a chance to explore my background.*
>
> *My total compensation package has ranged between <$> and <$>.*
>
> *Once we've had a chance to discuss the contribution I will make to the position, I'm sure we'll be able to agree on appropriate compensation.*

Including Your Resume

Your resume forms the image you present before the potential employer has met you. The resume by itself won't get you a job; it's a door opener to get you an interview.

Include

- Professional highlights
- Business experience
- Educational background
- Community involvement
- Foreign language(s) relevant to the position
- Dollars or percentages that quantify your contribution

Omit

- Objective (Save that for the cover letter. Start with professional highlights instead.)
- "References will be furnished on request." (No one will check your references until after they have met you. Bring a list of references to the interview.)
- Personal information such as "I'm reliable" and "I have a good personality" (Who would say they're unreliable or have a bad personality?)

Using Letterhead and Writing Resumes

Create letterhead on your cover letter that matches the heading on your resume. This gives a very professional look to your package.

- Example 6-1a shows a cover letter from a highly experienced professional that uses bullets to highlight three key accomplishments. This letter is in response to a job posting on the company's website. Example 6-1b is the accompanying three-page resume. There's no rule on resume length, provided you capture the reader's attention on the first page and all the ensuing pages add value.

- Example 6-2a shows a cover letter from a business systems analyst making reference to a personal contact. Example 6-2b is the accompanying two-page resume.

- Example 6-3a is a cover letter from a recent college graduate in response to a newspaper job listing. Example 6-3b is the accompanying one-page resume.

Using Keywords

When you write your resume or broadcast letter (more on broadcast letters later in this chapter), be sure to pepper it with words such as the ones below that bring to mind a range of transferable skills.

accelerated	converted	installed	sold
achieved	created	instructed	solved
administered	defined	launched	spearheaded
attained	demonstrated	managed	specialized
augmented	empowered	mentored	strengthened
balanced	enlarged	negotiated	structured
budgeted	generated	organized	supervised
built	headed	reduced	systematized
chaired	implemented	resolved	taught
coached	increased	saved	updated

Submitting Your Resume via E-mail

In this electronic age, more and more jobs are sought online. With companies receiving thousands of applications for each job, they often scan online resumes to narrow down the list of appropriate candidates. Some programs scan the full resume; others, only the first 100 words. It's for that reason that you should include near the top of your resume a list of keywords. These are the words that relate to

(continued on page 117)

Jon Allen
117 Higgens Street, Marlborough, MA 01752

jonallen@att.net
(508) 229-5556

August 20, 20—

Mr. Casper Michaels, President
Shrewsbury MicroSensors Company
333 Caldon Street
North Grafton, MA 01536

Dear Mr. Michaels:

Subject: Position of Applications Manager

The core of my vast experience in managing semiconductor process engineering is directly applicable to the position of Applications Manager posted on your website. Following are highlights of my background that indicate how I could contribute to the success of Shrewsbury MicroSensors Company. For more details, I have enclosed my resume.

- At Applesmith MicroSystems, I managed the process engineering group of 42 people in support of the company's volume production line.
- At Well's Solid State Electronics Division, I managed sustaining and development groups for thin films, etching, and sensor processing, including magnetic sensors and thin-film resistors.
- As director of applications for Orangeburg Research Corporation, I developed a unique sputtering planarization process on their Eclipse system, as well as reactive sputtering for TiN barriers.

This combination would be uniquely valuable to SMC. There's more to my experience and leadership skills than one sees in my resume. Therefore, I will call you next week so we can arrange for a personal meeting.

Sincerely,

Jon Allen

Enclosure

Example 6-1b: Resume that accompanied the letter in 6-1a

Jon Allen

117 Higgens Street, Marlborough, MA 01752

jonallen@att.net
(508) 229-5556

Applications Manager

Career Summary

Extensive hands-on experience in engineering and management responsibilities for Applications Development for semiconductor manufacturing capital equipment. Creative problem solving for customer applications and beta site development. Product characterizations to enhance marketing campaigns.

- Developed and characterized a wide range of semiconductor manufacturing processes including multilayer metallization, wafer bumping for flip chip and TAB assembly, and thin film resistors.
- Partnered with marketing by publishing application notes, delivering technical presentations, and supplying technical support at trade shows for leading semiconductor equipment vendors.
- Applied semiconductor device physics to the solution of wafer-fabrication process problems.

Experience

COOKLINE TECHNOLOGIES, INC., Foxboro, MA
Project Manager responsible for process and applications development for innovative wafer bumping technologies (1997–2001)

- Directed the applications efforts for Metal Jet system and Stencil Printer for solder bump depositions on semiconductor wafers.
- Guided marketing teams with technical reports, trade show participation, customer samples, and characterizations.
- Organized a cross-sector development program for improvements in solder paste formulation, stencil manufacture, and printer machine design to extend printing into 250-micron pitch technology.

APPLESMITH MICROSYSTEMS, Worcester, MA
Process Engineering Manager for bipolar and BIMOS semiconductor wafer production (1992–97)

- Managed all sustaining process engineering support, with 4 directly reporting section heads and 45 engineers and technicians.
- Resolved CMOS threshold problems with improved interpretation of CV tests.

Example 6-1b: Resume that accompanied the letter in 6-1a

APPLESMITH MICROSYSTEMS, Worcester, MA (continued)

- Implemented minority carrier lifetime testing for improved PNP beta control.
- Directed the process engineering participation on cross-functional teams achieving ISO 9000 and QS 9000 certifications for the wafer fab.
- Devised and implemented a Quick Response Team approach to production crises for yield enhancement.
- Developed computerized system for nonconforming material disposition and problem solving.

WESTON CORPORATION, SEMICONDUCTOR DIVISION, Beverly, MA
Manager of Sputter Process Development and Applications (1990–91)

- Managed engineering team for customer demonstrations of advanced sputtering system.
- Implemented laboratory techniques for structural analysis and prepared application notes.

ORANGEBURG RESEARCH CORPORATION, Orangeburg, NY
Director of Applications (1986–90)

- Managed applications engineers for bringing advanced sputter systems and magnetron ion etcher to market.
- Authored the key process patent to penetrate multilevel metal technologies with planarized aluminum depositions.
- Prepared and delivered technical presentations for potential customers in support of marketing efforts.
- Drove key software and hardware improvements for the Eclipse sputter system.
- Developed reactive sputtering for titanium nitride depositions.
- Expanded the applications laboratory to a staff of 18 with a satellite lab in Japan.

WELLS SOLID STATE ELECTRONICS DIVISION, Plymouth, MN
Thin Film Process Engineering Manager (1976–86)

- Managed the sustaining engineering and development for deposition and etching processes for metal, polysilicon, oxide and nitride for near- and submicron bipolar and CMOS processes.
- Directed the development of thin film processes for solid state sensor application and integration with analog technologies.

Example 6-1b (continued)

WELLS SOLID STATE ELECTRONICS DIVISION, Plymouth, MN (continued)

- Resolved contact resistance stability problems with the implementation of a barrier metallization technology.
- Managed a three-year program to develop an advanced three-level metallization process for high-speed bipolar technologies.

Education

M.S., Materials Science & Engineering, University of California, Berkeley, CA
B.S., Metallurgical Engineering, California State Polytechnic University, San Luis Obispo, CA

Professional Associations

Electrochemical Society, American Vacuum Society (AVS), American Society for Metals, American Association for the Advancement of Science, Materials Research Society.

Selected Patent Awards

"Planarization Method" (U.S. Patent No. 4,994,162)
"Acoustic Microphone" (U.S. Patent No. 4,495,385)
"Method of Forming a Dielectric Layer Comprising a Gettering Material"
    (U.S. Patent No. 4,515,668)
"Integrated Circuit Bimetal Layer" (U.S. Patent No. 4,566,026)
"Dielectric Barrier Material" (U.S. Patent No. 4,713,682)

Selected Publications

"Stencil Printing Holds High Promise for Wafer Bumping," presented at IMAPS conference, Boston, September 2000.
"Test Chip for the Evaluation of Surface Diffusion Phenomena in Sputtered Aluminum Planarization Processes," presented at International Conference on Microelectronics Test Structures in Kyoto, Japan, March 1991.
"Step Coverage Enhancement by the Multi-Step Deposition Process," Application Note, January 1991.
"Cross Sectioning Technique for Metallization Step Coverage Analysis," Application Note, June 1990.

Example 6-1b (continued)

Jason Randall
10 James Road, Ipswich, MA 01938
978-356-2231

September 12, 20—

Mr. James Coogan
Human Resources Director
AL & M Insurance
334 Topsfield Road
Sterling, MA 01564

Dear Mr. Coogan:

Subject: Position of Business Systems Analyst

Jon Roberts, your IT manager, mentioned that you have an immediate opening for a business systems analyst. Jon and I worked together at Blue Cross and Blue Shield of Massachusetts. He can attest to my qualifications and strong work ethic.

I am experienced in systems development, implementation and production support and have extensive experience with writing conversion specifications and with developing and executing user test plans and data quality analysis. I am also skilled in Oracle SQL, TOAD, TOra, Crystal Reports, COGNOS, and MedStat. For more details please see the enclosed resume.

Next step
I will call you next week to set up a mutually convenient time for us to meet. Thank you.

Sincerely,

Jason Randall

Enclosure

Example 6-2a: Cover letter mentioning referral source

Jason Randall
10 James Road, Ipswich, MA 01938
978-356-2231

Summary: Business Systems Analyst experienced in systems development, implementation, and production support. Extensive experience with writing conversion specifications, developing and executing user test plans, and data quality analysis.

Technical Summary: Oracle SQL, TOAD, TOra, Crystal Reports, COGNOS, MedStat

Accomplishments

- Represented actuarial division on corporate-wide project implementation teams. Major projects included implementation of two new medical claims processing systems within one year, implementation of new reimbursement methodology (DRG), implementation of third-party medical claims reporting application (MedStat), definition of corporate data warehouse requirements.
- Discovered design issue that stopped implementation of third-party software release. Prevented erroneous data evaluation and reporting used for provider reimbursement, account reporting, and product evaluation. Also resulted in a financial settlement with the software vendor.

Professional Experience

ABC SALES AND SERVICE CORPORATION   2000–03
Product Specialist/Account Manager

- Developed project plans, coordinated engineering and quality assurance resources, and developed release schedule for data integration application. Successful releases of application provided a tool used for billable process customization, resulting in increased customer satisfaction.
- Supported high-profile customers through implementation and on-going production use of supply chain software. Customers included Sears, Sears Canada, Staples, Payless Shoes, and others.

BLUE CROSS AND BLUE SHIELD OF MASSACHUSETTS   1980-2000
Business Systems Analyst IV/Actuarial Systems

- Represented Actuarial/Underwriting on various corporate-wide project teams, ensuring data accuracy to support account rating and regulatory reporting.
- Developed monthly testing of Non-Credible Group Rating system, ensuring accurate processing of annual billing of over 5000 non-credible groups.

Example 6-2b: Resume that accompanied the letter in 6-2a

- Provided direct user support via administration of system security, development of system documentation, and data consultation.
- Supported management special projects via ad hoc reporting using SQL and in-house reporting applications.

Business Systems Analyst III/MedStat Medical Reporting System

- Represented Actuarial/Underwriting on various corporate-wide project teams, ensuring data accuracy to support account reporting, product analysis, provider performance analysis, and reimbursement. Communicated impact of source system changes to user community and division management.
- Defined conversion specifications, developed and implemented test plans in support of a DB2 database and front-end reporting application. Acted as liaison between user community and development team to ensure user information needs were met.
- Provided support to user production and ad hoc reporting. Provided support to management special projects via ad hoc reporting using SQL and in-house reporting applications.

Analyst III/Actuarial and Statistical Systems

- Represented Actuarial/Underwriting on various corporate-wide project teams, ensuring data accuracy to support account rating, reporting, and billing; regulatory reporting; and product performance analysis.
- Defined conversion specifications, developed and implemented test plans in support of corporate statistical files.
- Provided consultation services to users throughout the company concerning data quality, availability, and use.

Education

Brandeis University, Waltham, MA
Bachelor's Degree in American Studies, with a minor in Education

Example 6-2b (continued)

Masha Lawrence
14 Lorenz Lane   Spring Valley, New York 10977   (914) 362-1994

March 2, 20—

Dr. Dennis Becker and Dr. Paula Becker
The Speech Improvement Company
1614 Beacon Street
Brookline, MA 02446

Dear Doctors Becker:

Subject: Position as Research Assistant

Sparked by your need for a research assistant, as advertised in the *Boston Globe*, I've enclosed my resume for your review. I believe I have the qualifications you're looking for.

While I was in college, I held many internships. This gave me insight into the business world, into working in laboratories, and into working with other professionals. I would like to use the skills I have acquired and build my career at The Speech Improvement Company.

Next step
I'll call you next week to set up an appointment.

Sincerely yours,

Masha Lawrence

Enclosure

Example 6-3a: Cover letter responding to a newspaper ad

Masha Lawrence
14 Lorenz Lane   Spring Valley, New York 10977   (914) 362-1994

Education	**Baldridge College, 1700 Union Blvd., Bayshore, NY** *Degree:* MS in Clinical Engineering *Graduation:* March 2000
	Baldridge College, Avenue J, Brooklyn, NY *Degree:* BS, Computer Science and Biology *Graduation:* June 1997
	Wellrock Community College, College Rd., Suffern, NY *Degree:* AA in Liberal Arts *Graduation:* 1994 *Honors:* Dean's List, Phi Sigma Omicron
Courses	Physiology for Engineers I and II; Genetics and Bioprocessing Laboratory; Genetics, Multivariate Analysis; Introduction to Research Methods; Microbiology; Biomedical Instrumentation; Medical Device Safety and Design; Mechanical Materials; Biomedical Engineering Laboratory; Electrophysiology Signal Processing; Business/Management Skills in Biomedicine
Professional Experience	**Nyack Hospital, Nyack, NY (10/99–1/00)** *Position:* Biomedical Intern *Responsibilities:* Preventative Maintenance, Maintenance of Hospital Medical Equipment
	North Star Research, Bayshore, NY (3/99–6/99) *Position:* Research Assistant *Environment:* R & D, Bioengineering *Responsibilities:* Research, Quality Control, Laboratory Maintenance
	Neuromedical Systems, Inc., Suffern, NY (12/96–9/97) *Position:* Customer Services Representative *Environment:* Client/Server *Responsibilities:* Customer Service, Database Maintenance, Software Troubleshooting, Training New Customer Service Representatives
Computer Skills	SQL and Assembly Programming

Example 6-3b: One-page resume for recent college graduate

your experience and the job you hope to land. Example 6-4 shows how to include keywords in an e-mail resume.

To: Dave.Bryant@abccompany.com
Subject: Process Engineering Manager

Robert Conway
One Andover Street, Cupertino, CA 95014
408-974-1325
conway@worldnet.att.net

Keywords: Semiconductor, process engineering, thin films, PVD, PECVD, etching, silicon, applications, vacuum, solder bumping, flip chip

Career Summary: Extensive hands-on experience in engineering and management responsibilities for process development of semiconductor wafer fabrication and assembly. Creative problem solving with emphasis on thin films leading to process enhancements, six patents, and five publications for semiconductor

Example 6-4: Submitting your resume online

The first line of your e-mail message may read as follows: *I am responding to your online posting for a Web Developer and have enclosed my resume in Word.* (Then proceed as you would in a letter.)

▶ Following are some things to remember when you send your resume electronically:

- Whether you cut and paste your resume into the text box or attach it, save it as a Text Only [*.txt] file. Keep the formatting simple, and don't use fancy fonts. If you do, your resume may appear garbled on the reader's screen.

- Don't bore your reader with the file name resume.doc or resume.txt. You stand out from the pack by using something more creative. Consider Lastname_Firstname_ Job.txt, as in Jones_Ray_Engineer.txt. If you have a long name, consider using an initial instead of your first name. You can also abbreviate the job title.

- Include a compelling subject line so that your resume will jump off the screen and shout, "Read me." Dare to be different. For example, instead of writing a subject line that says, "IT Manager," consider writing a subject line that says, "Your Next IT Manager." ◀

Switching Gears

On occasion it pays to get creative. Example 6-5 is an actual letter I wrote for a colleague. He saw an advertisement for a position for which he was overqualified. He used this as an opportunity to get his foot in the door and meet with the company president. He landed a three-month technical consulting position that led to his becoming manager of the engineering department.

Composing a Broadcast Letter

A broadcast letter is similar in style and content to a cover letter; see Example 6-6. The difference is that you send a broadcast letter *instead of* both a cover letter and resume, so you include all the information you want the reader to know. It's not necessary to limit a broadcast letter to one page. Although there's no guarantee that a broadcast letter is more successful than a cover letter and resume, it is becoming popular as the job market becomes more competitive and people look for new ways to be noticed.

Advantages	• Combines the cover letter and resume into one compact direct-mail piece.
	• Includes pertinent information at a glance that's not found in a typical cover letter.
Disadvantages	• Relies on getting the reader's attention at a glance.
	• May appear vague without details of your background.

▶ If you send a broadcast letter, prepare at least three bulleted items that best "sell" your professional strengths and accomplishments. In certain industries it might be appropriate to quantify your accomplishments. Here are some examples:

- Saved the company $760,000 during the first year of employment.
- Supervised a staff of 20, with 4 direct reports.
- Increased sales by 17% in the first quarter of last year.
- Managed a $2.6 million budget. ◀

Crafting a Networking Letter

Statistics show that most jobs are found through networks. Therefore, when you're in the job market, contact your friends, relatives, colleagues, and anyone else who

MALCOM GREENE   mgreene@att.net
117 Sudbury Street, Achille, OK 74720   (405) 339-8209

October 4, 20—

Mr. James Anderson, President
Utica Associates
22 Clinton Drive
Utica, OK 74763

Dear Mr. Anderson:

When I visited your website I recognized an excellent application for my skills in thin film engineering. Please review my resume to see how I can contribute to the success of Utica Associates. Following are a few highlights:

- Developed thin film processes on AMS's ECLIPSE sputter system for planarized aluminum and reactively sputtered titanium nitride; major contributions as director of the Applications Lab at MRC.

- Developed $PdSi_2$/TiW/AlCu multilevel metallization, CrSiN thin film resistors, and NiFe magnetic field sensors at FeellerSystem as Thin Film Process Engineering Manager.

- Developed processes for wafer bumping, including a novel solder jetting process for bump deposition, as Project Manager at Cobb Electronics.

I have complemented this unique set of experiences with management of process engineering staff, volume production engineering support, and effective problem-solving skills. I'd appreciate the opportunity to discuss with you how this skill set would meet your needs, either in permanent employment or in a consulting or contract role. I will call you next week to discuss our next steps.

Sincerely,

Malcolm Greene

Example 6-5: Letter serving as a door opener

ROBERT JOHNS
117 Salisbury Street, Saratoga, CA 95070

rjohns@aol.com
(408) 253-8209

January 23, 20—

Dr. James Goodwin, CEO
NORTA Systems
90 Vineyard Lane
Saratoga, CA 95070

Dear Dr. Goodwin:

The essential link between new product development and a growing, satisfied customer base is the Applications Team. These are the people who keep R&D on the track to successful marketing, and at the same time keep up a dialogue between the customer and the company to advance the products, capabilities and profitability. This team requires the strong, technically competent, and customer-oriented leadership I'd like to provide, on either a permanent or project basis.

I fulfilled this need for over four years at Chemco Research Corporation, which was then the leading manufacturer of advanced sputtering equipment. As the Director of Applications, I guided the ECLIPSE system to market leadership:

- Expanded the staff from 5 to over 18 engineers and technicians, adding responsibility for reactive ion etching equipment and an applications laboratory in Japan
- Developed a widely-accepted planarization process for aluminum metallization
- Delivered technical presentations for customers worldwide in support of sales and marketing efforts

The bulk of my career has been focused in semiconductor wafer fabs, both in a development/prototype mode and in volume production. I was responsible for equipment and process qualification for a $110M wafer size conversion for 3000 wafer-starts per week. These experiences supply the necessary background for representing the customers to your engineering, marketing, and sales teams.

There's more to my experience and leadership skills than can be captured in a standard resume. Therefore, I look forward to a personal discussion to explore opportunities with NORTA Systems.

Sincerely,

Robert Johns

Example 6-6: Broadcast letter

cares about you and may be willing to help. Example 6-7 is a note to a former colleague in the form of an e-mail message. Always follow up these messages with a phone call or meeting.

To: jim@abnet.com
Cc:
Subject: Making a job change. Hope you can help.

Dear Jim,

I know that we haven't talked in a while, but I want to update you on recent changes in my professional life. After five years with Sylex, there was a workforce reduction and my position was eliminated. This affords me the chance to change directions and move into technical sales, which I've been wanting to do. I'm very positive about this new direction and would appreciate running some ideas by you.

I've attached a list of 15 target companies and would be interested in your thoughts on which ones I should pursue. Also, I'd appreciate any information you have about their product lines, sales methods, reputation, policies, and anything else that would be helpful. If there's anyone you know at these companies, that would be a bonus.

I'll call you next week to catch up.

Regards,

Betsy

Example 6-7: Networking message to a colleague

As part of your networking activities, you always want to follow up and thank people for their help. Example 6-8 is a follow-up thank-you note. While an e-mail message is okay, a letter or handwritten note is more appropriate.

> Dear Jim,
>
> Thank you for the chance to meet with you last Friday. I appreciate the time you spent reviewing my target list and the information you gave me on those companies. I will follow up on the names you gave me and let you know my progress.
>
> I'm enclosing the article we discussed and will send you anything else I run across on the subject.
>
> Thanks for being such a great networking partner.
>
> Warmest regards,
>
> Betsy

Example 6-8: Follow-up thank-you networking note

Sending a Thank-You Letter

Employers say that a sincere, enthusiastic thank-you letter can tip the balance in your favor. This is of particular importance if two people are in close competition for the same position. A thank-you note doesn't ensure that you'll get the job or the second interview; however, the lack of one almost ensures that you won't. Some experts suggest that you send a handwritten letter; others suggest an e-mail message. E-mail has the advantage of timeliness, but a handwritten or typewritten letter is still the convention. Example 6-9 shows text for whichever method you use.

Express your appreciation for the interview, relate something you didn't get a chance to tell the interviewer, reiterate one of your accomplishments that impressed her, or reemphasize your desire to work for the company. Here are a few ideas:

> *My interview this morning was very educational. I knew that <company> was diversified, but I never realized the extent of that diversification until I met with you.*

Dear Barbara,

I very much enjoyed our meeting this afternoon to discuss the opportunity as IT manager. The chance to solve your IT problems is especially intriguing and a challenge I will enjoy. I'm sure that my ten years of experience in the industry will give me an opportunity to make an immediate contribution.

Next step

I am looking forward to returning for my next interview with the hope of sharing my enthusiasm and talents with your company.

Sincerely,

Jane

Example 6-9: Thank you for the interview

My visit to <company> yesterday was a pleasure. From the moment I entered the building, I sensed a genuine camaraderie that is rare in large companies today.

I hope you will consider my candidacy favorably. After meeting everyone, I'm more eager than ever to join your <department>.

I hope that you will invite me back to further discuss this opportunity.

▶ Try to collect a business card from everyone who interviews you, and send a thank-you letter to each with correct spellings and titles. ◀

Writing a Letter of Resignation

When you resign from a position, you want to do it without creating hard feelings. Therefore, you should present your intention to leave in a positive way. Even if you

May 1, 20—

Mr. Bob Myrtle
Zarak, Incorporated
200 Smith Drive
Abbott, WV 26201

Dear Bob:

I'm submitting my resignation effective May 2. My last working day will be May 16. My tenure at Zarak has been enjoyable, and I've been fortunate to work with capable and dedicated people. I have, in turn, performed to the best of my ability.

At this time, for the benefit of my family and my career, I have formally accepted a new position in another company. I'll be more than happy to train my successor to insure a smooth transition.

I wish you every success.

Sincerely yours,

Byron Aflack

Example 6-10: Letter of resignation

feel the company didn't treat you fairly and you were forced to look for a new job, present a positive tone. Check out Example 6-10 to see a letter of resignation. Include the following:

- Effective date
- Last day you'll report to work
- Your willingness to train your successor
- Your wish for the company's future success

Example 6-11 says goodbye to colleagues after you have submitted a resignation. Example 6-12 says goodbye to colleagues after you have been asked to leave.

To:	BU Colleagues
Subject:	Thank you and farewell

Dear Friends,

I'm sure you've heard the news about my leaving the university. After much consideration, I did accept a position at Georgia Tech. It offers me a wonderful location, a promotion, and a chance to specialize in advising and teaching graduate students. It's with mixed emotions that I resign my office. I have enjoyed being part of Boston University and will always look to my years here with pride, respect, and appreciation for my growth as an educator.

When you leave a place, some of it you take with you and some of yourself you leave behind. I've made many friends in my years here and will always cherish these relationships.

Warmest regards,

James

Example 6-11: Leaving by choice and saying goodbye

To:	Sudbury Colleagues
Subject:	Good-bye

Hello everyone,

I'll be leaving the Sudbury Company effective April 4. I enjoyed working with all of you and appreciate the wonderful friendships we developed. This is a small industry, and I know many of us will cross paths. I hope so.

Good luck to all of you,

Daniel

Example 6-12: Being asked to leave and saying goodbye

Acknowledging Receipt of a Resume

As a professional in human resources or otherwise involved in the hiring process, you should acknowledge the receipt of all resumes. It's very disheartening for job seekers to feel that they're sending their resumes into black holes. A rejection at least can provide closure.

If the application was made online, it's appropriate to send an online acknowledgment. If the application was hard copy, a simple card, such as the one you see in Example 6-13, will suffice:

This is to acknowledge receipt of your resume for the position of IT Manager. We've had an overwhelming response to our advertisement, and you can be assured that each resume will be given careful consideration.

Once this process has been completed, we will contact each candidate whose background matches our needs. Thank you for considering <name of company>.

<name and title>

Example 6-13: Acknowledging someone's resume when there is interest

If the applicant's credentials don't match the opening, it's still proper to send an acknowledgment. A letter such as Example 6-14 may suffice:

LETTERHEAD

December 3, 20—

Ms. Gwyn Hollis
56 Cove Road
Stanhope, NJ 07874

Dear Ms. Hollis:

Thank you for your recent application to The Kayne Company. Although your resume is very impressive, we've received resumes from people whose backgrounds more closely match our needs. We will, however, keep your resume on file in the event that a suitable position should become available.

Good luck in your job search.

Sincerely,

Patsy George
Human Resources Director

Example 6-14: Acknowledging someone's resume when there isn't interest

Denying a Request for an Interview

A precarious situation can result when friends or colleagues ask for your help in getting someone an interview with your company. If you think the person is a viable candidate, there's no problem. If you don't think she's suited for the position, the request can place you in an awkward position. Example 6-15 is a note that shows you how to decline graciously:

Dear <name>,

Your friendship is very important to me and I hope you won't be too disappointed that I can't arrange for you to come in to meet with <name>. I believe you would have done a wonderful job for us. However, <name> felt that your qualifications better fit a more junior position.

In the meantime, don't stand still! You have great qualifications and need to get your resume out there. I'll continue to keep my eyes open for a position at my company that might be right for you.

Warmest personal regards,

Example 6-15: Denying a request for an interview

Extending a Formal Job Offer

Job offers are generally written, not verbal, to avoid any misunderstandings as to the terms and conditions. At the bottom of the letter, allow a place for the applicant's signature in accepting the terms. See a sample in Example 6-16. Formal job offers should include any or all of the following:

- Salary, bonus plan, and any other forms of compensation

- Relocation benefits, if applicable

February 9, 20—

Mr. George Gleason
100 Besen Parkway
Abanda, AL 36274

Dear Mr. Gleason:

Congratulations: You're our choice for Engineering Manager
It's with great pleasure that we offer you the position of Engineering Manager, reporting to Sara Cohen, Engineering Director. We look forward to having you start on February 20, 20—.

What this offer includes
- A starting salary of $75,000.
- Three weeks' vacation the first year; four weeks after five years.
- Company-paid relocation from San Diego to Boston.
- Profit sharing, 401k, plus health and dental. All are outlined in the enclosed benefits package.

What this offer is contingent upon
- A satisfactory physical examination and drug test.
- A satisfactory security check.

We look forward to having you join us
Please indicate your acceptance by signing the bottom of this letter. Return one copy to me by <date> and keep the second copy for your records.

Please call me at extension 202 if you have any questions.

Sincerely,

<Your name>

I accept the above offer: _____
                          Name   Date

Example 6-16: Formal job offer

- Vacation and holiday policies

- Insurance benefits

- Anticipated starting date

Accepting a Job Offer

If there isn't a place on the letter for you to show your acceptance, write a formal acceptance. Here are some phrases to consider:

> *I truly appreciate the confidence you've shown in me by selecting me to be your next <position>. I'm delighted to accept.*

> *I'm delighted to accept your offer to become your company's next <position>.*

> *I look forward to becoming your next <position> starting on <date>.*

> *I'm delighted to accept your offer and look forward to the challenges that the position of <position> offers.*

> *Please accept this letter as my intention to accept the position as your next <position> starting on <date>, with the terms you have outlined.*

Revising a Job Offer

On occasion, it may be necessary to revise a job offer. You want to be congenial to foster a good working relationship, so keep the lines of communication open. See Example 6-17.

Rejecting a Job Offer

When you reject a job you were offered, put the rejection in writing. Examples 6-18a and 6-18b give the reasons for the rejection.

> ▶ If you have a candidate in for an interview and don't hire her, send a letter of rejection. Although a rejection letter isn't something anyone welcomes, it's good business and the right thing to do. *Your current job candidate may be your next prospective client or customer.* Your letter can resemble Example 6-19, with the proper modifications. ◀

LETTERHEAD

June 12, 20—

Mr. Patrick O'Maley
5 Cinder Circle
Wabaco, KY 40385

Dear Mr. O'Maley:

Thank you for responding to the job offer so promptly. We realize that there are a few details to work out, but they are manageable.

I spoke with Brad Williams, and we can't increase the base salary of $55,000 that we offered. We would, however, be willing to offer a sign-on bonus of $2,500, and $1,000 to cover your relocation expenses.

Please get back to us early next week. We look forward to having you join our company.

Sincerely,

Graham Collins
Vice President, Engineering

Example 6-17: Revising a job offer

LETTERHEAD

August 3, 20—

Ms. Edith Dowling
Cornwall Company
54 Magnolia Lane
Manhasset, NY 11030

Dear Ms. Dowling:

I very much appreciate your offering me the position of Administrative Assistant. When I met with you, I was hoping to receive such an offer. However, I just learned yesterday that my husband is being transferred to California and, of course, I'll be going with him.

It would have been a wonderful opportunity to grow with a company that's growing so fast. I wish you good luck in finding another candidate.

Sincerely,

Jessica Morse

Example 6-18a: Rejecting a job offer

March 5, 20—

Mr. Robert Clark, President
Dowd Conservation Company
100 Maple Drive
Oakdale, IA 52319

Dear Mr. Clark:

Thank you for your generous offer. The position of computer programmer sounds like a real challenge for the right person. However, I don't feel that I'm that person. As I mentioned during the interview, my real interest lies in IT, and I'm hoping to secure a position in that area.

May I extend to you and the Dowd Conservation Company my sincere wishes for success.

Sincerely,

Alex Greenberg

Example 6-18b: Rejecting a job offer

LETTERHEAD

April 8, 20—

Ms. Stephanie Sachs
20 Baxter Avenue
Lock Springs, MO 64654

Dear Ms. Sachs:

We enjoyed meeting you on April 1 and thank you for your interest in joining our company. Although we believe you would do a wonderful job for us, we are selecting a candidate whose background matches our needs more closely.

We wish you the very best of luck in finding a position that would be a good match for your talents.

Sincerely,

Mike Josling
Human Resources Director

Example 6-19: Rejecting a candidate you interviewed

Sending a Letter of Recommendation

Be wary of giving out any information about an employee or former employee if the recommendation is less than favorable. We've become a very litigious society, and a number of employers have been sued for making unfavorable remarks. It's for this reason that many companies have a policy of merely verifying a person's length of employment.

If you should be asked to have your name used as a reference and you don't feel that you can honestly give a favorable recommendation, you'd be wise to decline. However, if circumstances force you to terminate a valued employee, the employee may ask for a letter of recommendation. That's quite appropriate and often done.

When you respond to a written request for information about a former employee, be certain to mark the response "Confidential." Outline facts about the employee that will give a new employer an accurate picture. Try to separate opinions from facts.

Fact   Ms. Lavin took charge of the smooth running of our office and was always professional in her approach. She is an excellent administrative assistant.

Opinion   Ms. Lavin will make an excellent administrative assistant.

Paint a fair and accurate picture of the employee that includes the employee's position or job title while in your employ, major contributions or admirable qualities, and reason(s) for release, provided they aren't negative.

ON THE LIGHT SIDE …

Richard Lederer had a wonderful article in the April/May 2002 *Mensa Bulletin* entitled "Liar, liar, pants on fire." In it he quips:

- If the person has been habitually absent from work, you can write, "A man like him is hard to find."

- If he is afflicted with alcohol or drug problems, "We remember the hours he spent working with us as happy hours."

- If he has a criminal background, you may say, "He's a man of many convictions."

Introducing a New Hire

Some employees join companies and blend in with the woodwork—they go virtually unnoticed. Don't let this happen to your employees. Make a new employee feel welcome by sending a notice to everyone so coworkers know who they are. You can place the notice on a bulletin board or send it via e-mail. Include the person's name and position, a short bio, and her starting date. Example 6-20 is a simple message that does the job.

To:	Customer Service Department
Cc:	
Subject:	Please welcome Beth Greenberg on March 3

Hi Everyone,

Beth Greenberg will be joining our company on March 3. She'll be in Room 303. Please stop by and make Beth feel welcome. She brings to our company 15 years of experience as a customer service manager and has a degree from the University of Massachusetts.

I'm confident that Beth will be a big asset to our company and help us deal with many of the service problems we now have. To learn more about Beth, check out ‹link› on our company's intranet.

Regards,

Sara

Example 6-20: Announcing a new employee

If a small to midsize company were to increase its customer retention rate by 5 percent, its profits would double in about 10 years.

—BAIN & COMPANY
Boston-based consulting firm

CHAPTER 7

Customer Relations

There are a number of ways to bolster relations between you and your customers. Even though your sales department is directly responsible for making sales and keeping customers satisfied, everyone who has customer contact plays a vital role in customer relations.

Survey for Satisfaction

When you send a customer satisfaction survey along with a self-addressed, stamped envelope for an easy return, you let your customers know that you value their business. Make sure the survey asks the tough questions so you learn if you are exceeding, meeting, or not meeting their expectations. Unless the survey is very short (short being just a few questions), it's wise to mix up the questions between true and false, yes and no, numerical ratings, and fill-ins. Always thank respondees for participating in the survey.

Examples 7-1 through 7-4b illustrate a range of survey-related communications.

WHAT'S IN THIS CHAPTER

- *Survey for satisfaction*
- *Holiday greetings*
- *Reminders for events or deadlines*
- *Apology for employee's action*
- *Making quick and amicable adjustments*
- *Writing a tactful claims letter*

March 20, 20—

Ms. Barbara Baxter
10 Cardinal Drive
Justin, TX 76247

Dear Ms. Baxter:

We at Justin Memorial Hospital are dedicated to providing our patients with the highest quality care and services. To help us accomplish this, we would like to hear about your experience with us. What did we do right? How can we improve?

Please take a moment to fill out the customer satisfaction survey that we've enclosed and return it in the self-addressed, stamped envelope.

Thank you for helping us to continue to be of service to the community.

Sincerely,

Amy Nurse, Customer Relations

Enclosure

Example 7-1: Cover letter accompanying a customer satisfaction survey

August 22, 20—

Mr. Glen Madison, President
Madison Construction Co.
300 Crandall Court
Avondale, MO 64010

Dear Mr. Madison:

As part of our ongoing effort to add to the value of our services to our clients, we solicit feedback. Won't you please take a moment to let us know your evaluation of working with us to develop your website? Simply return this survey in the self-addressed, postage-paid envelope.

1. Was working with us a positive experience? Please explain why or why not.

2. What impact do you expect your new website to have on your business?

3. Did we [ ] exceed, [ ] meet, or [ ] not meet your expectations? (Please check one.)

4. Is there anything we could have done better or differently?

5. Do you have any other comments?

Most of our business comes from referrals; therefore, we'd appreciate your letting us know of any of your colleagues who may benefit from our services. Thanks!

Name and title: _____ Phone No: _____
Company: _____ Location: _____

Name and title: _____ Phone No: _____
Company: _____ Location: _____

Sincerely yours,

James Ball, Vice President

Example 7-2: Letter serving as a customer satisfaction survey

ESSENTIAL FAMILY CHIROPRACTIC SURVEY

In our ongoing effort to provide better service to you, we'd appreciate your taking a few moments to fill out the following questionnaire. Thank you.

OFFICE APPEARANCE

	Yes	No
Do you find the waiting room to be neat and clean?		
Do you occasionally take home or share with friends and family any of the informational pamphlets in the waiting room?		

On a scale of 1–10 (with 10 being the best), how would you rate the following:

_____ Lighting   _____ Scent in the office
_____ Layout of adjusting room   _____ Office carpeting
_____ Comfort of tables in adjusting room _____ Overall interior

On the above list, if you would recommend one change, what would that be?

_____

THE DOCTOR

	Yes	No
Do you feel confident in the doctor's abilities?		
Do you feel comfortable discussing personal health concerns with the doctor?		
Do you feel that the doctor listens to your concerns attentively?		
Do you feel that the doctor does a good job explaining your condition?		
Are you comfortable referring your family and friends to the doctor?		

If there's one thing you would recommend that your doctor change in order to serve you and your family better, what would that be?

_____

How would you describe the doctor's adjusting techniques? Please choose all that apply.

_____ Gentle   _____ Uncomfortable
_____ Forceful   _____ Painful
_____ Comfortable

Example 7-3: Comprehensive patient satisfaction survey

OFFICE COMMUNICATIONS Yes No

	Yes	No
Is the person at the front desk professional?		
Does the person at the front desk make you feel welcome?		
Do you get appointments when they're convenient for you?		
When you miss an appointment, do you like to get a reminder call that day?		

PATIENT INFORMATION Yes No

	Yes	No
Are you currently under active care (including regular maintenance)?		
Do you believe that maintenance care is important to preventing your condition from returning after the initial intensive phase of care?		

If you are no longer under care, is it due to any of the following?

_____ Cost of continued care
_____ Skepticism about chiropractic care
_____ You didn't get the results you expected
_____ Other reasons (Please explain below)

If you haven't referred others to our office, please let me know if there's a reason.

_____ Skepticism because of previous chiropractic experience
_____ Cost of chiropractic care
_____ You don't feel comfortable explaining chiropractic to others
_____ You would, but there hasn't been an opportunity

On a scale of 1–10 (with 10 being the best), how would you describe your overall experience at Essential Family Chiropractic? _____

ONGOING EDUCATION Yes No

	Yes	No
Would you like to receive our monthly electronic newsletter?		

If yes, please fill in your e-mail address. _____

Thank you for taking the time to fill in this questionnaire.

Dr. Eric Lindsell, Essential Family Chiropractic

Example 7-3 (continued)

Dear Guest:

To assist our ongoing effort to add value to the services we offer all our guests, please take a moment to let us know what you enjoyed about your experience and how we might improve.

_____

_____

_____

_____

Thank you.
Customer Satisfaction Department

Example 7-4a: Guest satisfaction card

Dear Guest:

Thank you for taking the time to share your thoughts about your visit to the Manhassett Museum. Please know that your comments and suggestions have been forwarded to the appropriate members of our staff for review.

Comments such as yours help us in our ongoing effort to improve your experience each time you visit us.

Thank you.
Customer Satisfaction Department

Example 7-4b: Thank-you card to respondee

Holiday Greetings

When you remember your customers during the holidays with a handwritten note rather than a traditional card, they'll remember you. There are more holidays than those that fall at the end of December. Don't forget Thanksgiving, the Fourth of July, Labor Day, and others. To make the greeting heartfelt, don't include any promotional material. If your mailing even hints at being a marketing ploy, you will have lost the impact of sincerity.

> ▶ If you send a holiday card to a business associate at home, include his spouse or partner on the envelope. If you send it to his office, address it to the associate alone. ◀

Examples 7-5 through 7-7 offer sample messages.

Dear Friends and Colleagues,

I wish you and your employees all the best this holiday season. We hope that you are blessed with customers as wonderful as you.

Thank you for helping to make us one of the leaders in our industry. Our fondest regards to all of you.

Happy holidays,

<Name>
<Company>

Example 7-5: End-of-December holiday greetings

Dear Friends,

During the Thanksgiving season my thoughts turn warmly and gratefully to those who help make my business such a pleasure. I truly give thanks for your trust, loyalty, and friendship.

Happy Thanksgiving!

Sheryl Lindsell-Roberts

Example 7-6: Thanksgiving greetings

Management Strategies Group

Consultants to organizations in transition

December 20—

Dear Clients and Friends:

As we've done for several years, instead of sending holiday cards to our clients and friends, we've made a contribution on their behalf. This year we've contributed to America's Second Harvest, an organization dedicated to "rescuing" perfectly good unsold food from grocery stores, food manufacturers, food distributors, and corporations. This food helps to feed hungry people across the United States. We believe that this is a very worthwhile organization and cause. America's Second Harvest believes that there should never be rampant hunger, especially among children.

I want to convey my best wishes to you and your family for a happy and peaceful holiday season and for a healthy and prosperous new year! Many thanks for your continued friendship and support.

With warm regards for a Happy Holiday season,

John A. Haas, Ph.D.
President

Example 7-7: Donation to charity as an expression of gratitude

► You don't have to wait for a holiday to express appreciation to your customers. Example 7-8 shows how to extend your appreciation for your customer's business any time during the year. ◄

LETTERHEAD

May 1, 20—

Mr. and Mrs. Conrad Brady
543 Broad Haven Drive
Chattanooga, TN 37412

Dear Mr. and Mrs. Brady:

I'd personally like to express my appreciation for your continued business. It's because of valued customers like you that we continue to be the leading sporting goods business in Chattanooga.

The next time you visit us, please bring this letter with you and get 15% off any purchase up to $100.

Sincerely yours,

Pat Sembler
General Manager

Example 7-8: Thanks for your patronage

Reminders for Events or Deadlines

You probably receive reminders from your doctor and dentist to make sure you don't miss your scheduled appointment. Reminders, however, don't have to stop with appointments you scheduled. Sending clients reminders about events or deadlines is a good way to foster better relations. Example 7-9 is a card my accountant sends to remind her clients that it's time to pay quarterly taxes. Although I never forget to send my check to Uncle Sam, I always appreciate the fact that Denise takes the time to remind me.

REMINDER
from
Denise Cataldo, CPA, P.C.
6 Simpson Road
Marlboro, MA 01752

Your ___ Qtr. individual tax estimates are due _____15, 20—
Make sure you pay Federal and/or State, as applicable.

Example 7-9: Reminder that quarterly taxes are due

Apology for Employee's Action

Despite your best efforts, it is likely that not all of your employees will be exemplary. Occasionally an employee may rub someone the wrong way (or worse) and you hear about it from the customer. Check out Example 7-10 for a response to action that resulted in a reprimand, and 7-11 for action that resulted in termination. Here's how to respond to a letter complaining about an employee's action:

- Thank the writer for bringing the matter to your attention.
- Apologize for the problem.
- Tell the writer what action you're taking.
- Send compensation, if appropriate.
- Ask subtly for continued business.

October 4, 20—

Ms. Renee Easton
5 Speen Street
Rockbridge, IL 62081

Dear Ms. Easton:

Thank you for bringing to our attention how disturbed you were that Nancy Madison was more interested in conducting a personal telephone conversation than she was in being of service to you.

We discussed this with Nancy and she acknowledged that during the past few weeks personal issues have occupied her time. We reemphasized to her that customers always come first, and we believe that she will be a better employee because of the conversation we had.

Nancy has asked me to personally convey her apologies to you. I hope you will visit us again and have a very pleasant experience.

Sincerely,

Glenda Murphy
Manager

Example 7-10: Notification of corrective action resulting in a reprimand

November 12, 20—

Mr. John Grouch
33 Knox Road, Apartment 3
Vortex, KY 41301

Dear Mr. Grouch:

Subject: My personal apology

Please let me personally apologize for the unfortunate treatment you received from George Green on November 1. Because of this situation, we have asked Mr. Green to leave his position, and he is no longer with our company.

We value you as a customer and apologize for the embarrassment you felt. To make sure this isn't repeated with others, we are implementing a training program that all employees must attend.

Please accept the enclosed $50 gift certificate as an expression of our apology. Thanks for understanding and for bringing this to our attention.

Sincerely yours,

Samuel Smithson
President

Enclosure

Example 7-11: Notification of corrective action resulting in termination

Making Quick and Amicable Adjustments

Customers who submit claims (a better term than *complaints*) are golden. They take the time to let you know there's a problem because they want to continue doing business with you. For every person who submits a claim, there are likely many others having the same problem who simply take their business elsewhere. Therefore, when you receive a claim letter from a customer, view it as something positive—an opportunity to serve him better.

When you send a quick response, it makes your customers feel important, keeps them coming back, and defuses potentially unpleasant situations. Even if you can't help the customer immediately, write to let him know his claim is being addressed and when he can expect an answer. If the claim must be studied before you give an answer, let the customer know that his claim is being investigated. If you need additional information before you can help the customer, ask for it with a smile, as Example 7-12 illustrates.

Granting an Adjustment

When you grant an adjustment, it's generally a "good news letter" and isn't too difficult to write. The following suggestions will be helpful:

- **Acknowledge the claim and tell the reader the adjustment is being granted.** Don't dwell on the customer's complaint and don't give the impression that you're making any special concessions—even if you are.

  It's easy to understand your frame of mind, <name>; please accept my apology. To make amends, we are ...

  As your letter of <date> pointed out, <issue> was indeed in error. The discount of <percentage> does apply to your latest purchase, and a revised invoice will be sent to you shortly. Please excuse the mistake, and thank you for calling this to our attention.

- **Stress the effort the company is making to prevent the problem from happening again.** Accept the blame gracefully, and don't denounce an employee.

  As you can imagine, we are grateful that you suffered no injuries, and we wish to extend our apologies for this unpleasant experience. We are taking additional precautions to make certain that this doesn't happen again.

- **End the letter on a positive note that will lead to future dealings.** Don't reiterate the incident that necessitated the adjustment. And don't overlook the possibility of promoting future sales.

  I am pleased to send you a <dollar amount> gift certificate toward the purchase of any merchandise in our catalog.

February 10, 20—

Mr. Paul Arden
5422 Woodhill Avenue
Greenwood, DE 19950

Dear Mr. Arden:

Subject: Please send us your Invoice No. 344

Thank you for your letter of February 7, 20—, calling our attention to the discrepancy in your invoice. I'm investigating the situation and hope to have an answer for you within the next two weeks. Because of customers like you who let us know when problems arise, we're able to serve all our customers better. For that we thank you.

Action requested
In the meantime, please send me Invoice No. 344. This will give me the additional information I need to process your claim quickly.

Sincerely yours,

Evelyn Gwinhurst
Customer Service Manager

Example 7-12: Requesting additional information

When you need <specific> equipment, you'll find everything from....You can continue to rely on our motto: "Satisfaction or your money back."

Scenario 1: On April 1 you receive an irate letter from a long-standing customer. He states that the door is no longer open to your salesman Vic Torian. Apparently Mr. Torian has been pushy and rude and has presented a series of ridiculous schemes. The irate customer concludes with: "We no longer want your <product> or any further contact."

Your response may be:

Dear <name>:

Subject: Please accept my sincere apologies

I'm very sorry to learn of the problem you had with our salesman, Vic Torian. All our salespeople attend a one-week training program because we expect them to be honest with and courteous to all our customers. Please accept my apology. We've taken corrective action regarding Vic Torian, and you can be assured that he won't be calling on you again.

<Customer's name>, your business is important to us, and we are anxious to continue our long-standing relationship. I'll call you personally next week to see how we may continue to offer you the fine service you've received over the last several years.

Most sincerely,

Scenario 2: You receive a letter from an irate customer whose order for a five-pound box of chocolate arrived in damaged condition.

Your response may be:

Dear <name>:

A new box of chocolate is on its way!

Thank you for taking the time to write us. We know it must have been a big disappointment to receive the box of chocolate in damaged condition. Our guess is that the damage occurred in transit. You don't need to do anything about the parcel post claim; we'll take care of that here.

We mailed a new five-pound box to you today and trust that this one will arrive safely. We are proud of our candies and want you to be completely satisfied. We have also included a gift certificate for a two-pound box to be used at your convenience.

Thank you for bringing this matter to our attention.

Sincerely,

Denying an Adjustment

Sometimes the customer is wrong and you can't grant an adjustment. It's not always easy to write a letter of this nature and keep the customer's goodwill, but you must try. Check out chapter 3, Step 2 for more information on sequencing your information for an unresponsive reader. The following suggestions will be helpful:

- **Start with a buffer that acknowledges the customer's point of view.** Show that you understand the problem and are trying to be fair.

  Thank you for relating the story of the delayed delivery of the <item> you pur-chased for <intended user>. We are sorry that the delay caused you both so much anxiety.

- **Give the explanation before the decision.** Stress what, if anything, can be done. Don't blame or argue. And avoid expressions such as "your com-plaint," "your error," "we refuse."

  Our one-year guarantee is made to cover only defective parts and workman-ship. We had one of our engineers inspect the computer, and she found that the floppy drive had been damaged. We wonder if perhaps the computer had been dropped.

  At present, all my student teachers are carrying very heavy workloads. Asking them to participate in a study, no matter how worthwhile, would be unfair to them. I compliment you on the topic you chose . . .

- **Be courteous, even if the customer wasn't.** Otherwise you lose both your self-respect and the customer.

- **Try to end on a friendly note.** This is especially important because the customer thinks he's right.

Scenario 3: You receive a letter asking for a refund based on a misunderstanding.

Dear <name>:

We pride ourselves on our policy not to be undersold. You must be completely satis-fied with any merchandise you purchase from us—for both quality and price.

 When I looked closely at the advertisement you sent from On-the-Cheap Computers, I noticed that the offer was for Model 123A. Your receipt is for Model 123B. It's certainly easy to confuse the two.

 We do appreciate your bringing this matter to our attention, and thank you for your support and patronage.

Sincerely,

Scenario 4: You have just received a letter from Ms. Bergstein, president of Bergstein & Associates. Ms. Bergstein is quite upset because invitations she ordered for the celebration of the retirement of the company's CEO weren't delivered on time. This forced her to invite her guests to the retirement dinner via Mailgrams. Ms. Bergstein would like to meet with you to reach an amicable settlement of this claim. She wants a full refund.

Your response may be:

Dear Ms. Bergstein:

Your certified letter has just been handed to me. I know how important these invitations were to you and want you to be assured that our company did everything in its power to deliver them to you on time. Following are the circumstances that led to the delay:

1. Mr. Green, your director of advertising, held the proofs for two weeks before returning them. That put us behind schedule initially.

2. Mr. Green approved the proofs with June 15, not June 16, as the day of the event. (We had no way of knowing that the 15th was incorrect.)

3. We scheduled an overtime shift and met your deadline.

4. After we delivered the invitations to you, Mr. Green noticed that the date was incorrect. He asked that the invitations be reprinted. Due to other scheduling commitments, we were unable to meet your deadline.

Next step
I'll be out of town for the next week and will call you when I return so that we can arrange a mutually convenient time to discuss this matter. Once again, I'm sorry that you were unable to use the invitations, but I believe once we have an opportunity to review all the details, you'll see that we were not responsible for the delay.

I value our relationship and look forward to discussing this with you in person.

Sincerely,

Scenario 5: An irate customer has just dropped by the Customer Service Department with a nine-year-old lawn mower that is no longer working. He had a five-year warranty on the mower and is now demanding that it be fixed free of charge. You must tactfully refuse.

Your response may be:

Dear <name>:

You are right to expect top-quality merchandise from us. We've always prided ourselves on giving our customers the best merchandise for the best prices, and we stand behind everything we sell.

Thank you for bringing the lawn mower back to our store. After many hours of testing, our service manager has determined that the mower's <specific parts> need to be replaced. It would appear that the lawn mower hasn't been maintained according to the instructions that accompanied it. The repairs would total $190. Would you like us to repair it?

Since the lawn mower is nine years old, you might consider replacing it. Please look for our flier in the mail next week. It will be advertising some "early bird" spring specials that you might want to consider. We're certain that, with proper care and maintenance, a new mower will give you longer service than the old one did.

Sincerely,

Scenario 6: You have just received a letter from Leslie Atchinson, and you're not sure if Leslie is a male or female. Leslie is complaining about a hairpiece he/she purchased and wants to return for a refund. Federal law doesn't allow the return of hairpieces.

Dear Leslie Atchinson:

Thank you for your letter of August 21 indicating you wish to return a hairpiece you recently purchased. Generally we accept return of all merchandise that's in reasonable condition and whose return is in compliance with state laws. Hairpieces, however, like underwear and bathing suits, fall under federal health regulations and cannot be accepted for resale.

Please visit our local store, <name and address>, and for a nominal fee, Mr. Wong, the store manager, will adjust your hairpiece to fit properly. We are confident this will enable you to have a hairpiece you'll be proud to wear.

Very truly yours,

Following are the words of a sign posted at the Freeport, Maine, headquarters of L.L. Bean. This attitude about the customer is one reason that L.L. Bean is so successful.

What is a customer?

A Customer is the most important person ever in this office ... in person or by mail.

A Customer is not dependent on us ... we are dependent on him.

A Customer is not an interruption of our work ... he is the purpose of it. We are not doing him a favor by serving him ... he is doing us a favor by giving us the opportunity to do so.

A Customer is not someone to argue or match wits with. Nobody ever won an argument with a Customer.

A Customer is a person who brings us his wants.

It is our job to handle them profitably to him and ourselves.

Writing a Tactful Claims Letter

Despite a company's best efforts to do everything right, occasionally something goes awry. The smart company is one that values hearing about mistakes, defects, disappointments, or dissatisfactions with products or services. This gives the company the chance to discover, analyze, and correct these problems—and ultimately serve their customers better. Why? Because customers who submit claims want to continue doing business with you. Otherwise they wouldn't send a letter.

▶ Before you send a letter, always call to get the name of the person in charge of the department you're contacting. In that way, you're assured that your letter reaches the right person. ◀

Grinning, not Grunting

When you have a claim, take time and reflect. Don't mail the first letter you write because it probably shows your anger. Look at the letter objectively after you cool down. Be polite, because a lot of people may be shown the letter, and the person who is reading your letter probably isn't the one who caused your anger.

In order to maintain the goodwill of customers, businesses do try to solve customers' problems quickly and fairly. It's generally better to write a letter than to make a phone call, because a letter creates a paper trail. Check out Example 7-13 for a claims letter requesting an amicable settlement, and Example 7-14 for

March 3, 20—

Ms. Pearl Klein
Go Away Travel Agency
100 Main Street
Abanda, AL 36274

Dear Ms. Klein:

Subject: Dissatisfaction with a trip booked for a client

On January 4, 20—, I booked a trip to Aruba for Mr. and Mrs. Cleveland Jones of 203 Green Street, Abanda, AL. As you had advertised, the reservations specified a five-day stay at the Golden Hotel from February 21 through February 25.

Mr. and Mrs. Jones have just returned from their trip, and they're quite disturbed. When they arrived at the Golden Hotel on the morning of February 21, they were told that there were no reservations in their name. The hotel was booked for a convention, and the only hotel in the area that had any vacancies was the Heartbreak Hotel. Mr. and Mrs. Jones would not have objected to staying at the Heartbreak Hotel, but it is in no way comparable to what they were expecting. My clients are requesting the return of the $1500 they paid for their stay at the Heartbreak Hotel.

Action requested
Please call me immediately so that we can arrange for an amicable settlement of this matter.

Sincerely,

Fred O'Hara
Travel Specialist

Example 7-13: Requesting an amicable settlement

September 16, 20—

Ms. Mary Addison, President
The Savings Bank of Minnesota
3 Maple Avenue
Preston, MN 55965

Dear Ms. Addison:

Subject: Correcting an error

Recently I had the following problem with your bank. I deposited a check for
$500 in the ATM on the morning of September 12. On that same day, you
returned a check in the amount of $250 payable to Green Markets marked
"insufficient funds." My bank statement indicates that the $500 deposit was
made on September 12 and I have the receipt. Please check your records
again. As a result of this error, I was charged $12 for the returned check and
have suffered embarrassment with Green Markets.

Action requested
I believe you should remedy this in the following ways:

- Refund me the $12 I was charged for insufficient funds.
- Send a letter to the Green Markets, 4 Wayland Drive, in Preston,
  explaining that my account was not overdrawn and it was a bank error.
- Send me a letter of apology for my embarrassment and expense.

I await your comments. Thank you.

Very truly yours,

Melinda Parker

Example 7-14: Requesting specific remedies

a claims letter asking for a specific remedy. When you seek an adjustment, remember the following:

- **Send your claims letter as soon as the problem arises.** If you wait too long, you weaken your case.

- **Contact a person in a position to help you.** Get the name of someone in the company who is in a position to act on your claim. It might be the vice president of Sales or the director of the Customer Service Department.

  > *As the director of Customer Service, I'm certain you can help me solve the problem I'm having with <details>.*

- **Start with the assumption that the company is anxious to satisfy you.** Don't be negative, sarcastic, threatening, or hostile. Following are examples of positive and negative approaches:

  Positive   *There apparently is a great deal of confusion about this account, and I hope that you'll recheck your figures.*

  Over the last several years, every time I've visited <facility>, your staff has been extremely courteous. That is why I am so surprised.

  The sign on your door says, "A satisfied customer is our main concern." I believe you.

  Negative   *Your product stinks.*

  Your competitors offer better service. Why should I do business with you?

- **Present the details in logical order, offering as many facts and documents as possible.** Assume you'll be treated fairly. Include a description of the original transaction and a clear explanation of your disappointment. Supply names, prices, and dates. Send copies of invoices, sales slips, canceled checks, or other relevant documentation to validate your claim. Keep the originals.

  > *On <date> I purchased a <item> at your store. Enclosed is a copy of the invoice with all the information you should need. The <item> was delivered on <date>, and we have had it in our home for two months. Already, the <problem>.*

  > *On <date> I ordered <items> from your store and charged them to my <credit card information>. The <items> were delivered on <date>. <State problem>.*

- **Ask for a fair adjustment.** If you have a specific adjustment in mind, let the reader know exactly what it is. If you're not sure, ask the reader to be fair. Or, if you don't seek an adjustment and this is merely FYI, make that clear.

> *I've checked the warranty, which guarantees the material and workmanship for one year. Therefore, please have someone call me as soon as possible so that we can arrange to have a new <item> delivered.*

> *I am returning the <items> via UPS. Please either send me a new <item> or credit my account.*

▶ There may be occasions when you seek an adjustment for merchandise that was never guaranteed or is no longer covered by the guarantee. Your job as a dissatisfied customer is to convince the reader that he should accept responsibility and rectify the problem. In addition to outlining the details that would be included in a standard claims letter, it's important to establish a good reason why the company should accept responsibility. It might be for general customer satisfaction, company reputation, or the like. You could simply start with the following:

> *A long-time customer is a reliable customer, and I qualify on both counts. I've been coming to your store for more than ten years, and ...* ◀

Credit buying is much like being drunk. The buzz happens immediately and gives you a lift ... the hangover comes the day after.

—DR. JOYCE BROTHERS

CHAPTER 8

Credit and Collections

h a a a r g e! That's a common cry in our free-enterprise system. About 90 percent of our buying and selling is done with "plastic." Some people even suggest that we're on the verge of becoming a cashless society. Wherever you shop, you can sign up for a credit card and charge purchases on the spot. All you need is a pen, a semi-decent credit history, and a would-those-eyes-lie kind of look.

WHAT'S IN THIS CHAPTER

- *Credit fosters more buying*
- *Collecting your debts*
- *Rewarding prompt payment*
- *Apologizing for erroneously sent collection letter*

As charge accounts flourish, businesses burgeon and the mail carrier collapses under the weight of consumers' end-of-the-month billings. This chapter takes you through the pros and woes of credit buying, including customers who keep telling you, "The check is in the mail."

Credit Fosters More Buying

Credit is beneficial for consumers because they can buy now and pay later, avoid carrying large amounts of cash, and exchange or return merchandise more easily. Businesses obviously profit from higher sales, but they do experience a downside.

Credit increases the cost of doing business, ties up capital, and accumulates losses from bad debts. Therefore, businesses must be cautious before extending credit to any customer who requests it. Credit is based on the 4-Cs:

Character	A sense of dealing honestly and ethically
Capacity	The ability to pay
Capital	Tangible assets
Conditions	Business trends or demands.

Soliciting Customers

Businesses solicit credit customers so they don't have to rely solely on walk-in trade to build an ample base of qualified charge customers. Solicitation can take the form of sending a general mailing, welcoming a new family to town, or announcing a store celebration or seasonal sale. Following are some aspects of a successful solicitation letter. Check out Example 8-1 to apply these aspects.

- **Project a courteous and friendly tone.**

- **Extend an invitation to come in and browse and to fill out a credit application.**

    When you come in, please stop by and fill out an application for a convenient <your company> charge account.

    Won't you give me a call at your earliest convenience so that we can arrange to meet personally to discuss how our credit arrangements can serve you?

- **Entice the customer with information about your merchandise or services.**

    <Company> has a treasure trove of merchandise waiting for you. We hope you'll stop by to browse and delight in the unusual merchandise you find.

    You'll continue to enjoy these exclusive advantages that are unavailable to other shoppers:
    - *Courtesy Certificates to create your own sales*
    - *Previews of sales and exclusive storewide events*
    - *A 90-day 0% finance charge.*

- **Stress the advantages of buying on credit.**

    It's so much easier to shop when you can just write a check once a month.

- **Call for action.**

    We know that you'll enjoy the privilege and convenience of being a <your company> charge customer. Why not stop by soon and let us serve you?

LETTERHEAD

July 1, 20—

Mr. Glen Hamilton
54 Annurack Road
Allston, MA 02134

Dear Mr. Hamilton:

Subject: Managing your credit so wisely

Congratulations on having managed your credit so wisely. It's for that reason that you've been selected as a candidate for our valuable credit card. Here's how the card can save you money:

- ☑ *Low interest rates and cash advances.* With a 5.5% variable APR, our credit card can save you many percentage points over other cards. In fact, this is one of the few cards available today to offer such a low APR on both purchases and cash advances.

- ☑ *No annual fees.* While some low-APR cards look good at first glance, beware of the fine print. Annual fees can be as high as $— per year. With ours, there is never an annual fee.

- ☑ *Sizable credit line.* You'll hold a powerful credit line of up to $1500. Our card lets you take your total available credit line in cash for any reason you choose.

- ☑ *Grace period for purchases.* Some lenders charge interest immediately on the amount of your purchases. Not us. We allow you a 30-day, interest-free grace period for payment on purchases.

- ☑ *Special privileges.* You'll be notified of advance sales and private sales that are exclusively for credit customers.

Next step
Just fill out the enclosed credit application today and enjoy the advantages that our credit card has to offer.

Sincerely,

Laura Kelley, Manager

Enclosure

Example 8-1: Selecting Customers for Credit

Extending Credit Privileges

Let's assume that a credit check has revealed the customer to be creditworthy. The first step in establishing the credit relationship is to send a "good news" letter extending credit privileges. Following are some aspects of such a letter. Check out Example 8-2 to apply these aspects.

- **Approve the credit cheerfully.**

  Welcome to our family of satisfied customers who come into <your company> and say, "Charge it!" On behalf of everyone at <your company>, I'd like to thank you for your trust and loyalty.

- **Explain specific terms of the account.** (Embed this portion of the letter in the middle because it detracts from the friendly tone. However, it is necessary information.)

- **Delicately encourage more buying.**

  The catalog contains several order forms and return envelopes that will make it easy for you to place your orders.

- **Express appreciation for the customer's patronage, encourage open communication, and/or discuss company services.**

  At <your company> we regard you as our top priority. We look forward to serving you as our customer for years to come.

Refusing Credit Privileges

Let's assume that a credit check has revealed the customer is *not* creditworthy. This is a very delicate situation, because you want to persuade the customer to deal with you on a cash basis and not discourage buying. Tell the customer you're unable to extend credit right now, but leave the door open. Following are some aspects of a letter refusing credit.

Check out Example 8-3 to apply these aspects.

> ▶ Because of the sensitivity of a letter of this nature, it may be wise not to use a subject line. In that way you can deliver the message gently and maintain goodwill. ◀

- **Express appreciation for the customer's interest in the company.**

  Thank you for requesting credit with <your company>. And thank you for completing and returning your application forms so quickly.

December 10, 20—

Ms. Helen Black
5 Kane Park
Hickory, NC 28601

Dear Ms. Black:

Subject: Please enjoy the convenience of your new credit card

Welcome! We are pleased to present your new Stella's Boutique Credit Card—
your entree to a world of special privileges reserved exclusively for you. You can
be sure that our sales associates will do everything possible to make your shopping a pleasant and satisfying experience. If you have any special needs—just ask!

Starting now, you'll be invited to attend private sales and enjoy savings that aren't
advertised to the general public. You'll be notified by mail in advance of selected
sales in all your favorite locations—from fashions to home furnishings and much
more.

We look forward to seeing you at Stella's Boutique, where the exciting world of
shopping awaits you!

You can count on us,

Stella Steele
President

P.S. If you have any questions about your account or would like to apply for a
higher credit limit, please call me at Ext. 456.

Example 8-2: Welcoming a new credit card customer

March 14, 20—

Ms. Danielle Radner
10 Powder Hill Road
Verona, NJ 07044

Dear Ms. Radner:

We thank you for your request for credit; it's a compliment to us. Your references have all agreed that you've been very cooperative and are always willing to discuss the details of your account.

Our experience has taught us that next to credit references, the most important aspect affecting business success is cash on hand. This is especially true for new businesses such as yours. We always encourage our customers to maintain a cash balance that will allow them to sufficiently cover salaries and expenses for at least six months. We are certain that within the next few months you'll be able to increase your average cash balance. It is, therefore, for your benefit as well as ours that we suggest that you reapply for credit when your cash position is somewhat stronger.

Enclosed you'll find our latest sales brochure. You'll notice that an additional five-percent discount is offered to any customer who pays cash. Just fill out the order blank, enclose your check, and your order will be on its way.

We will be more than happy to review your credit request in the near future, and we look forward to having you join our family of satisfied customers.

Sincerely,

Bob Hanscom
Vice President

Enclosure

Example 8-3: Refusing credit tactfully

- **Refuse by first mentioning favorable observations, putting your refusal of credit at the end.**

  Your references unanimously agreed that you are one of their most cooperative customers. After carefully reviewing your many obligations, we feel that we cannot open a credit account for you at this time. While you are working through your obligations, however, we can still be of service to you.

- **Offer alternatives such as reapplying at a later date and buying on a cash basis in the meantime.**

  In the meantime, we'd be delighted to fill your orders on a cash basis and to review your credit request as soon as some of your obligations have been satisfied.

- **Assure the person that you want her business and are willing to work with her.**

- **Sound sincere, not degrading.**

Encouraging Credit Buying

The purpose of extending credit to customers is to increase sales. Therefore, an active account is an advantage to your customers and to you. If an account goes unused for an extended period, ask yourself these questions: If I were a credit customer …

- What would it take for me to reactivate my account?
- Would I like to hear "We miss you"?
- Is there something special waiting for me?
- Is there is a store celebration or seasonal sale?

Never play up "use your credit," or you risk sounding greedy. Write your letter in such a tone that you express appreciation for the customer's business. Check out Example 8-4 for a letter encouraging credit buying.

> ▶ It's important to motivate return business from a customer as soon as an account is opened. Some companies send thank-you letters to customers who pay on time; others offer them discounts. ◀

April 12, 20—

Mr. and Mrs. Eugene Rourk
144 Westford Place
Saunderstown, RI 02874

Dear Mr. and Mrs. Rourk:

We've missed you!

It's a pleasure to have you as one of our valued customers, and we want to continue giving you the kind of service you deserve. Why not stop by to take advantage of the special once-a-year inventory sale that will be offered during the week of July 1? We're here to help you whenever you visit us.

Sincerely,

Example 8-4: Encouraging the customer to come in and spend

If you owe $50, you're a delinquent account.
If you owe $50,000, you're a small businessman.
If you owe $50 million, you're a corporation.
If you owe $50 billion, you're the government.

—LYNN TOWNSEND WHITE, JR., American historian

Some people and companies do not meet their financial obligations. Excuses for not paying bills are as varied as people themselves. They range from "I've run out of checks and the printers are on strike" to "I'm in jail and will pay you in two years when I get out." There was even a fellow who placed his own obituary in the newspaper and mailed a copy to all his creditors.

Credit managers, or people who deal with debtors on a regular basis, realize that the longer an account is outstanding, the less likely it is to be paid. Also, the sooner the customer pays the bill, the sooner she'll make additional purchases. So it behooves everyone to settle an account quickly.

Collection letters are generally written in a series, ranging from gentle reminders to the threat of turning the matter over to a collection agency or an attorney. This section will address the following types of letters:

1. Gentle reminder

2. Stronger reminder

3. Request for an explanation

4. Appeal for payment

5. Last call for payment.

> ▶ Typically collection letters are sent three to four weeks apart. However, you may not have the patience or the cash flow to take this process through five attempts, especially if the customer has a poor track record. Your options are to accelerate the succession of letters to one every two weeks or to decide how long you're willing to wait to put on the pressure. ◀

Giving a Gentle Reminder

It's quite possible that this reminder and the payment will cross in the mail. Or perhaps the customer just forgot. Following are ways to create a gentle reminder:

- Send a preprinted reminder card.

- Attach a sticker to the original invoice.

- Write a note on the bottom of the second invoice.

Following are some aspects of a gentle reminder. Check out Example 8-5 to apply these aspects to a preprinted card and Example 8-6 to apply them to a personalized letter. (You may want just to resubmit the original invoice and handwrite any of these comments near the bottom.)

- **Call attention to the oversight.**

  We haven't received payment for the <date> invoice. If it's on its way, thanks. If not, please send it out today.

- **Urge prompt payment.**

  Won't you drop your check in the mail today? We've enclosed a self-addressed envelope for your convenience.

- **Suggest merchandise that may be of interest.**

  The prediction for this winter is cold and snowy. Have you considered purchasing a snowblower? <Your company> is offering a preseason sale on ABC snowblowers during the next three weeks, or as long as the supply lasts. Once your account has been satisfied, wouldn't it be nice to know that you'll never have to shovel your driveway again?

Occasionally we all need a little reminder to do something we had intended to do, but just forgot.

Won't you please take a moment to send us your check for $_____ today? If this card and your check crossed in the mail, thank you for your payment.

Thank you.

<Name>

Example 8-5: Gentle reminder card (preprinted)

March 3, 20—

Mr. I. O. Hugh
100 Slow Lane
Candor, NC 27229

Dear Mr. Hugh:

Subject: Invoice No. 345

We know that the due date of your payment has slipped your mind and that by now your check for $750 is probably in the mail. If so, we thank you.

More helpful hints, such as the ones included in your recent shipment, are available to you upon request. If there is any other way that we can be helpful to you, please let us know.

Sincerely,

Michael Bigelow
Manager

Example 8-6: Gentle reminder letter

Giving a Stronger Reminder

Even your fast-paying customers may overlook a payment. If the customer ignores the gentle reminder, send a stronger reminder three to four weeks later. Following are some aspects of a stronger reminder. Check out Example 8-7 to apply these to your collection letter.

- **Reaffirm the good relationship you've enjoyed.**

- **Stress the customer's financial obligation.**

- **Employ sales tactics.**

    When you mail your payment of $—, due <date>, why not send your summer order?

- **Offer to make payment easy.**

    Please slip your check into the self-addressed envelope we've enclosed.

Requesting an Explanation

Send this third letter in the collection series to customers who've ignored the previous reminders but who generally keep their accounts current. This reminder assumes that something out of the ordinary prevents the customer from making payment. It also offers to open the lines of communication. Following are some aspects of a request for an explanation. Check out Example 8-8 to apply these aspects.

- **Request communication from the customer.**

    I would like to talk to you about the circumstances that have caused your bill in the amount of $— to become three months overdue.

    Can you help us? We are wondering about the circumstances that have caused your bill in the amount of $— to become three months overdue.

- **Suggest that perhaps there might be an error in the bill or some good reason for the delay.**

    You've always paid your bills so promptly that we're wondering if there may have been an error in the bill or if there may have been some other problem.

    Because you have always been such a fast-paying customer, we're wondering if there is some reason why you are unable to make full payment at this time.

- **Show sincere interest in settling the account.**

    Be assured that we'll cooperate in any way we can. If you're having financial difficulties, we will be more than happy to work out an easy-payment plan.

April 3, 20—

Mr. I. O. Hugh
100 Slow Lane
Candor, NC 27229

Dear Mr. Hugh:

Subject: Invoice No. 345

You've always been one of our valued customers, and we look forward to being of service to you for many more years. As a businessperson yourself, we know you appreciate those who meet their financial obligations in a timely manner. We do too. Won't you please send us your check in the amount of $750 in the enclosed self-addressed envelope?

Within the next two weeks you'll receive our catalog displaying our new line of winter merchandise. Our sales representative will call you shortly thereafter to help you determine your needs.

Sincerely,

Michael Bigelow
Manager

Enclosure

Example 8-7: Second, stronger reminder

May 3, 20—

Mr. I. O. Hugh
100 Slow Lane
Candor, NC 27229

Dear Mr. Hugh:

Subject: Third reminder of unpaid balance

After three months we still haven't received your check in the amount of $750 or any explanation as to why your bill has not been paid. Since you've always paid so promptly, we're wondering if perhaps there are extenuating circumstances or if there is some error in your statement.

Next step
If either is the case, please contact us so that we can work together to retain your good credit standing. Or, return your check for $750 in the enclosed envelope.

Sincerely,

Michael Bigelow
Manager

Enclosure

Example 8-8: Third reminder: request for an explanation

- **Make it easy to for the customer to respond.**

  Next step
  An explanation? Your check for $——? A payment plan? Please put one of them in the enclosed self-addressed envelope today.

Appealing for Payment

Several months have passed, and it's now time to apply pressure. Never suggest that the customer should pay because your company needs the money; it's her responsibility to pay her debts. Because you still want to retain the customer's business if possible, the following are some aspects to use in your appeal for payment. Check out Example 8-9 to apply these aspects.

- **Recap the history of the account.**

  Your account is now four months past due and you've ignored all our prior notices.

- **Appeal to the customer's pride or sense of fair play, or employ any psychological appeal you feel may work. Don't be sarcastic or insulting.**

  By sending your check today, you'll be able to maintain your fine credit reputation and continue to order without having to include a check each time.

- **Warn of further action.**

  You're putting your good credit reputation at risk. Please don't force us to take this matter further.

- **Indicate your faith in the customer's intention to pay.**

  We know you understand the importance of a good credit reputation. Why not put your check in the mail today, while it's fresh in your mind?

Making a Last Call for Payment

About five months have passed and you'll make one last appeal. The customer has ignored all your efforts and you're not willing to be patient any longer. The customer will be given one last opportunity to pay before you turn this matter over to an attorney or collection agency. Even at this late date, you'd like to salvage the relationship. Following are some aspects of a last call for payment. Check out Example 8-10 to apply these aspects.

- **Set a firm deadline—usually five to ten days.**

  If we don't receive payment in full within ten days from the date of this letter, we will turn this matter over to our attorneys for collection.

June 3, 20—

Mr. I. O. Hugh
100 Slow Lane
Candor, NC 27229

Dear Mr. Hugh:

Subject: Fourth reminder of unpaid balance

Have you ever considered that your credit reputation is much like an insurance policy; it protects you against loss? The loss of buying on credit can be devastating to your business for the following reasons:

- It affects your cash flow
- It limits your ability to replenish your stock
- It costs you the goodwill you have worked so hard to establish.

Your account is now four months past due, and you've not responded to any of our requests for payment. By sending your check in the amount of $750 today, you'll ensure the privilege of maintaining the good credit reputation you now have. Take a moment now to drop your check in the mail.

Required action
We hope it won't be necessary for us to take this matter further, because you are one of our valued customers.

Sincerely,

Michael Bigelow
Manager

Example 8-9: Fourth reminder: appeal for payment

July 3, 20—

Mr. I. O. Hugh
100 Slow Lane
Candor, NC 27229

Dear Mr. Hugh:

Subject: Final notice

For five months we've been writing to you in an attempt to clear up your unpaid balance of $750. You've chosen to ignore all our efforts. If you send your check for $750 today, you can continue your good credit reputation.

Action demanded
Unless you send us payment in full within ten days from the date of this letter, we'll turn this matter over for collection. The choice is yours. If your check reaches us by July 13, your credit reputation will remain intact, and we'll be able to continue doing business with you on a credit basis.

Sincerely,

Michael Bigelow
Manager

Example 8-10: Fifth reminder (pay up or else)

- **Outline the action you will take.**

  Don't make it necessary for us to take legal action. Put your check in the enclosed envelope and mail it today.

- **Stress the importance of a good credit reputation.**

  <Name>, we have been more than fair. For the last five months you've ignored all our efforts to contact you. As an upstanding member of the business community, your credit reputation is of great value. You are now in danger of placing a permanent blemish on that record.

- **Offer a final chance for payment.**

  This is the last time you will hear from us directly. Please put your check in the mail today to avoid legal action.

▶ Sometimes a longtime, valued customer is delinquent and you want to take special care in addressing the situation. You can write a letter such as you see in Example 8-11 at any point in the collection cycle. Mention your pleasure in the relationship, write a neutral subject line, and provide the customer with some way to save face. ◀

Requesting Additional Payment

Collection letters may deal with problems other than nonpayment, such as you see in the examples that follow. Example 8-12 requests payment for shipping charges the customer neglected to include in her payment. Example 8-13 is an initial letter requesting payment for an unearned discount. Requesting additional money can be touchy, especially if the customer represents a large account.

Rewarding Prompt Payment

Customers who pay promptly help your cash flow, and you want to encourage them to continue paying promptly. Just as you dun customers who are delinquent, you should reward customers who pay promptly. In some cases, thank you is enough, but an incentive to continue paying promptly really packs a wallop. Following is a list of possible incentives. Example 8-14 issues a small discount for prompt payment.

- Discount for continued prompt payment
- Coupon for a dollar amount
- Notice of special offer to preferred customers only

March 3, 20—

Mr. I. O. Hugh
100 Slow Lane
Candor, NC 27229

Dear Mr. Hugh:

Subject: Account No. 3455

Over the last several years, our business relationship has been a source of great pleasure to me. Please understand that my reason for writing is to foster our relationship.

Your account is in arrears, and that is causing our accounting department some concern. I know that your business is seasonal and that cash flow is a problem for you at this time of the year. We have always been willing to work with you during these times.

Please call me when you receive this letter so we can work out a mutually agreeable way for you to pay this account. I know you will understand that my motive is to continue our special relationship and to help you get through this tough situation.

Sincerely,

Michael Bigelow
Manager

Example 8-11: Collection letter to a longtime, valued customer

April 23, 20—

Ms. Brianne Smith
3 Church Street
Kaufman, TX 75142

Dear Ms. Smith:

Subject: Adjustment to your last payment

Thank you for your recent order and for your prompt payment. When you sent us your check in the amount of $100, you neglected to include the shipping charges of $5.50.

Please note that, rather than ask you to send us another check, we'll add that balance to your next statement.

Sincerely,

Michael Bigelow
Manager

Example 8-12: Requesting payment for shipping

September 3, 20—

Mr. Paul Giannetti
Giannetti & Sons
200 Central Avenue
Winthrop, MA 02152

Dear Mr. Gianetti:

Cash discounts always contribute to the bottom line. That's why we offer our customers a 1% discount when they pay us within 10 days from the date of the invoice. It benefits them as well as us.

We notice that your discount period expired August 15 and your check was dated and mailed on August 20. Won't you please put a check in the mail today in the amount of $25, and your account will be paid in full.

Thank you for your continued business.

Sincerely,

Michael Bigelow
Manager

Example 8-13: Requesting payment for an unearned discount

LETTERHEAD

November 2, 20—

Mr. Kevin Kelley
One Williams Avenue
Providence, RI 02903

Dear Mr. Kelley:

You are a valued customer

We just received your check for $500 in payment of your March invoice. We have noticed that for the past six months you've paid well in advance of the 15th due date.

Rewarding your promptness

Starting with your April invoice, you may deduct 1.5% when you pay by the 15th of each month. We thank you for your continued loyalty.

Best wishes,

Michael Bigelow
Manager

Example 8-14: Thanks for prompt payment

Apologizing for Erroneously Sent Collection Letter

When you send a collection letter in error, acknowledge the mistake as soon as it's brought to your attention. Example 8-15 offers a sincere apology.

LETTERHEAD

January 22, 20—

Ms. Jane Ordway
1 Corriander Street
Glenwood Springs, CO 81601

Dear Ms. Ordway:

Subject: Your account is in good order

We apologize for the collection letter we sent you last month. These mistakes don't happen often, and we are red-faced, to say the least.

We're especially sorry that this happened to a good customer such as you. We hope that this error didn't cause you any embarrassment or inconvenience and that it won't damage the wonderful relationship we've established over the years.

Sincerely,

Michael Bigelow
Manager

Example 8-15: Apology for erroneously sent collection letter

President Coolidge invited some Vermont
friends to dine at the White House. They were
worried about their table manners and decided
to do everything President Coolidge did. The
meal passed smoothly until coffee was served.
Coolidge poured his coffee into a saucer. The
guests followed suit. He added sugar and cream,
and the visitors did likewise. Then, Coolidge
leaned over and gave his saucer to the cat.

—*Curmudgeon's Corner,* as reported in
an Ann Landers column

CHAPTER 9

You Are Cordially Invited

In business, you will come across various opportunities to extend invitations to colleagues, associates, customers, and others. Whether you invite them to a black-tie affair, a seminar, or a country hoedown, you want your invitation to be "inviting." This chapter gives you suggestions on issuing invitations to business associates for a variety of events you may host—formal, semiformal, and informal.

WHAT'S IN THIS CHAPTER

• *Come one, come all*
• *Invitation by letter*
• *Formal invitations*
• *Invitation to a seminar*

Come One, Come All

The invitation forms your guests' first impression about your event, and it should make the recipient look forward to coming. The invitation establishes the tone for the celebration and generates excitement for the event. The color, size, design, and texture of the invitation must all work together to reflect your image and the nature of the function. Invitations come in all shapes and sizes—anything from the $5.00 packet you buy at a stationery store to the formal engraved invitation. I once received a jigsaw-puzzle invitation from a computer company. When I put it together, it looked like a computer, and the monitor showed the invitation. Both related to the business of the company, and the whole was very creative.

> ▶ The invitation is a statement about you and the type of event you're hosting. Is a formal printed invitation better than a letter invitation? That's like asking, Is Max Factor better than Mary Kay? It's strictly cosmetic. ◀

What the Invitation Includes

No matter what kind of function you host or what kind of invitation you send, there are certain things you should include on the invitation:

Host(s)   Name of host, host company, and/or company logo, if appropriate.

Inviting phrase   Here are a few formal and informal inviting phrases:

- Requests the pleasure of your company
- Cordially invites you to
- Would like to have you join us
- Please celebrate with us
- Stop by for wine and cheese

Guest of honor or purpose of event   Why are you hosting this event?

- To introduce, meet, or honor …
- It's Christmastime or picnic time
- To mark a special anniversary
- Moving to a new location
- To show customer appreciation

Date   The formality of the date depends on the tone appropriate to the event.

Formal: Friday, the eighth of April, Two thousand … (spelled out)

Less formal: Friday, April eighth, 20—

Informal: Friday, April 8, 20—

Time	Time follows the date.
	Formal: At eight o'clock
	Less formal: At 8 o'clock
	Informal: At 8 p.m.
Address	Put the city and state on a line below the address.
Refreshments	Mention what meals or refreshments (if any) you plan to serve. You may be serving cocktails, lunch, dinner, wine and cheese, a buffet, and so on. If you ignore the issue, the reader assumes you're not planning to serve anything. (You don't want people to show up with thermoses and snacks.)
Dress	(This isn't a *yes* or *no*.) If you don't mention dress, the reader will use his own discretion.
	• If you're planning a formal affair, you might say "Black-tie optional."
	• If you're planning a pool party, you might say, "Please bring bathing suits."
Cost	If the reader is expected to incur a cost, be sure to mention what it is. No one likes last-minute surprises; they create ill will. If you expect attendees to pay for their own alcoholic beverages, you might say something such as, "Soft drinks will be provided and a cash bar will be available."
Response	Let people know how to respond. It may be by phone, e-mail, or response card (for formal events). Some hosts ask for Regrets Only, instead of RSVP. This means that the host wants to hear only from those who plan not to attend. The disadvantage is that people tend to be forgetful and may not respond even though they won't be attending. If you want a reasonably accurate head count, ask people to respond either way.

Timing Is Everything

The rule of thumb is to give people as much notice as you can; they have busy schedules and their calendars fill up quickly. Also, if people are coming from out of town, they may need to make travel arrangements. Following are guidelines for how far in advance to send invitations. If you need to have invitations printed, factor in time for printing, addressing, and mailing.

Function	Lead time
Company picnic	4–6 weeks
Evening reception	4–6 weeks
Cocktail party	2–4 weeks
Christmas party	Around Thanksgiving
Seminar	As soon as it's scheduled

▶ If you receive a group invitation by e-mail and it asks for a response, reply only to the person who sent the invitation; *don't reply to all.* (Many people reply to the group, rather than just the sender.) ◀

Company Event

If you host a company event—such as a picnic or holiday party—consider posting the announcement on the company's intranet. Send e-mails to everyone and include a link to the page. Example 9-1 is an e-mail message announcing an annual holiday party that has a link to the company's intranet. Example 9-2 is the link with all the information. Example 9-3 is an e-mail invitation to the staff for the celebration of a job well done.

To:	**Distribution**
Cc:	
Bcc:	
Subject:	**Holiday party on December 12**

Hi everyone,

Click on www.mayberry.com/holiday to get the lowdown on the annual Christmas party.

Regards, Betty

Example 9-1: E-mail message about holiday party with link

Mayberry Associates cordially invites
you and a guest to its
Annual Holiday Party
at the
Renaissance Century Hotel
Nyack, New York

Saturday, December 12, XXXX
At 8 PM

RSVP by calling Sweeny Todd at extension 344
By December 5

Example 9-2: Holiday party invitation at link

Hi Gang,

I invite all of you to share in "Sundaes on Friday" this Friday at 3:00. We'll meet around the picnic tables and enjoy a little ice cream and socializing. You've all been working very hard and I appreciate your efforts.

I don't want anyone to report to work over the weekend and will padlock the doors. Make your own sundaes, then go home and enjoy the beautiful weather promised for the weekend.

Thank you all for an outstanding job!

Jake

Example 9-3: E-mail invitation to a celebration to show appreciation to employees

Invitation by Letter

A letter invitation is less formal than a printed invitation. The one thing to keep in mind when sending a letter invitation is that you want to make sure people recognize it as an invitation. Don't make the mistake of assuming everyone reads your "pearls of prose" closely enough. Example 9-4 is a letter to customers inviting them to a buffet to show appreciation for their loyalty.

Formal Invitations

Formal invitations are printed professionally. They're generally printed or engraved in black on white or ecru stock. Formal invitations are generally accompanied by response cards and return envelopes. Example 9-5 is an invitation from a board of directors to selected guests to celebrate the opening of new offices.

> ▶ The outer mailing envelopes should be handwritten. If you have the money and the inclination, you might hire a calligrapher for an elegant touch. ◀

July 6, 20—

Mr. Milton Goldstein, President
Parador Enterprises, Inc.
405 Madison Avenue
Peru, OH 44847

Dear Milt,

Join us for a buffet dinner so we can thank you for your loyalty!

You've played an important role in the success of our company, and we want to thank you personally. Please join us for a buffet dinner. Dress casually and bring a big appetite.

> *Where:* Commodore Hotel
> *Date:* August 12
> *Time:* 8 p.m.

Please call me by August 5 to let me know if you'll be joining us. We look forward to welcoming you.

Most cordially,

Dan Gleason

Example 9-4: Letter invitation to a customer-appreciation dinner

> *The Board of Directors*
> *of*
> *Marric Consulting Corp.*
> *cordially invites you to a cocktail reception*
> *on the occasion of the opening of its new offices.*
>
> *Friday, the eighth of April,* < year written out >
> *at eight o'clock*
> *24 Besen Parkway*
> *New Holland, PA 17557*
> *(Black-tie optional)*
>
> *RSVP by March 15, 20—*

Example 9-5: Put on your best bib and tucker

Response Card and Envelope

It's a sad commentary on today's society that you need to ask for a response; people should respond to any invitation. But people are people, and—even with the best of intentions—they're often hopelessly remiss when it comes to responding to invitations. When you send out a formal invitation, ask people to fill out a response card such as the one you see in Example 9-6. You need to know how many people will attend. After all, you wouldn't want to have too many monkey-brain canapés left over because there weren't enough victims to eat them. Also include a self-addressed, stamped return envelope such as the one in Example 9-7. The return address appears on the back flap.

> ▶ Here are a few tips for responding:
> - If you're unable to attend don't write merely "will not attend." You show a lot of class when you add a little note giving a reason. *Will not attend because we'll be out of town. Thanks for inviting us.*
> - Be sure you answer by the expected date. Respond immediately or mark your calendar to respond before the deadline.
> - If you happen to meet your host on the street and say, "I just received your invitation, and I'll be there," that doesn't suffice for a response. ◀

Please respond on or before
March 15, 20—

*M*_____

will _____*attend*

Example 9-6: Formal response card

Marric Consulting Corp.
24 Besen Parkway
New Holland, PA 17557

Example 9-7: Front of response envelope

Special Instructions and Inserts

Include any special messages in the lower portion of the invitation. If you say something is enclosed, make sure to enclose it. Here are a few examples of special messages:

- Valet Parking

- Rain date

- Map

- Please present this invitation at the door

Canceling an Event

If you have to cancel an event, notify each guest personally and give the reason. If there is enough time, write a personal letter; if time is short, phone each guest. Example 9-8 shows how a cancellation letter might read.

Invitation to a Seminar

Before you invite people to a seminar, answer question 3 on your Start Up Sheet, "What's in it for my reader?" Why should the reader spend his time (and/or money) on your seminar? Examples 9-9 and 9-10 show two examples of invitations to seminars.

May 12, 20—

Mr. and Mrs. James Nelson
345 Potake Lane
Medusa, NY 12120

Dear James and Sally,

Need to reschedule the May 15 open house

It's with deep regret that I must cancel the open house scheduled for Friday evening, May 15. My mother is ill, and I'll be flying back to Columbia this evening.

I'll reschedule this when I return.

Sincerely,

Bob

Example 9-8: Canceling an event

Author Dr. Bard Williams
Shares the Excitement of the Web

Radison School hosts Dr. Bard Williams, author of *The Internet for Teachers,* 3rd ed. (part of the Dummies Series), by IDG Books Worldwide. Dr. Williams is a "technology evangelist" who has been sharing the excitement of classroom technology with educators for years. Join us for this free seminar!

Date: September 16, 20—
Time: 2:00 p.m.
Place: Foster City Campus

Benefit from Dr. Williams's Keen Industry Insights

If you're like most educators, you are anxious to explore the brave new world of the Internet. Dr. Williams will strip away all the "technobabble" and teach you how you can harness the power of the Internet in your classroom. Here are some of the topics that he'll cover:

- Explore Web page production and find out how to use powerful Web page creation tools.

- Build your own strategies for teaching and learning with the Web.

- Uncover tips on marketing your Web pages.

- Find out about Java and JavaScript and how they can liven up your Web pages.

At the seminar, you'll also learn about the exciting new programs offered at Radison School, and you'll have a chance to meet many of the faculty members.

How to Reserve Your Seat

If you haven't already done so, please make your reservation now. Seating is limited.

Register on the Web at **www.radisonschool.com** or
Call us at **1-800-RADISON, ext. 476**

Example 9-9: Invitation to a seminar

Energize Your Business Writing!
Practical, Effective Marketing for Business

Quarter Savings Bank is proud to announce our next Business Success Seminar

No matter what you write—letters, memos, e-mail, proposals, reports, brochures, and more…this mini-workshop is a must. In just two hours, you'll learn to write strategic documents your readers read first…documents that get results… documents that deliver a persuasive message.

This workshop will cover:

- ✓ *Writing a compelling and descriptive subject line*
- ✓ *Karate chopping your way through writer's block*
- ✓ *Understanding your audience, purpose, and key issue*
- ✓ *Using e-mail etiquette*
- ✓ *Psychology of punctuation*

Please bring a document to work on—one that's in your hand or in your head! It can be a letter, brochure, website, proposal, e-mail or anything you need to write.

Sheryl Lindsell-Roberts, Principal of Sheryl Lindsell-Roberts & Associates (Marlborough, MA) has earned numerous awards and national recognition in her 20-year career as a business-writing expert. She's written 18 books, including *Business Writing for Dummies.* Companies and universities throughout the United States have acclaimed Sheryl's workshops.

Please join us on Tuesday, October 21st, 20—
8:30 AM – 11:00 AM
Continental breakfast served

**Hemenway Outdoor Center, 275 Forest Ridge Road, Nashua, NH
at the Beech Cliff Hotel**

Space is limited!
For reservations, Call Grace Miles at (603) 225-3061, by October 17th

**Quarter
Savings Bank**

Example 9-10: Invitation to a seminar

People forget how fast you did a job—but they remember how well you did it.

—HOWARD W. NEWTON
American advertising executive

CHAPTER 10

Placing and Acknowledging Orders

People juggling jobs, errands, and families don't always have time to stroll through the malls and do leisurely shopping. Therefore, mail order has become big business. It offers convenience, detailed information, excellent guarantees and return policies, and generally good service. This chapter provides insights into the process, from placing orders by mail to responding to orders.

WHAT'S IN THIS CHAPTER

- *Placing orders*
- *Acknowledging and filling orders*
- *Following up*

Placing Orders

As a mail-order customer, you probably either complete and mail an order form, phone the company, or order directly from the company's website. However, there may be instances when those avenues aren't available and you need to send a letter. Following are tips on information to include so the company can fill your order promptly and accurately.

- **Open with a courteous request.** When you start the letter with a smile, you get results.

    Please send me the following . . .

    I'd like to order . . .

- **Mention the source.** If there's a date or number on a catalog, mention that.

- **Send a complete description of the merchandise.** Include quantity, page number, color, grade, size, weight, model, price, extended price, or other special distinctions, or whatever is appropriate. Include local tax, insurance, and shipping and handling, if applicable.

- **State the method of payment.** If you enclose a check, mention the date and check number. If you use a credit card, give the account number and expiration date. Never send cash through the mail.

- **Give the shipping address.** If the shipping address differs from the address on your letterhead (or if you're not using letterhead), be sure to specify the delivery address.

- **Specify the method of shipment.** If you need the order in a hurry, let the company know that you're willing to pay for expedited delivery. If not, the company will select the method of shipment.

> ► The United States is one of the few countries that doesn't use the metric system. When you order something from another country, always include the metric equivalents. (Check out Appendix D.) ◄

Acknowledging and Filling Orders

An order processor's job is never easy, especially during crunch times (such as the final hours of the Christmas rush). Can you imaging trying to fill an order for the following customer at the beginning of April when the Northern folks are coming out of winter hibernation and getting into gardening mode?

Dear Sir or Madam:

Several years ago I ordered five plants from you, and I'd now like to order five more. I can't remember the name of the plants, but they have big green leaves, small pink flowers, and bloom in the summer. I can't seem to find the catalog either.

Please send me five more of the plants I just described and send me a bill. Thank you.

Very truly yours,

Clueless in Coconut Grove

What's missing? Just about everything the order processor needs to fill the order. If you think this is uncommon—think again. This happens more often than you can imagine. Ask any prematurely gray-haired order processor you know.

Brimming with Customer Service

Public-relations-minded business people acknowledge all orders they can't ship immediately. Example 10-1 shows a simple acknowledgment card that makes customers feel important. They fill in the blanks by hand for an added personal touch.

We are delighted to fill
your order for _____, which will
ship on _____.

It's our pleasure to serve you, and we
hope you will give us that privilege again soon.

<Name>

Example 10-1: Card acknowledging an order

Gimme Details

Orders that omit critical information are so common that many order processors reply by using form letters or cards that list all the possible reasons why they can't process an order. In Example 10-2, the order processors merely place a check mark next to the applicable reason(s). If you prepare such a letter or card, include some of the following:

- **Start with an upbeat opening.**

  Yes, you will have your order in time for Christmas.

- **Tell the customer exactly what information you need.**

  Before we can ship your order, you must let us know . . .

- **Make it easy for the customer to reply. Send a postage-paid reply envelope or card.**

The *hydrangeas* you ordered are among our best buys of the season. Please give us the following information, and we'll ship your plants immediately.

☐ Catalog number _____

☐ Quantity _____

☑ Color _____

We hope you'll get many years of pleasure from the plants you order from us. Remember that we offer a one-year money-back guarantee.

Garden of Eden Delights

Example 10-2: Card asking for more information

Other Getting-in-Touch Situations

Other circumstances may require you to touch base with a customer. When one of the following reasons applies, send the customer a letter immediately. (Don't send something that's preprinted, as then it may look as if you have these problems often.)

- **You can only fill part of the order.** Let the customer know what she will receive and when. Give the customer appropriate options, and apologize for any inconvenience.

- **You need to substitute one item for another.** Always notify the customer when you must substitute one item for another, even if the substitution is minor.

- Explain the reason for the substitution.
- Specify what you'd like to offer as a substitute.
- Give her the option of refusing.
- **You can't fill the order immediately**. Write to the customer promptly, citing the reason for the delay. A customer will understand a logical reason for a delay, but won't tolerate long and silent waiting periods.

Example 10-3 is a letter to a customer advising of a delay. The customer is given the option of accepting either partial shipment of the order or a substitute item. Example 10-4 also informs the customer of a delay, but doesn't offer any choices.

Following Up

The epitome of customer service is to follow up on your sales. This holds true for established customers as well as new customers. Example 10-5 thanks a customer for her business and discreetly gives her an incentive to buy more.

March 3, 20—

Ms. Margaret Matheson
300 Prospect Street
Milldale, TN 37171

Dear Ms. Matheson:

Subject: Your order for brushes

On March 10 we will be shipping your order for No. 4 and No. 27 brushes; however, No. 15 is on backorder and won't be available until May.

The choice is yours: Do you want to wait until we have No. 15 in stock, or would you like us to substitute No. 16, which is very close in size?

Please call us at 800-123-4544 and let us know. We look forward to serving you.

Sincerely,

Morris Pratt, Manager

Example 10-3: Letter offering a substitute item

March 3, 20—

Ms. Margaret Matheson
300 Prospect Street
Milldale, TN 37171

Dear Ms. Matheson:

Subject: Your order for brushes

Thank you for your interest in brush No. 15. Because of the unexpected demand, we've temporarily exhausted our supply. We're in the process of placing an order, and we should have your brushes to you by the end of May.

We thank you so much for your order and hope this won't cause you any inconvenience.

Sincerely,

Morris Pratt, Manager

Example 10-4: Letter explaining a delay

LETTERHEAD

March 3, 20—

Ms. Margaret Matheson
300 Prospect Street
Milldale, TN 37171

Dear Ms. Matheson:

Subject: Special buying plan

We want to thank you for your recent order and hope that you are enjoying your new brushes.

As a new customer, you should know about our special buying plan. If you buy more than $500 in merchandise within a six-month period, you will receive a gift card for $25 good on any purchases for the following year.

If at any time you have questions or want to discuss an order, please call me personally. I look forward to being of service.

Sincerely,

Morris Pratt, Manager

Example 10-5: Follow-up thank-you letter

Show me an avid note writer, and 9 times out of 10, I'll show you a success.

—BOB BURG
Endless Referrals

CHAPTER 11

Personal Business Notes

Business writing touches upon very personal matters and reaches people in a very human way. Letters of friendship in the business world may be exchanged between old friends, new friends, or people you met briefly. A personal note takes only a few minutes to write, and its influence may be lasting. Look for opportunities to send personal business notes or letters.

> **WHAT'S IN THIS CHAPTER**
>
> • *Attributes of a personal note*
> • *Asking for and declining favors*
> • *A note of thanks*
> • *The art of giving and receiving gifts*
> • *Words of encouragement*
> • *Extending congratulations*
> • *Offering apologies*

- Acknowledge a gift or favor.

- Thank a colleague for a job well done.

- Express regrets to a colleague who's experiencing difficulties.

- Extend condolences for the loss of a loved one.

- Send an apology.

Personal business letters build bridges. Each time you add a personal sentiment to a business letter, you turn it into a letter that creates goodwill.

> ► When you send a personal note, don't use company letterhead, as it detracts from the warmth of your message. Instead, use plain paper or personal notepaper. It's rarely appropriate to send such a note via e-mail. ◄

Attributes of a Personal Note

When you write a personal business letter, type it or handwrite it. Following are some suggestions:

- **Keep the message brief.** Even a single sentence, such as "I'm delighted for you," is appropriate.
- **Be thoughtful, honest, and prompt.**
- **Avoid exaggerations and trite expressions such as, "I'll bet you a million bucks that you ...."**

Asking for and Declining Favors

It's often best to put requests in writing. This is especially true if there's a chance the reader may not be able to grant your request, as the reader then can say no without giving you the evil eye.

Requesting a Favor

Open with a personal message, give the reader the opportunity to refuse, and personalize the closing. When asking for a favor that's out of the ordinary, send a handwritten note. A note such as you see in Example 11-1 goes a long way.

Dear <name>,

It was delightful seeing you and Grace at the Sullivan's party last week. Those wonderful tans were certainly an indication that you're finally taking time to get away.

I'd like to ask you a big favor, and I certainly understand that this is last-minute notice. <Detail all the information.>

Again, I understand that this is the last minute and you may already have prior commitments. In any event, please send my warmest regards to Grace.

Cordially,

Example 11-1: Requesting a favor

Declining a Favor

Open with an expression of your inability to do the favor asked, give a short explanation, offer an option if that's appropriate, and close by saying that you hope you can be of assistance in the future. Check out Example 11-2 to see how this is done graciously.

Dear <name>,

It isn't easy to refuse someone who's been so kind to me. I'll be out of town next week, but I've taken the liberty of calling Allan to see if he'll be available. Allan will be glad to help you out, so please give him a call at 508-222-3354.

I hope that the next time you need me, I can be there for you.

Regards,

Example 11-2: Expressing your regrets

Expressing Thanks for a Favor

When someone does you a favor, go on record immediately with a thank-you note. If you wait, you may forget. When you are known as someone who says thank you, people regard you as thoughtful and well mannered. They then will be more inclined to say yes to you. Example 11-3 is a brief note of thanks.

Dear <name>,

Your lending me your car this morning when mine wouldn't start was a lifesaver. I made it to the client's office in time for the meeting and was able to close the deal.

Thanks. I really owe you one!

Bill

Example 11-3: A note of thanks for a favor

A Note of Thanks

As you learned at your mother's knee, a little thank-you goes a long way. Little did you know that your mother was preparing you for the business world. Find opportunities to thank people for referrals, special favors, jobs well done, something they did unexpectedly, or just about anything else. Write promptly, be sincere, and make the person who did the nice deed feel like a million dollars. Example 11-4 is an informal thank-you note written on a personalized card.

> ▶ If you're at a loss for words, start with "What a <wonderful luncheon>, <fantastic evening>, <thoughtful gift>, <great surprise>" and the words should flow from there. ◀

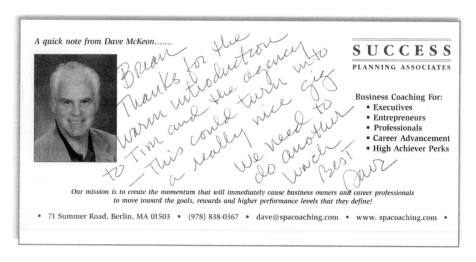

A quick note from Dave McKeon.......

Brian,
Thanks for the warm introduction to Tim and the agency — This could turn into a really nice gig. We need to do another lunch. Best, Dave

SUCCESS
PLANNING ASSOCIATES

Business Coaching For:
• Executives
• Entrepreneurs
• Professionals
• Career Advancement
• High Achiever Perks

Our mission is to create the momentum that will immediately cause business owners and career professionals to move toward the goals, rewards and higher performance levels that they define!

• 71 Summer Road, Berlin, MA 01503 • (978) 838-0367 • dave@spacoaching.com • www. spacoaching.com •

Example 11-4: Personalized thank-you note

The Art of Giving and Receiving Gifts

People give business gifts for a variety of reasons: to say thank you, I'm sorry, congratulations, and to express a host of other sentiments. A gift can be a turkey for Thanksgiving, tickets to the theater or a ball game, an expensive product, or a free trip. Whether you give a gift or acknowledge one, the sender always appreciates a personalized note.

Sending a Gift

When you send someone a gift, be certain to give it in the right spirit, and don't expect anything in return. Example 11-5 shows a note to send with a gift of appreciation.

Dear <name>,

Today <company name> will distribute $1 million in Performance Incentive Awards among employees in recognition of their contributions to our success in the year 20—. Without the individual efforts of each of you, we wouldn't be able to provide high-quality services to our customers. Congratulations!

Please accept this gold pen as a token of our appreciation for your outstanding team efforts. Thanks to your hard work and dedication, we should meet our corporate objectives and provide the high quality of service our clients have come to expect.

Sincerely,

Example 11-5: Sample note to accompany a gift of appreciation

Acknowledging Appropriate Gifts

Always acknowledge gifts with a thank-you that you send in a timely manner. Example 11-6 does this.

Dear <name>,

When you laid the little gift on my desk two days before my birthday and said it was a "little remembrance," I must admit I had all I could do to wait until my birthday to open it. Thank you so much for the wonderful book and for your good taste.

Most sincerely,

Example 11-6: Acknowledging an appropriate gift

Acknowledging Inappropriate Gifts

When someone gives you an inappropriate gift or a gift that's in bad taste, you should still acknowledge it. Notice how Example 11-7 differs in tone from Example 11-6.

Dear <name>,

It was a pleasant surprise to receive the nice gift from you. I appreciate the thought and send you and your family my best wishes.

Most sincerely,

Example 11-7: Acknowledging an inappropriate gift

Refusing Gifts

In many companies, it's against policy to accept a gift under any circumstances. If you have to return or refuse a gift, you must be very tactful. Check out Example 11-8.

Dear <name>,

It is so kind of you to remember me during this Christmas holiday. Your gift is so generous and thoughtful. However, it's against company policy to accept gifts of any sort; therefore, I must return it. I know how much thought went into selecting <gift>, and I greatly appreciate it.

I want to wish you a very wonderful holiday and success in the new year.

Sincerely,

Example 11-8: Refusing a gift

Words of Encouragement

A personal note can be very comforting to a colleague in distress. And without getting too personal, you can let someone know you care by saying the following:

> *I can't help but notice that you haven't been yourself lately. I'm not trying to pry. I just want to let you know I care. If I can be of any help, please don't hesitate.*

Extending Condolences

People often hesitate to write condolence notes because they don't know what to say. Here are a few suggestions:

- **It's okay to use the word *died*.** You don't have to sugarcoat what happened.

- **Describe something you remember about the deceased that was special.** Check out Example 11-9.

Dear <name>,

I'm so very sorry to hear of Jack's death. Through the years, we always looked forward to Jack's visits. He was a gentleman in every sense of the word. There aren't many people in this industry who have his depth of knowledge or such a warm and sincere regard for others.

Everyone who knew Jack will truly miss him.

Warmly,

Example 11-9: Note of condolence when you knew the deceased

- **If you didn't know the deceased well, focus on the impact of his death on the family or coworkers.** Check out Example 11-10.

Dear <name>,

I don't know what to say, except that my heart is breaking for you. Although I didn't know <name of deceased> well, I've always heard of her devotion to you and the family and of all the wonderful work she did for charity. She will certainly be missed.

Please accept my condolences.

Warmly,

Example 11-10: Note of condolence when you didn't know the deceased

- **Consider any of the following messages:**

  I was shocked to learn of the death of <name>. Although he had been ill for a while, I was still taken by surprise.

  I was shocked to hear of the death of <name>. Such losses defy understanding.

  Please accept my deepest sympathy on behalf of everyone at <company>.

  Please accept my condolences on the untimely passing of <name>.

  Our deepest sympathy to you and your family on the death of <name>.

  I was saddened to hear the news that <name> died last week, and I wish to extend my sympathy.

Responding to Condolences

Many people respond to expressions of sympathy. Some people send preprinted cards; others personalize the message. It's a matter of choice. Example 11-11 shows a personalized note.

> Dear <name>,
>
> The memories you shared about my husband were a great source of joy for my family and me. Thanks so much for sharing them and for being so thoughtful.
>
> Messages such as yours mean a great deal.
>
> Thank you.

Example 11-11: A thank-you for a message of condolence

Losing a Job

Losing a job is a shattering experience, regardless of the reason. Example 11-12 offers support without prying.

> Dear <name>,
>
> I just heard the news. I know this is a terrible blow to you at the moment, but try to focus on all the experience you gained and how you'll be able to plug your talents into a company where you'll be fully appreciated. Please let me know if there is anything I can do to help. Review your resume? Run you through a mock interview? Be an ear?
>
> Remember that you're a winner and will land on top!
>
> Sincerely,

Example 11-12: Note for loss of a job

Extending Congratulations

Congratulatory notes are probably the nicest to write. Take advantage of these opportunities; they are innumerable. When congratulating someone, be enthusiastic and sincere without showing envy. Stick to the accomplishment or the occasion. If you don't know the person very well, you may consider sending these via e-mail; see Examples 11-13, 11-14, and 11-15. Examples 11-16, 11-17, and 11-18 are of a more personal nature. Example 11-19 is a message inside a birthday card. Many professionals such as doctors, accountants, financial planners, and others send birthday cards to their clients. Example 11-20 compliments someone on a speech, and Example 11-21 congratulates someone on a personal triumph.

To: gretchensmith@abcco.com
Subject: Congratulations on your promotion

Gretchen,

It didn't take the company long to recognize your talents. Eight years is an extremely short time to burn a path from Director to President. You've worked hard, gained everyone's respect, and now you've made it to the top.

You can count on my cooperation whenever you need it.

Mike

Example 11-13: Congratulations on your promotion

To: glenn_golan@boxwooco.com
Subject: Congratulations on your new job

Glenn,

I read in the company's newsletter about your appointment to the position of Vice President of Marketing of the Tyson Company. I'm sure you're excited about the challenges that await you at Boxwood Industries.

Lots of success and happiness in your new job. Please stay in touch.

Best wishes,
Michael

Example 11-14: Congratulations on your new job

Pat,

The Gibson project would never have been completed without your 150% effort during the last several months. Congratulations on the excellent work you and your team did. I know the many sacrifices you and your families made in order to bring this project to completion. On behalf of all of us, thanks for your dedication above and beyond.

Best wishes,
Molly

Example 11-15: Congratulations on your hard work

Dear Bob,

We're just delighted to hear that Emily Ann arrived on March 1. We're looking forward to seeing pictures of her and perhaps to seeing the baby herself at the company picnic.

My best,
Molly

Example 11-16: Congratulations on the birth of a baby

Dear Jackson,

Congratulations on the new addition to your family. We're looking forward to meeting little Jack and hope you'll bring him by the office so we can say "hello."

My best,
Molly

Example 11-17: Congratulations on the adoption of a baby

Dear Paula,

I want to send my very best wishes to you and Bill on the occasion of your wedding. I understand that you're going to Hawaii for your honeymoon, and I hope you return tanned and rested.

My best,
Molly

Example 11-18: Congratulations on a marriage

When you were a child, did you dream of what
life would be like?

Did you ever imagine the people you'd meet
and the lives you'd touch?

Life tends to change us. There are friends you've made, friends
you've yet to find, people you've left behind, and
ones still on the path to where you're going.

I, for one, am glad that our paths have crossed. I hope you have a
wonderful birthday and that all your dreams come true.

May your life go according to plan.

Brooke Riley

Example 11-19: Birthday greetings from a financial planner

Dear Max,

I was in the back of the room last night and you probably didn't see me. Not only did you deliver your talk with punch and conviction, you also delivered a very important message. I had no idea that you had traveled so extensively.

Congratulations on a first-rate job.

Regards,
Sarah

Example 11-20: Compliments on a speech

Dear Brian,

Congratulations on your victory! All your friends at the office rejoiced when it was announced. Although you were a dark horse, none of us had any doubts about your overwhelming qualifications. Apparently, the voters didn't have any doubts either.

I wish I could have videotaped our reaction. We'll certainly miss you, but our loss is their gain.

Warmest regards,
John

Example 11-21: Congratulations on a personal triumph

Offering Apologies

No matter how hard you try to always do the right thing, sometimes you mess up; it's part of being human. When you commit a faux pas, own up to your mistake and apologize immediately. Never apologize on the phone. Do it in person, if you can. If not, send a handwritten note such as the one in Example 11-22.

Dear Margie,

This is one of the most difficult letters I've ever had to write, because I know that I've hurt you. My remark this morning was terribly insensitive, and I am very sorry. I hope you will show me the mercy I seem to be lacking.

Never again will I even think, much less make, a remark like that. I hope that you can find it in your heart to forgive me.

Sincerely,
Pat

Example 11-22: A note of apology

If you think publicity doesn't pay—we understand there are 25 mountains in Colorado higher than Pikes Peak. Can you name one?

—ANONYMOUS

CHAPTER 12

Media Relations

In our media-oriented society, your survival and growth are often connected to media exposure—and it's often free in newspapers, magazines, or on television. Never waste an opportunity to get your name out there when you have something of importance to share.

Hiring a Public Relations Agency

If you prefer not to write your own media materials, consider engaging a public relations (PR) agency. PR agencies have ongoing relationships with the media, so they may give you a better chance of getting published.

WHAT'S IN THIS CHAPTER

- *Hiring a public relations agency*
- *Writing a press release*
- *Placing articles in publications*
- *Acknowledging an article you've read*
- *Promoting a recently published book*
- *Asking for a correction*
- *Responding to an article or editorial*

Example 12-1 is a letter offering to retain a PR agency. Example 12-2 is a letter terminating a relationship with a PR agency. Not all terminations will be as friendly as this one, but you should always avoid negativity. This letter follows a telephone conversation—news such as this shouldn't be broken in a letter.

LETTERHEAD

August 12, 20—

Ms. Patsy Cleiner
Cleiner Public Relations
304 Second Street
Los Gatos, CA 95030

Dear Patsy,

Congratulations!

The newspaper, magazine, and broadcasting coverage you outlined for us is the best we've had proposed. We're especially impressed with your firm's track record for working with midsize clients in the biotech industry. So, we're delighted to let you know that we're giving you our account.

We'd like to offer you a one-year contract, and we are anxious to get our show on the road. I'll call you next week so we can discuss this over lunch.

Sincerely,

Marc Allan, President

Example 12-1: Offer to retain a PR agency

LETTERHEAD

August 12, 20—

Ms. Patsy Cleiner
Cleiner Public Relations
304 Second Street
Los Gatos, CA 95030

Dear Patsy,

As I said in yesterday's conversation, I am deeply sorry to let you know that we won't be using your services after September 14. We have recently been acquired by Atlas Company and find it necessary to streamline our operations dramatically. Our public relations and advertising will be handled by the parent company in New York.

We are sorry to give you this news, because you have done a wonderful job getting us in the right newspapers and magazines. If I hear of anyone needing the services of an outstanding PR firm, I will be sure to give them your name.

Warmest regards,

Martha Morgan
Vice President of Marketing

Example 12-2: Terminating a relationship with a PR agency

Writing a Press Release

When you have the know-how, you can write your own press releases and send them to the editor of a newspaper, magazine, and/or broadcasting station. In written publications, you find the names of editors on the masthead of the publication.

> ▶ To maximize your chances for publication, use the Questioning Technique (from chapter 3) and include all the key information in the first paragraph. Following are ways to get your press releases noticed and printed:
>
> - **Build an accurate database of media contacts.** You don't want to send a press release on robotics to a gourmet foods magazine.
>
> - **Send copy that's error free.** You build trust with the media when you send accurate information that has no typos or misinformation.
>
> - **Include a photo.** People's eyes are drawn to graphics and text more than to text alone.
>
> - **Give complete contact information.** Be sure to include up-to-date names, addresses, and phone numbers.
>
> - **Remember that journalists may work faster than you do.** If the journalist calls with a question, respond immediately. Timeliness is everything. ◀

See how this is done in the following examples. These are just a smattering of ways to publicize your business.

- **Example 12-3:** Moving your office or opening a new office.

- **Example 12-4:** Introducing a new product line or new business direction.

- **Example 12-5:** Opening a practice.

- **Example 12-6:** Adding a new employee or principal.

FOR IMMEDIATE RELEASE

####

ARCHITECT OPENS NEW OFFICE

Marc A. Lindsell, president of Marc Lindsell Architects, is pleased to announce the opening of his new office at 501 Cortland Street in San Francisco. Marc settled in the Bay Area twelve years ago after graduating from Georgia Tech's College of Architecture.

Marc started his career designing schools and municipal buildings, and opened his own firm nine years ago, specializing in new-home design and remodeling. Marc's uniquely designed homes have been featured in the Sunday Home Section of the *Boston Globe* and the *Architectural Record*, a prestigious publication for architects. Marc is also the winner of several awards presented by the National Association of the Remodeling Industry (NARI) for remodeling projects. You can contact Marc at 415-826-5459.

(116 words)

# # # #

Example 12-3: Press release announcing the opening of a new office

ISO 9000 NETWORK CHANGES FOCUS FOR CHALLENGING TIMES

For the past 15 years, the ISO 9000 Network, a Wayland, Massachusetts–based company, has been successful in helping companies achieve certification for the ISO 9000 Standards. The company prides itself on its guarantee that companies will achieve certification if they follow its program.

As businesses face constant change during these challenging times, however, they're forced to continuously improve all aspects of their operations. They realize that compliance with the Standards is only one step toward this goal. The ISO 9000 Network has answered the call and has expanded its business to include Continuous Improvement programs that are making companies more effective, more efficient, and more profitable.

Companies who join the Continuous Improvement initiative are increasing sales and profits because of better performance, quality, and delivery. They're retaining employees and attracting more highly qualified employees. They're also experiencing higher morale.

The ISO 9000 Network has extensive experience in helping manufacturing, service, and distribution organizations to be more efficient and more profitable through Continuous Improvement programs. They help companies to implement time-tested methods to measure performance, analyze data, and apply the appropriate process changes.

For more information, contact William Noz or Hal Greenberg at 888-476-6389.

(192 words)

####

Example 12-4: Press release announcing a new business direction

For Immediate Release

####

Essential Family Chiropractic comes to the village of Owen Brown. Dr. Eric Lindsell is an active member of the community and enthusiastically brings "Optimal Health Through Chiropractic" to Howard County. His office will be located at 7270 Cradlerock Way, just off Brokenland Parkway.

<u>**About Dr. Eric Lindsell**</u>

When Dr. Lindsell graduated from Palmer College of Chiropractic West, it was the fulfillment of a lifelong dream to become a chiropractor. At his graduation, Dr. Lindsell was awarded the distinctive Certificate of Clinical Excellence. He's a member of the prestigious Pi-Kappa-Chi fraternity.

One year ago, Dr. Lindsell successfully treated a woman for migraine headaches that had plagued her for ten years. Her husband was so grateful for the incredible improvement in her health and their marriage, that he nominated Dr. Lindsell as one of 1998's "Outstanding Young Men of America." Dr. Lindsell is especially proud of bringing about such dramatic lifestyle changes to his patients.

<u>**For more information . . .**</u>

For information about the special room set up for children or any other questions about the wonderful effects that chiropractic care can have on your family's total well-being, please call Dr. Lindsell at (401) 290-6596. He'll be delighted to talk with you.

(206 words)

####

Example 12-5: Press release announcing the opening of a practice

For Immediate Release

####

DENISE CATALDO, CPA, PC
ADDS TO STAFF

The accounting firm of Denise Cataldo, CPA, PC, Marlborough, MA, is proud to announce that Michele Whyte, CPA, has joined the staff. The firm offers accounting and financial advisory services. They maintain a dynamic, flexible, and creative environment to develop fully the success of each client.

Michele has 15 years of accounting experience, including SEC reporting for multinational corporations. She has a broad range of public and private experience that includes assisting with mergers and acquisitions, raising capital, dissolving and selling companies, implementing accounting systems, and developing policies and procedures for start-up corporations.

Michele holds a Bachelor of Arts and a Master of Science, and is a member of the Massachusetts Society of CPAs and the American Institute of CPAs. Michele lives in Sudbury with her husband and daughter. She's also a runner and a certified yoga instructor.

For financial solutions that add up, check out www.cataldocpa.com or call 508-485-3811.

(148 words)

####

Example 12-6: Press release announcing a new employee

Placing Articles in Publications

An article is far more influential than an ad because it positions you as an expert. When you have pearls of wisdom to share, writing an article is a wonderful way to market your business. All you need is a good idea, a target publication, a dynamite query letter, and lots of determination.

Getting to Know the Publication You're Targeting

Before you write a query letter, read at least a half-dozen back issues of the publications you target. This will give you an idea of what types of articles the journals publish, what writing styles they use, how long the articles are, and other useful information.

Check the masthead at the front of the publication that lists publishers, editors, phone numbers, e-mails, and other good stuff. If the e-mail address is given, submit your query electronically.

> ▶ You increase your chances of getting published when you send for the manuscript guidelines from the magazines or journals you're considering. Simply state your request in a short letter. (Note that SASE is publishing speak for "self-addressed, stamped envelope.")
>
> Please send me a copy of your manuscript guidelines. I've enclosed a SASE. Thank you. ◀

Writing a Query Letter or E-mail

When you send the query to an editor, describe the subject matter, mention if it represents something new or insightful, and tell why it would be of interest to readers. Include a call for action. Don't send the article itself yet—this is merely an inquiry to find out if there's any interest. See Example 12-7 for a query that worked for me. Here are some hints:

- Keep the letter to one page or the e-mail to one or two screens.
- Create an interesting opening paragraph.
- Convey your knowledge of the publication.
- Tell why you're qualified to write the article.
- Be positive and enthusiastic.
- State the length of the article.

> ▶ Journalists have built-in hogwash detectors, so be sure you sound credible and have valuable information. ◀

What to say: Include a brief statement that tells what the article does: *This article relates four case studies ... This article charts the progression of ... This article examines the impact ... This article compares ....*

What not to say: Avoid weak statements such as *May I impose on you to read this?* or boastful statements such as *Here's an article you'll just love.*

> ▶ Even if everyone in your target market doesn't see your article when it runs, high-quality reprints become key items in your marketing arsenal. ◀

To: patsamuels@unified.com
Subject: Proposed article: "What's in a Name? It's Absolute Lunar Sea"

Dear Mr. Samuels,

A favorite conversation among fellow sailors has always been boat names. Each boat owner likes to share "his story." Therefore, I believe *At Sea* would be an ideal publication for boat owners to do just that.

"What's in a Name: It's Absolute Lunar Sea"
I sent out questionnaires to dozens of sailboat owners and have acquired many funny and heartwarming stories. "What's in a Name? It's Absolute Lunar Sea" would make wonderful reading for your sailing audience. Please let me know if you'd be interested in seeing my 1500-word manuscript with a view toward publishing it. In addition to stories, many boat owners sent photographs that would be ideal to include.

Next step
I look forward to hearing from you and to sharing these wonderful stories with your readers.

Sincerely,
Grace White

Example 12-7: Query offering an article for publication

It's acceptable to send multiple queries. Example 12-8 shows a postcard that makes it easy for the publisher to close the loop, even if it is with a rejection. (If an editor is interested, you may get a letter or phone call.) On the front of the postcard, type your name and address. On the back, type the following:

<Title of Manuscript>

[ ] Yes, I'm interested in reading your manuscript with a view towards publishing it.

[ ] No thanks. Your idea doesn't fit into our current marketing plans.

<Name of Publication>

Example 12-8: Postcard to expedite response

Writing a Cover Letter

If an editor is interested in reading your article, send a copy with a cover letter, such as the one in Example 12-9. This can be hard copy or electronic, depending on the editor's preference. Here's what to cover:

- Indicate that she asked to see your article.
- Write a brief description of the article.
- Include permission to use any copyrighted material, if applicable.

Requesting Use of Copyrighted Material

You need to get permission to use copyrighted material. Example 12-10 is such a request. Here's what to include:

- The title of the article and the source where it originally appeared;
- The graphic or portion of the text you want to use;
- Where you intend to publish it;
- The cost for its use, if applicable.

LETTERHEAD

March 3, 20—

Ms. Edie Tor
The Corporate Weekly
200 Corporate Drive
Quail Ridge, NC 27330

Dear Ms. Tor:

Subject: Manuscript you requested, entitled "Communicate to Collaborate"

Thank you for asking to see the enclosed article. I've been a reader of your publication for several years and always enjoy your interesting and informative articles. That's why I'm glad to have a chance to contribute.

To my knowledge, no other publication has addressed the lack of communication between collaborators to this extent. The article points out the benefits of adopting dimensions of each other's concepts to create a more cohesive dialogue and reach a meeting of the minds.

I look forward to hearing from you.

Sincerely,

Beth Writer

Enclosure

Example 12-9: Cover letter accompanying an article

March 2, 20—

Ms. Allison Wilcox, Editor
Just Right Magazine
400 Third Avenue
Yewed, OK 73728

Dear Ms. Wilcox:

Subject: Permission to use copyrighted material

I'm writing an article tentatively titled "Going Home," to be published in *Oklahoma Weekly,* and am requesting permission to use the following. I will certainly give you and the author proper credit and will send you a copy of the article once it's published.

> **Author:** Leslie Marlow
> **Publication date:** June 2, 20—
> **Pages:** 100–102

If you consent, please sign the bottom of this letter and return it to me in the enclosed SASE. Thank you.

Sincerely,

Barton Grogan

I (we) give permission for you to use the material requested.

_____
Name   Date

Example 12-10: Requesting permission to use copyrighted material

Acknowledging an Article You've Read

When you read an article written by someone you know, it's nice to send a congratulatory note. Example 12-11 shows you how. You can generally get in touch with an author through the publication.

Dear Blanche,

I very much enjoyed your article in the May 23 edition of Paramount. I am a distributor for one of the <details about what you sell> for <company>, and I completely agree with your premise.

I'd like to speak with you about some of the points you raised. The publisher wouldn't give me your telephone number, so I'd appreciate your calling me next week.

Sincerely,

Example 12-11: Enjoyed your article

Promoting a Recently Published Book

Many people publish books through conventional publishers or self-publish channels. In either event, you want to get as much publicity as you can in newspapers and magazines and on radio and television stations. Local publications and stations are always looking for good material, especially success stories from local people. Example 12-12 alerts a local television station of your recently published book.

Asking for a Correction

Although publications try very hard to be accurate, inaccuracies do occur. This is more prevalent in newspapers, where they're under the gun to generate a daily publication.

December 1, 20—

Mr. Marvin Cox
WTCI
20 Chester Avenue
Zutphen, MI 49426

Dear Mr. Cox:

Subject: My book entitled *The Trouble with Henry*

I recently published a book entitled *The Trouble with Henry.* I believe the topic would be of wide interest to your listeners, and I would be interested in discussing highlights of the book on your show. The premise is that <give a brief explanation of the value to listeners>.

I have enclosed a biographical sketch, a synopsis of the book, and a press release from the publisher.

Action requested
I hope you'll have a chance to consider this opportunity, and I'll call you next week to discuss the possibility of moving forward on it.

Sincerely,

Katie Kahn

Enclosures

Example 12-12: Letter to a TV station about promoting a recently published book

▶ I once sent a press release to a local newspaper announcing the publication of one of my books. The paper misreported where I lived and the gender of my two children. (At least my name and the name of the book were correct.) Example 12-13 is the letter I sent to the publisher asking for a correction. They made the correction, and I got my name in print twice. ◀

LETTERHEAD

February 2, 20—

Mr. Samuel Salesor, Editor
The Daily Rag
20 Maple Avenue
Nilak, AK 99666

Dear Mr. Salesor:

Subject: Correcting inaccurate information

I appreciate your including my press release in the February 1 edition of your publication. I always enjoy reading your publication because it's informative and timely. When you printed my article, however, you inadvertently reported the following

> Inaccurate: I live in Pomona with my two daughters.
> Accurate: **I live in Monsey with my husband and two sons.**

Action requested
I'd very much appreciate your printing a correction in the next edition. Thank you.

Sincerely,

Sheryl Lindsell-Roberts

Example 12-13: Requesting a correction

Some errors are grievous and require that you write a strong letter, such as the one in Example 12-14. When you write a letter demanding a correction, keep the following in mind:

- Limit the letter to one page.

- Be specific about what was wrong and what is right.

- Offer to give substantiation, if that's appropriate.

- Keep your emotions under control. (Have someone else look at the letter before you send it to make sure it's not too harsh.)

- Request personal contact with the editor, if that's appropriate.

Responding to an Article or Editorial

You often read articles and editorial comments that you may or may not agree with. Responding to these articles creates another opportunity to get your name in print. Editors often use these letters in the editorial column. Example 12-15 is a positive response; Example 12-16, a negative response.

LETTERHEAD

June 18, 20—

Mr. Robert Coran, Editor
The Weekly Publication
One Smith Cove
Yellow Pine, ID 83677

Dear Mr. Coran:

Subject: Demanding a retraction

In the June 17 issue of *The Weekly Publication,* your writer Dean Johansen reported that <elaborate on the erroneous information that was printed>. This report is inaccurate, misleading, and has caused us much embarrassment.

I'm enclosing <what you're sending>, which should set the matter straight.

Action demanded
I demand that you print a retraction in the next edition in a prominent place. If you would like to discuss this further, call me at <phone number>.

Sincerely,

Val Glicker

Enclosure

Example 12-14: Strong demand for a correction

May 5, 20—

Ms. Nancy Peters, Editor
Monthly Chronicle
10234 Harvey Place
Hubbardton, VT 05749

Dear Ms. Peters:

Subject: Kudos on your article "No Free Lunch"

I wish to commend you for the stand you have taken against <issue>. I strongly support you because <state your feelings>.

Thank you for supporting my position and those of many of my colleagues.

Sincerely,

Laureen Katz

Example 12-15: Positive response to an article

May 5, 20—

Ms. Nancy Peters, Editor
Monthly Chronicle
10234 Harvey Place
Hubbardton, VT 05749

Dear Ms. Peters:

Subject: Your article "No Free Lunch"

Although I generally agree with the articles you publish, I must strongly disagree
with the one entitled "No Free Lunch." <State your opposition and the reason
for it>.

I hope you will realize how your readers feel about these issues before taking
such a strong stand. Thank you for understanding our position.

Sincerely,

Laureen Katz

Example 12-16: Negative response to an article

The volume of paper expands to fill the available briefcase.

—JERRY BROWN
former governor of California

CHAPTER 13

Professional Potpourri

Companies send out gazillions of letters that don't fall into any specific category. This chapter contains a sampling of the orphan letters, memos, and e-mail messages that were relegated to the miscellany chapter.

Soliciting Donations

Asking for a donation is never easy, especially if you're not offering a free meal, discount airline tickets, or anything that's tangible, but here are some phrases that tug at people's heartstrings:

> *You can say with pride, "I've made a difference."*
>
> *With your gift of <…>, we can now <…>.*

WHAT'S IN THIS CHAPTER

- *Soliciting donations*
- *Winning proposals*
- *Asking for and writing testimonials*
- *Issuing a sexual harassment prevention policy*
- *Recommending a colleague for membership in an organization or club*
- *Responding in someone's absence*
- *Announcing a merger*
- *Renewing a membership*
- *Dealing with internal communications*
- *Booking a meeting or conference facility*
- *Showing appreciation for great service*
- *Giving specific directions, procedures, or instructions*

Your tax-deductible gift will help us to continue our vital research.

Your gift can help <…> to survive.

Without your help, all the gains of the last few years would have evaporated.

We desperately need your help.

We cannot continue this fight alone.

The future of <…> depends on you.

Together we can <…>

Help us to meet this crisis.

Your generous contribution will <…>

This is your chance to help <…> to meet the challenges of the coming years.

Check out the following letters and announcements soliciting donations:

- **Example 13-1:** Flier soliciting donations for a building fund.
- **Example 13-2:** Letter soliciting funds for charity. (This was written by a patient with the particular illness. It's a letter that prompted me to make a sizable donation.)
- **Example 13-3:** Letter soliciting funds from individuals.
- **Example 13-4:** Letter soliciting funds from companies.
- **Example 13-5:** Flier from a professional holding an event open to the public.
- **Example 13-6:** Announcement from an organization sponsoring a blood drive.

Following are tips for increasing your chances of success:

- Identify the charity or institution.
- Tell the reader why the donation is worthwhile.
- Stress the satisfaction the reader will get from making a contribution.
- Talk about the progress you've made because of prior donations, if applicable.
- Include the percentage that goes directly to the charity (if it's large or applicable).
- Mention whether or not the donation is tax deductible.

▶ Save the solicitation letters you get. Notice the teaser on the envelope, the special words and phrases that tug at your heartstrings, and what moves you to put a check in the mail. Also notice what doesn't move you. ◀

Please Help Us Turn a Good Library into a Great Library

My Library was dukedom large enough.
—WILLIAM SHAKESPEARE, *The Tempest*

The new Parnassus Public Library Foundation was established in 2002 as the latest addition to our library family. The Foundation includes trustees, staff, friends, volunteers, and Parents' Council, who will continue to partner with the City of Parnassus to provide you and your family with the best possible library and services.

The Foundation is a 501(c)3 nonprofit corporation whose primary mission is to raise money on behalf of the library. Take a trip to the library and you'll see why we need funding. Although the library is quite functional, there are many areas where we need to improve.

- There's little room for new books.
- We have little space for visitors to come in to relax and read.
- Our popular programs are crowded with no room to expand.
- Parking is very limited.

Goal of the Foundation

Our residents deserve a state-of-the art library they can be proud of. The primary goal of this foundation is *to raise money through our fund drive* (along with city and state funds) *to build a new library*. This will be a major enhancement to the City of Parnassus and provide residents with a clear-cut, tax-exempt path for major financial donations. Once the new library is built, the Foundation will provide an ongoing endowment for the library to keep pace with new technologies, expand its collections, and continue upgrades to the public space.

Please Help Us to Help You

Your generous contribution will help to build a strong and enduring future for all the residents of the wonderful City of Parnassus.

Example 13-1: Soliciting funds for a new building

Dear Friend,

Going to friends' funerals is sad enough, but it's really heartbreaking when a family member says, "If I had only known, I would have helped."

That's why I've worked hard since I was diagnosed with <illness> in <year> to encourage my family, friends, and neighbors to understand this terrible illness and band together to support me. No one understands what it's like to wake up each morning feeling <symptoms>, not knowing whether you can make plans for the next week.

But I'm lucky, because my friends, family, and neighbors are there for me on the days I need help. Too many others are struggling with this illness alone and without the funds to get the proper care. When you send your donation, you know that 87% of your contribution goes directly to helping people fighting <illness>.

With friends like you, no one suffering from <illness> needs to be alone. Thank you from all of us.

Sincerely,

Example 13-2: Letter soliciting funds for a charity from someone afflicted with the illness

LETTERHEAD

Dear Friend,

Subject: Please help us to reach our goal

Things are rapidly changing in the health care profession, except for the funds that are so badly needed to meet the demands of tomorrow. Today's health care institutions are facing unprecedented challenges as well as exciting opportunities involving ideas and programs that will offer new advances in health care.

As you know, <institution> has always tried to offer the community the latest in quality health care. We are completely autonomous and nonprofit, and we can't do without your help. We have reached 75% of our goal for <where money will be spent>, but we need additional funds. Won't you please help us reach our goal of <dollar amount>? You can take your contribution as a tax deduction and be part of the team dedicated to providing the finest health care in the community.

Please give from your heart

Please put your check for whatever you can afford in the envelope that's enclosed. We thank you so much for your support.

Gratefully,

Example 13-3: Letter from a charity soliciting funds from individuals

LETTERHEAD

December 1, 20—

Mr. Peter Smith, President
Kaaawa Supply Company
4 Creek Circle
Kaaawa, HI 96730

Dear Mr. Smith:

Subject: We need your help

<Requester> is starting its annual drive on <date>. We realize that there are many demands on your resources and those of your employees, but we hope you will once again support this worthwhile cause. In the past, your company has been one of the leaders in this drive. We realize that your employees' dollars aren't stretching as far as they used to, and ours aren't either.

Please let us count on the giving spirit of your generous employees to help us make a difference to so many who need our help. This year we're hoping that each company will open its heart and match the contributions of its employees.

When you send in your tax-deductible donation, you can be assured that you are helping members of the community who desperately need the care we provide.

Thank you so much for your continued support.

Warmly,

Example 13-4: Letter from a charity soliciting funds from companies

KIDS' BOOK BONANZA

—★★★— Dedicated to bringing kids & books together —★★★—

Don't miss our First Annual Kid's Book Bonanza

EXCITING EVENTS AND TONS OF WONDERFUL BOOKS FOR ALL AGES!

➢ Meet your favorite fairy tale characters! (featuring the Mt. Excelsior Drama Club)

➢ Readings every half hour by local children's authors!

➢ Write and illustrate your own storybook!

➢ Stump the Storyteller! Interactive fun with local storyteller Tony Toledo

➢ Craft fun! Make a leaf for your favorite book to hang on the Book Tree

➢ Free balloons, face painting, fortune telling, and washable tattoos!

BRING A BOOK / TAKE A BOOK

Find the perfect book for you at our

"Swap Till You Drop!"

all-day book exchange!

WHEN: Saturday, June 30 ☆ 11:00 A.M. to 3:00 P.M.
WHERE: Mt. Excelsior Public Library
DONATION: $3.00 per family

Sponsored by: The Flying Cow Children's Bookstore
For information call: 781-599-6951

All proceeds to benefit the Children's Room at the Mt. Excelsior Public Library

Example 13-5: Announcing an event open to the public

Please join us for our semiannual blood drive
and help to save precious lives

When: <date or dates>
Times: <hours of operation>
Where: <address>

Everyone is invited to join us for refreshments
that will include pizza, hot dogs, and more.

You can call <phone number> to make an appointment or just drop by.
Either way, we look forward to welcoming you.

<Organization>
<website>

Example 13-6: Announcement from an organization sponsoring a blood drive

Expressing Thanks for Donations

When someone sends a donation or volunteers, always respond with a personalized thank-you letter, such as the ones in Examples 13-7 and 13-8.

Dear Phil and Geena,

We very much appreciate your generous gift to the <institution> fund. The building is nearly complete, offering a wonderful addition to our facility. We have reached 90% of our goal, and your contribution is making the completion a reality.

Thank you for your generosity, and we look forward to seeing you at the ribbon cutting, which we plan for <date>.

Cordially,

Example 13-7: Letter expressing thanks for a donation

Dear Elijahu,

Our awards banquet would never have taken place if you and your staff hadn't pitched in so eagerly. I will never be able to thank you enough for supplying the brains and brawn, which were sorely needed.

My staff and I thoroughly enjoyed working with you. Because of everyone's good nature and sense of humor, we got through one crisis after another. You were my White Knights who came to the rescue.

I owe your staff a lunch and will call next week to set one up.

Cordially,

Example 13-8: Handwritten note of thanks to a volunteer

Winning Proposals

Although every proposal is unique, all contain similar basic information. If the proposal is formal or lengthy, send it with a cover letter that confirms everything outlined in the request for proposal (RFP). Here's the minimum information to include in a proposal:

- An introduction that states the purpose and scope of the project, when the project will begin and end, special benefits, and the cost.

- An itemization of products or services, procedures, and materials; a time schedule; and a breakdown of the cost.

- Specifics about what's covered in the cost and what isn't.

> ▶ Realize that a proposal is basically a sales/marketing piece. You must convince the reader that you're the right person or company for the job. Therefore, consider including one or two testimonials that serve as third-party endorsements. ◀

Simple proposals can be sent in the form of a letter; complex proposals should include a cover letter. In each of the following examples, notice how the headlines tell the story:

- **Example 13-9:** Simple proposal for training sent in the form of a letter.

- **Example 13-10:** Cover letter for a very large fixed-price contract. (This is the cover letter for a proposal I wrote that paved the way for an architectural firm to close a $70-million contract.)

- **Example 13-11:** Proposal/agreement I use for my business writing seminars.

November 14, 20—

Mr. Morgan Sterling
Sterling Chemical Company
College Station, TX 77840

ATTN: Bid Request Submissions

Dear Mr. Sterling:

SUBJECT: Proposal for Writing Workshops

It's with great pleasure that I submit my proposal for the following workshops that will help your employees to write with confidence and competence: *Grammar/Basic Writing Skills* (3 hours), *Technical Writing* (6 hours), *Business Communications—memos, letters, e-mails* (6 hours). Following is a sample of the rave reviews you can expect:

I was very impressed with your business writing workshop because you provided very practical ideas to help us organize our thoughts and express them more clearly (and with more energy). The class exercises and real-life examples you provided clearly reinforced the ideas you presented. The best compliment I can give you is that the day after the workshop I observed my staff implementing your ideas. They felt the time spent in class and the one-on-one sessions with you were most worthwhile. After looking for such a program for the past couple of years, I want to thank you again for helping me achieve my objective. You were wonderful.

<Name and company of person giving testimonial>

What's in the Folder
Please refer to the following documents to better understand why I'm the most qualified person to conduct these workshops:

- Professional biography that shows my extensive workshop and writing experience. Please note that I'm the author of 18 books, including *Business Writing for Dummies, Technical Writing for Dummies,* and *Business Letter Writing.*
- Synopsis of the three workshops.
- Testimonials from delighted clients.
- Case study from one of New England's high-technology companies that had a major breakthrough following my workshop.
- Sample certificate of completion and evaluation form.

Example 13-9: Two-page cover letter attached to a proposal responding to an RFP

Disciplines of Typical Participants
Typical participants come from the following disciplines: human resources, sales and marketing, finance, legal, government, architecture, public relations, academia, and more.

Certificates and CEUs
Each participant receives a certificate of completion and is eligible for CEUs.

Investment
My fee is $<amount> for each 3-hour session, and travel arrangements are negotiable. Clients typically reproduce the handouts.

Satisfaction Guarantee
I guarantee that participants are delighted with what they learn. I promise another workshop or a refund to anyone who doesn't find the workshop to be worthwhile—although I've never had to honor that.

Policy Information
If a client cancels a workshop 5 business days or more before the scheduled date, they owe me nothing except for travel expenses I've incurred. If they cancel between 3 and 4 business days before, they owe me half plus any travel expenses I've incurred. If they cancel 1 or 2 business days before, they owe me the full fee plus any travel expenses I've incurred. If I cancel at any time, they owe me nothing.

Dates and Class Times
I'm available during the months of August through December 20—, with the exception of the first week in November.

Next Step
I look forward to hearing from you and to helping the employees at <their company> to write documents that get results!

Most sincerely,

Janice Blythe
Principal

Example 13-9 (continued)

January 6, 20—

Ms. Cindy Hansen, Superintendent
Warrensville School District
Warren Street
Warrensville, NC 28693

Dear Ms. Hansen:

Subject: Proposal for School District Expansion

Thank you for giving <your company> the opportunity to submit this proposal for design services for the <name of project or group issuing RFP> in accordance with the guidelines outlined in your Request for Design Proposals.

On Time, On Budget
Our award-winning firm is proud to have completed more than 325 schools on time and on budget in its 24 years of experience. We partner with the community and school leadership to design buildings that blend with the fabric of the local architecture, while best meeting the needs of the children and the community.

... expertise, timeliness and service to the committee and town project manager, were combined with a willingness to listen and understand our community, incorporating their needs into the project.

<Name and company of person giving testimonial>

Professional Qualifications
The following are our qualifications as outlined in your RFP. We've included the corresponding page numbers, when relevant, so you can find additional information quickly:

1. North Carolina registration and licensing in all applicable disciplines. (page 8)
2. Thorough knowledge of procedures, requirements, and practices of North Carolina State Board of Education, School Governance Bureau, and other agencies related to the design and construction of schools.
3. Thorough knowledge of the North Carolina State Building Code and Regulations of the Architectural Barriers Board.

Example 13-10: Cover letter for a proposal that helped an architectural firm close a $70-million contract

4. Thorough knowledge and familiarity with the requirements of Chapter 579 and the Acts of 1980 (Omnibus Construction Reform Act).
5. Sufficient levels of staff to complete the project. (page 12)
6. A full-time local presence over the lifetime of the project.
7. Adequate insurance required prior to signing the contract. (page 18)
8. Prior experience in designing school and identification to the Building Committee of key persons, specialists, and individual consultants for this project. (page 21)
9. Other qualifications that the Building Committee and the School Committee may consider significant and consistent with the foregoing. (page 25)

What Sets Us Apart
In addition to providing a continuous tradition of architectural excellence since 1978, here is what sets us apart:

- We firmly believe that *your ideas are critical to the success of the project.* We listen carefully to feedback from the school administration, school committee, staff, parents, community groups, regulatory boards, and your committee.
- Our firm offers a broad range of planning and design services, including needs assessments, educational programming, feasibility studies, master planning studies, and the design of additions, renovations, and new school buildings.
- The school designs we submit are warmly received and praised for their sensitive relationship to existing buildings and the community context in which they are built.
- We construct successful buildings for our public-sector clients within their original budget.

Your Success Is Our Success!
We look forward to the interview to speak directly to your needs, understand your approach to your projects, and identify areas where we can help you to be successful.

Sincerely,

Example 13-10 (continued)

Sheryl Lindsell-Roberts & Associates   117 Sudbury Street, Marlborough, MA 01752
508-229-8209 • sheryl@sherylwrites.com
www.sherylwrites.com

Energize Your Business Writing Workshop

Dates   \<dates\>

Client	\<Client\>
Workshop	• Six-hour workshop, 9:00 to 4:00 • Class will be limited to 12 participants
Focus	Workshop will focus on the Six Steps to energized business writing: 1. Getting Started 2. Creating Headlines and Strategic Sequencing 3. Writing the Draft 4. Designing for Visual Impact 5. Honing the Tone 6. Proofreading
Fee	\<$ amount\> per class of 12 people
Workshop materials	• Client will photocopy worksheets • Client will supply overhead projector and flip chart
Cancellation policy	If you cancel the workshop 5 business days or more before the scheduled date, you owe me nothing. If you cancel between 3 and 4 business days before, you owe me half. If you cancel 1 or 2 business days before, you owe me the full fee. If I cancel at any time, you owe me nothing.

_____   _____
Client   Date

_____   _____
Sheryl Lindsell-Roberts   Date

Example 13-11: One-page proposal that serves as an agreement

Asking for and Writing Testimonials

When a client or customer raves about your product or service, it beats anything you can write or tell about yourself. Never hesitate to ask clients for testimonials. Satisfied customers are more than happy to sing your praises. Some may not know what to write and may need a little coaching. Example 13-12 prompts clients through the testimonial. Example 13-13 is a great testimonial letter.

To: jan_duryea@columbiainc.com
Subject: Thanks for offering to send me a testimonial

Dear Jan,

I very much appreciate your offering to send me a testimonial and am delighted that the project exceeded your expectations. As we discussed, here are some questions for inspiration in writing the testimonial:

- Why did you select me over my competition?
- What were some of the benefits of working with me?
- Did I meet, not meet, or exceed your expectations?
- Can you place a dollar value on your return on your investment?

Thanks so much.

Best regards,
Bill

Example 13-12: E-mail asking for a testimonial

Sheryl Lindsell-Roberts
117 Sudbury Street
Marlborough, MA 01752

December 21, 20—

Dear Sheryl,

I wanted to follow-up with you regarding some very positive feedback you received during your recent workshops that you delivered to our East and West Coast clients.

As a training professional at a $3 billion company with more than 12,000 employees worldwide, I am committed to maintaining only the highest quality instructors and courses for IDG employees. I am very pleased to see the consistent high level of energy, participation, and satisfaction that your sessions continuously draw. Participants are always very pleased with the concrete knowledge and information that you are able to deliver to them in such a clear, concise method.

Here are some specific comments that I thought you would appreciate hearing:

➢ "I feel that everything covered in the session was relevant and useful to so many aspects of my job. Sheryl is an excellent teacher and very informative and clear."

➢ "I will apply what I have learned to my e-mails, memos, letters – everything I do!"

➢ "Sheryl is top-notch! She knows her stuff inside and out. It was a pleasure to learn from her."

Due to the decentralized nature of IDG, I seek instructors who are willing and able to get to know and understand our diverse culture. One of the things that I appreciate most about working with you is that you have really taken the time to get to know the IDG community. Thus, you make a remarkable impact on each of your class participants, as they feel they and their environments are truly understood. Thank you for being such a pleasure to work with and for your continuous attention to your different audiences.

I look forward to a long working partnership with you.

Best regards,

Laurie Parsons
International Data Group
IDG Corporate Training and Development Specialist

INTERNATIONAL DATA GROUP

3 Speen Street / Framingham, Massachusetts 01701-9192 / (508) 875-5000

Example 13-13: Testimonial from a delighted client

Issuing a Sexual Harassment Prevention Policy

It's illegal to harass anyone or to make any man or woman feel uncomfortable in the workplace. Therefore, companies are required to issue sexual harassment policy statements such as the one you see as Example 13-14. The statements should contain the following:

- Definition of sexual harassment;
- Notification that sexual harassment is illegal;
- Procedures to be followed if someone has been victimized.

Recommending a Colleague for Membership in an Organization or Club

There are times when you may be asked to give recommendations for membership in organizations or clubs. A strong recommendation is easy to give because you obviously hold the person in high regard. Notice the difference between Example 13-15 and Example 13-16. If you don't think the person is worthy of membership, decline to give any sort of recommendation.

Responding in Someone's Absence

When someone is gone from the office for an extended period, someone else must mind the store. Promptly answering incoming mail is important to the company's image of caring about its customers. The administrative assistant (or the person designated to do so) should acknowledge mail in a timely manner. Example 13-17 shows a sample letter. Here are a few pointers:

- Explain why you're writing and not the addressee. Sign *your* name.
- Be careful about making commitments you're not authorized to make.
- Don't divulge personal reasons for the manager's absence (golf tournament or implants for baldness).
- Be gracious and willing to help.

Date: February 5, 20—
To: All employees
From: Human Resources Department
Re: Sexual Harassment Policy

Sexual harassment is illegal and will not be tolerated. Any employee who is found to have committed an act of sexual harassment will be subject to severe disciplinary action, which could result in termination.

What Is Sexual Harassment?

Sexual harassment at work occurs when an employee is subjected to unwelcome conduct based on his/her gender. There are two types:

1. Threats of termination, demotion, intimidation, or similar consequences made to an employee by anyone in authority for refusing sexual advances.
2. Creation of an abusive or hostile work environment or interference with an employee's job performance through words or actions.

What Is a Hostile Environment?

A hostile environment is created by unwelcome conduct such as the following:

- Discussing sexual activities
- Unnecessary touching
- Commenting on a person's physical attributes
- Telling off-color jokes
- Using demeaning or inappropriate terms and nicknames
- Displaying sexually aggressive pictures, calendars, photos, or more
- Using suggestive gestures
- Ostracizing employees because of gender
- Using crude or offensive language

Example 13-14: Sexual harassment policy

Page 2
Sexual Harassment Policy

Complaint Procedures and Responsibilities

Supervisors are responsible for preventing sexual harassment and maintaining a productive work environment. Should a report of harassment occur, supervisors are responsible for assisting in the investigation and resolution of the complaint.

An employee who feels victimized should report the incident immediately to his or her supervisor. If the immediate supervisor is the source of the harassment, discuss the incident or incidents with the supervisor's superior or someone in the Human Resources Department. All complaints will be treated with respect and confidentiality. Further, no employee will be subject to any form of retaliation or discipline for pursuing a sexual harassment complaint.

Example 13-14 (continued)

> **To:** Beth_Gross@alliedinc.com
> **Subject:** I wholeheartedly recommend Susan Warren for membership
>
> ---
>
> Dear Beth,
>
> I strongly recommend Susan Warren for membership in SamRob's Executives Club. It is my privilege to have known Susan for fifteen years and to have watched her career flourish. The attached biography details Susan's numerous accomplishments, as well as her membership and contributions to several nonprofit institutions.
>
> Susan has made an outstanding contribution to the field of nursing and has a reputation for being a person who cares about her community and *does something about it.* Susan is a wife and mother of two. She has managed to juggle her family and a distinguished nursing career with an expert sense of balance. I know of no one who would make a more suitable member of SamRob's Executives Club, and I hope the membership will look kindly on this proposal.
>
> Please feel free to contact me if I can add anything to facilitate Susan's membership.
>
> Cordially,
> Margaret

Example 13-15: A strong recommendation

> **To:** Allison_Brady@Cogson.com
> **Subject:** Recommendation for Susan Warren
>
> ---
>
> Dear Allison,
>
> In response to your request, I am addressing this letter to the Membership Committee of SamRob's Executives Club on behalf of my colleague, Susan Warren, who is very anxious to join. I have known Susan professionally for fifteen years and have enclosed a copy of her biography for your review.
>
> If any members of your committee would like to discuss Ms. Warren's qualifications and her suitability for membership, please contact me.
>
> Sincerely,
> Mort

Example 13-16: A lukewarm recommendation

October 1, 20—

Mr. Robert James
Cola International
203 Sandy Hill Road
Zora, MO 65078

Dear Mr. James:

I'd like to acknowledge that we received your October 1 letter. Mr. Grant will be away from the office until October 15, and I'll bring this to his attention as soon as he returns.

If there's anything I can do for you in his absence, please let me know.

Sincerely,

Pat Madison

Example 13-17: Responding in a manager's absence

Announcing a Merger

Companies are involved in mergers all the time. They merge with each other; they merge departments; and they merge work groups. Whenever a merger is imminent (and rumors have a way of preceding formal announcements), people go into a tizzy. Whether rumors are true or false, they invariably take on a life of their own and get distorted.

> ▶ Can you recall the game of telephone you played as a kid? The message at the end of the line would bear no resemblance to the original message. The same thing happens in business, and the results can be catastrophic. ◀

Here are two messages that stave off rumors and that manage the process:

- **Example 13-18:** E-mail message from the CEO to the staff, announcing the benefits of a merger. (Notice the word in the subject line is *benefits*.)

- **Example 13-19:** Memo from a CEO to the managers, letting them know what to expect.

To: Distribution@Cogson.com
Subject: Come and hear the benefits of the merger with Grayson Company

Good morning,

I'm pleased to announce that effective July 6, 20—, we will become a wholly owned subsidiary of Grayson. Principals at Grayson have asked me to let you know that they plan to continue operating this division as it now stands, and they plan to retain all the employees. There are many benefits to be gained by the merger, and I'd like to share them with you personally.

Date:	May 6, 20—
Where:	My office
Time:	1 to 3

Once you know all the benefits Grayson brings, I'm sure that you'll approve of the merger and strongly support it. This change is an opportunity to grow and to get out of old routines and ways of doing things.

Regards,
Susan

Example 13-18: E-mail message to the troops announcing the benefits of a merger

I F T T E R H E A D

Date: May 3, 20—

To: All VPs, Directors, and Managers

From: Jon Allen, CEO

Re: Merger with Grayson Company

So far we've been able to keep the plans of this merger at the top levels, but I'll be announcing it to the entire staff in an e-mail message I'll issue next week. Here are some things we must be thinking about to minimize the shock and maximize productivity during the transition:

- Prepare for a highly charged emotional response. Mergers are stressful times.

- Make employees feel valued so they'll remain loyal and productive.

- Re-recruit our good people. Once some start to leave, others think it's the right thing to do. This can drain us of wonderful resources.

- Make whatever changes you need to as soon as possible. Once the merger is announced, people sit around waiting for the ax to fall.

In the final analysis … Let people know that change is an opportunity to grow and get out of old routines and ways of doing things.

Thanks for your support.

Bill

Example 13-19: Memo to managers to put a plan in place for a merger

Renewing a Membership

People let memberships lapse for a variety of reasons. Sometimes they just forget and need a gentle reminder, as you see in Example 13-20. If appropriate, consider offering an incentive, as you see in Example 13-21.

We hope you'll renew your membership!

We miss you as a member. The enclosed renewal notice is sent with the club's gratitude for your past membership and with the hope that you'll rejoin us at this time.

We want you to know that dues will increase as of September 1, and because of your past membership, we invite you to rejoin now to qualify for the current rates.

We look forward to renewing your membership and thank you for your continued interest.

Leah Todd

Example 13-20: Postcard reminder to renew a membership

This card is worth **$50** toward renewing your membership

We miss you as a member of the spa and look forward to welcoming you back. We've purchased many new pieces of equipment and added many more classes and instructors.

Rates will be increasing on September 1. If you join now, you can take advantage of the lower rates and apply this $50 coupon toward our already low price.

Here's to your health,

Barb Bell

Example 13-21: Postcard offering an incentive to renew a membership

Dealing with Internal Communications

There are a variety of reasons to communicate with employees, on both individual and company-wide issues. Most often e-mail works better than memos because it allows you to reach employees at both your home office and dispersed locations.

Change in Vacation or Holiday Policy

When you make a change (especially a change that employees don't see as a plus), clearly state the nature of the change and why it's being implemented. See how that was done in Example 13-22.

To: **Distribution list**
Subject: **Change in Fixed Holiday Schedules**

To all staff members:

Many of our employees have asked us to change our fixed holiday schedule. We're glad to accommodate those requests. You still have 10 paid holidays. During 6 of them, our facility will be closed. The 4 marked with an asterisk are floating holidays.

Day of New Year's Eve*	Labor Day
New Year's Day	Thanksgiving
Good Friday*	Day after Thanksgiving*
Memorial Day	Day before Christmas*
Fourth of July	Christmas Day

How to Use the Floater
If you choose not to take a floating holiday, you can apply that day to a personal day or vacation day.

Janice Golden, HR Director

Example 13-22: Announcing a policy change

New Travel Requirements

When you suggest a change, let people know why and make sure you provide a forum for questions. Put changes in bullet format for easy reading. See Example 13-23.

To: **Distribution list**
Subject: **New Travel Expense Policy**

To our staff:

As our firm has grown, so has related business travel. It's for that reason that we've worked out an arrangement with GoAway Travel to keep our costs down. As of March 1, 20—, please make all travel arrangements though Jane Smith at the travel agency. You can reach her at 800-UGO-AWAY. Please follow these guidelines:

- Make airline reservations as soon as your trip is confirmed to get the best rates.
- Book lodging at Marriotts or Holiday Inns to get our corporate discount.
- If the hotel provides service to and from the airport, determine if you need to rent a car.
- Make every effort to keep meal expenses to $40 a day.

If you have any questions, please call me at x204

Example 13-23: Announcing a new travel expense policy

Policy Change from Outside

Be sure you let your readers know that you understand that burdens may accompany a policy change. Point out the reason for the change and the consequences of not complying, as in Example 13-24.

To: **Distribution list**
Subject: **New expense account procedures**

To our staff:

Our accounting firm has just informed us that we must be strict about our records for trip reimbursement. According to the IRS, we are required to have bills and receipts for any expense over $25. I realize that it's difficult to gather this information, especially on extended business trips. However, we must comply.

In order for you to receive any reimbursement, we must have originals or copies of all your bills and receipts. Unfortunately, we can't make any exceptions.

Thank you. Denise

Example 13-24: Announcing a procedure imposed by an outside company

Loss of Key Customer

Delivering bad news is never easy, but people appreciate being informed. Example 13-25 delivers the news directly, outlines what the company is doing to solve the problem, and promises to keep everyone informed. When you can, try to put a positive spin on the issue.

To: **Distribution list**
Subject: **Loss of Allied Corporation's Business**

To our staff:

I regret having to announce that Allied Corporation has opted not to renew its contract with us because its business is in financial trouble and it is changing its business model. For the past five years, Allied has provided 25% of our business, and the loss of this contract will reduce operating revenues. This means that we've had to lay off three technicians and two consultants.

The bright side

- We're in the process of negotiating contracts with several other companies and should know within the next month which will reach fruition. We'll keep everyone informed as we move through the process.

- Our company is recognized as a leader in the industry, and we will recover. I know that everyone will pull together to help us get back on track.

Thank you for your understanding.

Regards,
Ivan

Example 13-25: Announcing the loss of a key customer

Excessive Absences

When one employee takes advantage of a situation, it opens the door for others to follow suit. Example 13-26 is a formal warning about excessive absences.

Tom,

In my e-mail message of June 10, I informed you that you had already used your ten personal leave days and the year was only half over. Last week you called in sick on two additional days

Next step
We value you as an employee, but we must give you formal notice that these excessive absences are not acceptable. You will not be paid for the two sick days last week, and we must meet to discuss this problem. Please stop by my office tomorrow at 3:30.

Ben

Example 13-26: Warning about excessive absences

Terminating an Employee

When you terminate an employee, handle it delicately. You should first discuss this in person and hand the person the letter formalizing the termination. (Many companies escort terminated employees out the door immediately after notice is given to prevent outbursts or damage to property. Use your good judgment.) Example 13-27 shows you how.

Booking a Meeting or Conference Facility

Whenever you book an event, get all the particulars in writing and send a letter of confirmation. Example 13-28 is a letter confirming the details of a conference reservation.

Showing Appreciation for Great Service

People complain when service is poor, and they should also express appreciation when service is good. Send the letter of appreciation to the manager of the person you are commending and ask that the special employee be notified. (When you send a letter of appreciation, you help to assure great service in the future.) Example 13-29 expresses appreciation for wonderful service.

LETTERHEAD

Date: August 30, 20—

To: Zeb Greeland

From: Human Resources

To confirm our discussion, the downturn in the market is forcing us to close our State Street facility. As a consequence, many positions such as yours are being eliminated as of September 15. Here's what we're doing to help ease this burden:

- You will receive severance pay equal to three months' salary.
- The company will pay your medical insurance for the remainder of the year. After that time you will be eligible for COBRA.
- We've contacted New Start Group as an outplacement agency to help you through this transition.

We wish you the best of luck in finding suitable employment. Please feel free to use me as a reference.

Best wishes,

Barbara

Example 13-27: Terminating an employee

June 20, 20—

Ms. Nancy Oppenheimer
Customer Service
Heartbreak Hotel
One Pacific Street
Fairbanks, ME 04938

Dear Ms. Oppenheimer:

Subject: ABC Conference on September 15, 20—

I enjoyed speaking with you last Monday and want to confirm the details of the ABC Conference scheduled at your facility on September 15 from 9:00 to 5:00.

Cost and payment: $1200 for Suite 100. We are enclosing a 50% deposit and will pay the balance at the conclusion of the conference.

Lunch: Lunch will be served in Suite 102 from 12:00 to 1:00 at the price of $20 per person. I've attached the menu with our lunch selections.

Equipment: The cost of use of the following equipment is included in the price listed above:

- VCR and screen
- Internet hookup
- Two flip charts

Cancellation: If we cancel seven or more business days before the event, you will return half of our deposit and we will not owe you the balance.

Next step
Please sign the bottom of this letter to confirm your agreement. We look forward to working with you.

Sincerely,

_____   _____
Your name   Name of Facility Representative

Example 13-28: Confirmation of reservation of a facility

October 1, 20—

Ms. Sheila Gomez, President
Shindig, Inc.
100 Grove Place
Epperson, KY 42001

Dear Ms. Gomez:

Kudos: Marv Roy is one of your outstanding employees

Our firm held its annual meeting at your facility last week on September 26. Marv Roy greeted us when we arrived. He made himself available throughout the day and checked our needs frequently, yet unobtrusively.

When we had a minor crisis with a piece of equipment we had brought with us, he helped us with swiftness and good humor.

Marv is a great asset to your staff, and we want to commend him to you.

Sincerely,

Amanda Manners
Customer Service

Example 13-29: Kudos for great service

Complaining About Poor Service

Research shows that a dissatisfied customer tells an average of 13 people about the unpleasant experience, and those 13 people tell 5 others. Therefore, managers appreciate knowing when you're dissatisfied and why. Example 13-30 expresses disappointment for poor service. Here's what to include in such a letter:

- Tell of your dissatisfaction and with whom. Be specific.

- If you want reparation, ask for it. (Even if you don't, you may get reparation if the facility wants your repeat business.)

Giving Specific Directions, Procedures, or Instructions

When you write directions, procedures, or instructions, you're the teacher—the expert who needs to share information in a clear, easy-to-follow, step-by-step format. You must understand who your readers are, the level of detail they need, how they process information, and how they'll use the information. If you don't gather that information, your message will be as ineffective as the foreign-language directions that came with your VCR.

Examples A and B show two ways to write directions. If you send someone a message with the directions you see in Example B, he could put them on the passenger seat of his car and follow them step by step. If you send directions such as you see in Example A, your reader may hit a tree trying to follow them.

Example A: Difficult to follow

Get off Route 128 at Exit 26. Follow the signs to Marlborough. Drive 9.8 miles (toward Sudbury). When you reach that point, you see a sign that says "Wayside Inn" to the right. Take that right to Wayside Inn Road and follow it. Make your third right, which is Sudbury Street. My office is the second driveway on the right.

Example B: Easy to follow

1. Get off Route 128 at Exit 26 and follow the signs to Marlborough.
2. Drive 9.8 miles (toward Sudbury).
3. Take a right at the sign that says "Wayside Inn." (That's Wayside Inn Road.)
4. Make your third right, which is Sudbury Street.
5. Turn right at the second driveway.

LETTERHEAD

October 1, 20—

Mr. Saul Morton
Planned Catering
2 Salem Place
Zion, SC 29574

Dear Mr. Morton:

Our company has held its annual dinner at your facility for the past two years, and we were delighted with the quality of service. We wrote to you on each occasion, commending the people who went the extra mile to be of service.

This year, however, things were different. Following is what went wrong:

- The room hadn't been cleaned. We found dirty napkins and coffee cups on the tables, and no one answered when we called for service. We had to clean the room ourselves.
- The VCR wasn't working, and we had to improvise because there were no others available.
- Dinner was served 15 minutes late, which meant everyone had to rush through the meal.

I'm not asking for a refund or for any reparation, I just want to let you know why you won't be seeing us next year.

Sincerely,

Amanda Manners
Customer Service

Example 13-30: A letter expressing dissatisfaction with poor service

PART FOUR

Applying E-mail and E-marketing Know-how

Have you ever aspired to be a screenwriter? You probably do more writing on-screen (the computer screen, that is) than you ever dreamed you'd do. Of course, your professional on-screen endeavors may not be as lucrative as Steven Speilberg's, but you can write dynamic e-mail and e-marketing messages that shout Read me! *and increase your business and bottom line.*

Technology is a weird thing; it brings you great gifts with one hand, and it stabs you in the back with the other.

—C. P. SNOW
quoted in the *New York Times*

CHAPTER 14

E-mail Messages That Shout *Read Me!*

In the world of business communications, electronic mail (e-mail) is like the un-Cola: It's something like mail, but not quite. E-mail adheres to the guidelines of business communications, but it has a unique flavor. You can send e-mail messages to one person at a time or to gazillions simultaneously—whether they're across the room or across the world. Or you can send schizophrenic e-mail to another e-mail box, an Internet address, a fax machine, or as a letter in the postal mail.

WHAT'S IN THIS CHAPTER
• *Understanding the header*
• *Writing a compelling subject line*
• *Body building*
• *Are you ready to send?*
• *Privacy issues*
• *Dealing with spam*
• *Security issues*

E-mail is a serious business communications tool, and you should treat it with the same respect as any business letter you write. Just because the computer screen doesn't have the heft and feel of a sheet of paper, that's no excuse to abandon the good habits you learned for the print medium. Check out Example 14-1, which details the success a dynamic e-mail message achieved for one of New England's largest technology companies. (I have omitted the name of the company because of the delicate nature of relationships with the media.)

Sheryl Lindsell-Roberts

Conducts Workshop That Leads to Major Recognition for One of New England's Top Technology Companies

Background: Need to Capture Editor's Attention

Editors for newswire services work under very tight deadlines to report fast-breaking news. They can't possibly cover stories in depth as television news personalities do, so they rely on communications provided by public relations professionals. This communication—often in the form of e-mails—must capture the editor's attention at a glance, and the message must be clear and concise. Otherwise the story will be lost in the electronic messaging maze.

Situation: An Epiphany

The manager of Public Relations and principal spokesperson for one of New England's leading technology companies was sitting in my workshop when a primary competitor made an announcement that would have a major impact on the industry. The newswire service quickly issued a story before contacting the PR manager's company for comment. Because this story would likely be carried by major daily newspapers the next day, it was imperative for the PR manager to get his company's message to the editor of the wire service very quickly and very clearly, in the hope that the editor would issue an update.

The PR manager rushed back to his computer and implemented the strategy he had just learned at the workshop:

- He wrote a very compelling subject line that instantly captured the attention of the editor.
- He started the message with very solid "sound bites" to make sure that the key information would appear in his company's version of the breaking news story.
- He followed the key information with supporting comments about the sound bites.

By composing a strategic subject line and message, the PR manager quickly and accurately controlled his company's version of the story, which would be read by hundreds of thousands of readers. *Stories such as this one can make or break a company.*

Result: Company Gained Instant Credibility with Immeasurable Results

This technology-based New England company got its version of the story printed in the leading newspapers via the wire service. This gave the company instant credibility and educated readers as to how this company is superior to its competitor. The company's relationship with this editor and newswire service has continued to flourish, and the company is now recognized as the industry leader in its technology space. The power of a clear, concise, and well-written message cannot be overestimated.

Example 14-1: E-mail yields profits for a large technology company

▶ Before you begin to write an e-mail message, be sure to review the questioning technique in chapter 3. Many recipients will read your e-mail message on a handheld device that has a very small viewing screen. When you use the questioning technique to answer the questions your reader will have, you can give your reader the key information she needs at a glance. ◀

Understanding the Header

Headers differ from one e-mail service to another, but all have the following fields:

To: is where you enter the name of the recipient. This section can contain the addresses of a person, multiple people, or an entire group.

Cc: (which stands for *courtesy copy*, or to old-timers *carbon copy*) is the place where you indicate that the message is being sent as a courtesy to someone other than the recipient. Copy only those people who need to see the message, otherwise you're contributing to information overload.

Bcc: stands for *blind copy*. It's for situations when you don't want the addressees to know you're sending a copy to a third party. Use Bcc prudently, because it's a clear indication you're sending something unbeknownst to the person or people in the To field. Have you ever received an impersonal e-mail, such as the one that follows, with your name and many others' in the To or Cc field?

To:	Tobe Gerard; Steve Bardioe; Rick Fingerman; Mike O'Malley; Michael Goldberg; Mark Murdoch; Mark Goldstein; Marianne Brush; Margie D'aniello; Lunne Clifford; Linda Jackson; Laurie_Parsons@idg.com; John Haas; Jeffrey Schaffer; Jane Briscoe; Harry Pape; Harrison Greene; Hal Greenberg; Greg Eden; Eileen O'Brien; Diane Darling; Denise Russo; Denise Cataldo; Dave McKeon; Corinne Farinelli; Charles Nikopoulos; carol szatkowski; Brian Como; Bill Noz; Bill Loughlin; Anne Pace; Ann Coffou; Andy Sumberg; Amy Beaver; Susan Burns

Here's how to avoid that: When you send an e-mail message to groups of people, place their e-mail addresses in the Bcc field. The people whose addresses are typed in the Bcc field each get a copy of the message, but they don't see the names of the other Bcc recipients. Each recipient sees only her name. Following is an example:

The sender types:

Bcc:	Tobe Gerard; Steve Bardioe; Rick Fingerman; Mike O'Malley; Michael Goldberg; Mark Murdoch; Mark Goldstein; Marianne Brush; Margie D'aniello; Lunne Clifford; Linda Jackson; Laurie_Parsons@idg.com; John Haas; Jeffrey Schaffer; Jane Briscoe; Harry Pape; Harrison Greene; Hal Greenberg; Greg Eden; Eileen O'Brien; Diane Darling; Denise Russo; Denise Cataldo; Dave McKeon; Corinne Farinelli; Charles Nikopoulos; carol szatkowski; Brian Como; Bill Noz; Bill Loughlin; Anne Pace; Ann Coffou; Andy Sumberg; Amy Beaver; Susan Burns

The recipient sees:

To:	Tobe Gerard
Subject:	Deadline extended to September 30

Writing a Compelling Subject Line

The subject line is the most important piece of information in an e-mail message. It stands alone to pull in your audience without the benefit of context. Your words are trapped on the recipient's screen with competing subject lines, unable to set themselves apart by means of boldface, italic, or underscored type.

There are people who get hundreds of e-mail messages a day, and they can't possibly read them all. So, if your subject line doesn't seduce the reader, she may never open your message. If you look down the subject-line column of your inbox, perhaps you see subject lines, such as these, that give you absolutely no information and no reason to check the message:

Meeting
Two things . . .
About Jane
Something else
Can you help me?

I'm sure you've read *USA Today.* On the front page is a column called "Newsline" that offers informative headlines on what's happening around the world. You can read the headlines and get a snapshot of the major stories. Wouldn't it be informative to read the subject column of your inbox and get that same level of information?

Always include in your subject line a key piece of information, so your reader can get the gist of your message at a glance. Compare the following sets of subject lines. Notice that the second column is much more compelling.

HO-HUM	COMPELLING
Profit report	15% profit expected for Q2
Sales meeting	Rescheduling 5/5 sales mtg to 5/6
Contact you requested	Contact Jane Brown at Mellows Co.
June 5	Deadline moved to June 5
Possible dates	Does July 6, 7, or 8 work?
New hire	Brad Jones joining Mktg. Grp. 9/10
Credit cards	Now accepting all major credit cards
About Mark Jones	Mark Jones still interested, but not ready to sign

> ▶ When you abbreviate, be certain the recipient will understand your abbreviation. For example, in the United States, we recognize 5/6 as May 6. In Europe or in the military, they recognize 5/6 as June 5. ◀

Deliver the Message in the Subject Line, If You Can

If you can, deliver your message as the subject line and don't bother writing in the text box. For example, you may write, "I'll finish the report tomorrow morning—SLR," and not write anything in the text box. When you put your initials at the end of the message, your reader gets to know that the subject line is the message. Instead of your initials, you can use —END or —EOM (for end of message).

> ▶ I don't recommend this type of electronic shorthand when you write to someone you don't know. It's for colleagues with whom you communicate regularly. However, you should always use a descriptive subject line. ◀

Following is a series of e-mail subject lines I exchanged with a colleague. We rescheduled a meeting, and neither of us ever had to open the text box. Usually I don't recommend scheduling appointments via e-mail, because it's more efficient to schedule appointments when you're both looking at your calendars. However, I know my audience. This woman lives and breathes e-mail and doesn't return phone calls.

Mon. doesn't work. How's Tues? —SLR
Tues is NG. How's Wed? —MN
Wed. is fine. —SLR
See you Wed. at 3:15 —MN

> ► When I first started sending subject lines without a text box, several people "got it" right away and responded in the same manner. A few, however, let me know that they "didn't get my message." When I told them that I try to save my reader's time and deliver the message in the subject line when I can, they too started responding with this electronic shorthand.
>
> And don't be like the new breed of e-mail writers who send messages without subject lines. A message without a subject line is akin to a newspaper with the headlines cut out. The reader's eye is drawn, with annoyance, to the big gaping holes. ◄

Use Keywords in the Subject Line

Using a keyword at the start of your subject line can be helpful for when you want to forward a message to someone else or try to locate an old message on an important topic. Some keywords may be: MIS, Billing, Human Resources (HR), Meeting, New Products—or anything else that can serve as a trigger.

> ► When a co-worker answers a question or helps you in some way, send "Thanks for your help—Your Name" as the subject line. You've used good rules of etiquette and saved the reader an extra click. Check out chapter 15 for rules of e-mail etiquette. ◄

Change the Subject Line When Replying to a Message

When you reply to someone's message, change the subject line. To maintain continuity in a stream of messages, use the keyword in the subject line and add the change to the message. For example: "Billing: To be discussed at April mtg."

My colleague James tells the story of coming to work one foggy morning and noticing that a parked car had its lights on. He sent an e-mail to the entire distribution list with this subject line: "Lic. #234 ADB car lights on." Realizing that James was in the office, people took the opportunity to reply with their own messages. One person asked James to meet her for lunch; another wanted to find out when a seminar was being offered; and another wanted some other information. None of the people changed the subject line from "Lic. #234 ADB car lights on," although none of the messages had anything to do with the one James had sent.

> ► For in-depth information on e-marketing as it relates to subject lines, check out chapter 16. ◄

Greetings and Salutations

Start each e-mail message with a salutation and end with a complimentary closing. Unlike the formal salutations and closings you use in letters, e-mail salutations and closings can be less formal. Following are a few examples:

Salutations	Closings
Hi Ken,	Regards,
Hello everyone,	See you later,
Hi,	Best wishes,
Ken,	Thanks,

Body Building

If you're sending someone a simple message, of course, it isn't necessary to prepare a draft; otherwise, it's vital that you do. Here's how to structure the body of a message:

- **Structuring short messages:** A short message can be delivered in one or two screens. Check out chapter 3 to give your reader the who, what, when, where, why, and how (or whichever apply) on the first screen. If you need a second screen, it can carry supporting information.
- **Structuring long messages:** If the message is longer than two screens, prepare it in your word processor and consider sending it as an attachment. Or post it on the company's intranet.

Easy-to-read Text

Following are some tips for creating text that's easy to read on the screen:

- Never use ALL CAPS. That's akin to shouting at the reader, and it's hard to read.
- Limit paragraphs to no more than 7 to 8 lines of text, leaving one line space between each paragraph.
- Use action-packed headlines to call out key information.
- Use bullets and numbers when they're appropriate.
- Use normal sentence structure with standard capitalization.
- Use proper punctuation.

▶ Refer to chapter 3 and the questioning techniques in Step 1. It's important to think of the questions your reader will have and to answer those questions in the first paragraph—much as a reporter does. Remember that people often view e-mail messages on handheld devices that have a very small screen, so you must put the key information right up front. ◀

Examples 14-2 and 14-3 show two different versions of the same message. Example 14-2 has a descriptive subject line, and the key information jumps off the screen. Example 14-3 has a vague subject line, and the key information is buried in all the gobbledygook. In Example 14-3, the information about the luncheon doesn't even appear on the first screen, and the reader may not page down.

To:	Distribution list
Subject:	YES! We're merging with Ken–San

Effective: January 1st
Yes, we start the new year as a wholly owned subsidiary of Ken-San Company. We've worked hard for this and know it comes as good news.

Learn more over lunch
Barbara N. Arthur, from Ken-San, will be here at a company-wide lunch to answer any questions and assure you of Ken-San's sincere intentions to continue business as usual. <u>Attendance is mandatory.</u>

Date:	July 15
Time:	12 to 1:30
Place:	Apollo Restaurant

Example 14-2: Explicit subject line and key information jump off the screen

---

To:	Distribution list
Subject:	Rumors about merger

Rumors have been flying about the possibility of merging with Ken-San Company. Well, let me give you the facts. As of January 1 we'll become a wholly owned sub-sidiary of Ken-San Company. We've worked hard for this and know it comes as good news. There are two key advantages. This is what they are: We've added strength in terms of public acceptance and operating capital, and we'll be able to serve our customers more promptly, efficiently, and thoroughly. This is something every company should strive for, because the customers are the backbone of any business. We are sure you have a lot of questions, and we want to be sure that you get a chance to air them. We'll be sponsoring a company-wide buffet luncheon, which will give you a chance to have all your questions answered. Barbara N. Arthur from the Ken-San Company will be on hand to answer your questions.

I'm sure many of you are wondering about the future of your jobs. Ms. Arthur will be letting you know firsthand of the company's sincere intentions to continue operating this division autonomously. Here are the details of the luncheon. The luncheon will be at the Apollo Restaurant on July 15. It will start at

---

Example 14-3: Key information is buried

▶ Sender beware! If you think that an e-mail message isn't a legal document—think again. More and more courts are recognizing e-mail messages as legal documents, even though they don't have written signatures. Here's a case in point:

In Massachusetts, a seller sent an e-mail message to a potential buyer detailing all the issues and dollar amounts to be written into the purchase and sale agreement for the sale of his home. Shortly thereafter the seller reneged. The intended purchaser sued the seller, claiming that the e-mail message constituted a binding contract. The court agreed. ◀

Electronic Signatures

Prepare an electronic signature file that ends each message. (Check your software's Help screen if you don't know how.) This creates free advertising on every message you send and differentiates you from the crowd. For example, here's the one I use:

Sheryl Lindsell-Roberts

sheryl@sherylwrites.com
www.sherylwrites.com
508-229-8209

You make more dollars when you make more sense!
* Creative Business Writing
* Business Writing Workshops
* Business Writing Coaching

Are You Ready to Send?

Just because you keyed in the closing, doesn't mean you're ready to send your message. Before you send, ask yourself these questions. When you answer yes to all of them, you're ready to send.

- Is my subject line compelling and revealing?

- Is my message visually appealing?

- Have I established the right tone?

- Have I proofread, proofread, and proofread?

Privacy Issues

E-mail and *privacy* are mutually exclusive. *E-mail is not private.* You don't know what system your message is passing through or what system other people's messages are passing through. Also, there's nothing to stop a systems administrator from snooping through your mail.

E-mail has raised a lot of issues about privacy, and many cases have been brought before the courts. In 1986, the Electronic Communication Privacy Act (ECPA) upheld a company's right to monitor its e-mail. The premise is: The company provides it and pays for it, therefore the company owns it! So, it's prudent not to send anything that you wouldn't want posted on the company's bulletin board. Here are some reasons why:

- A large entertainment company was in the midst of bankruptcy proceedings. Vast numbers of files were confiscated. Among those files were incriminating e-mail messages that weren't meant for the public eye. This led to the firing of several high-level people.

- Jennifer was the new office manager of a large company. Her first day on the job, James sent an e-mail message to Sam saying that he thought Jennifer was "pretty hot." Over the next several weeks, James and Sam exchanged messages about Jennifer. The messages got increasingly descriptive.

  The gents in question weren't aware that "Big Brother was watching." Both were called in for disciplinary action under the company's sexual harassment policy. Even though neither one had ever said a word directly to Jennifer, both were reprimanded and their employment records blemished.

- In a small New Jersey town, the police seized the e-mail of a murder suspect in order to further their investigation of the homicide case. On the strength of the evidence they gathered, which included incriminating e-mail messages, the man was charged with the murder.

- A noted New York columnist was caught out by e-mail monitoring. When he responded to a bluntly critical e-mail message from a young ethnic female colleague by sending back a barrage of sexual and racial epithets, he was suspended for two weeks.

Dealing with Spam

It's unclear how a household meat product morphed into the name for unsolicited e–junk mail that accounts for nearly 50 percent of all e-mail messages. The possible inspiration is a comedy routine by Monty Python's Flying Circus in which the word is repeated incessantly. Spam can take the form of anything from merely annoying messages to get-rich-quick schemes to pornography. Here's how spamming works. There are little "robots" that crawl around the Internet looking for the names of unsuspecting victims. Often the spammers use false return addresses to avoid being traced. Learn more about spam in chapter 16. If you're barraged with spam, spam, and more spam, here are a few things to try:

- **Never open the message.** Even if the message says, "If you'd like to be removed from this list, …" ignore it. If you respond, spammers will then recognize yours as a live address and will continue to pester you.

- **Contact your e-mail provider.** Give the sender's address to your e-mail provider with the strong message that you don't want unsolicited mail from that sender. In many cases, the spamming will stop.

- **Consider using two addresses.** Give one to your friends, relatives, and business associates; save the other for online ordering and public messaging such as in chat rooms.

WARNING: DON'T GO PHISHING

Phishing (pronounced *fishing*) is one of the worst kinds of spam. Scam artists represent themselves as legitimate businesses such as banks, credit companies, online retailers, and others. They send e-mail messages that say your credit has been compromised, your account is overdrawn, or some other attention-grabbing message. They then direct you to their bogus website (that often looks authentic) and ask you to fill out a form with lots of personal information that may include your social security number, credit card number, driver's license, or perhaps a number from your bank account.

What you should do: If you get a message such as this, immediately call the institution to report the scam.

Security Issues

Teenagers have broken into Pentagon files on several occasions, so you really have to wonder how secure any system is. There are two things you can do, however, to try to safeguard your system. (The key word here is *try.*)

1. **Configure your system to remember your username and password.** And never, never, never give them out to anyone—even if you're tortured.

2. **Get a program that can encrypt mail.** This will apply both to mail that you send and mail that you receive.

*E-mail technology is marching forward too
fast for social rules to keep up, leaving
correspondents to police themselves and
sometimes commit gaffes that would make
Miss Manners wince.*

—JEFFREY BAIR
columnist

CHAPTER 15

E-mail Etiquette

When Alexander Graham Bell invented the telephone in 1876, he never anticipated how profoundly it would change the way people think and communicate. It was a remarkable invention that soon became the centerpiece of the workplace. And e-mail, since its inception, has continued to revolutionize the way people think and communicate.

E-mail is the main stop on the information superhighway—one of the primary tenants in cyberspace real estate. It has replaced many of the letters and memos business people used to write, but the ease of sending and receiving messages creates problems. People have a tendency to prepare e-mail messages on the fly and fire them off to everyone in the universe.

WHAT'S IN THIS CHAPTER

- *Know when to send e-mail*
- *E-mail isn't private*
- *Change the subject line when replying to a message*
- *Reply only to people who need a reply*
- *Forward selectively*
- *Include a salutation and complimentary closing*
- *Never send a Rambogram*
- *Use distribution lists appropriately*
- *Send one message per subject*
- *Don't be too casual*
- *Use international savvy*
- *Be mindful of sending attachments*
- *Inform people of a change of address*
- *Reserve "urgent" for pressing messages*
- *Break the chain*
- *Proofread until your eyeballs hurt*

E-mail etiquette (or *netiquette,* as it's known in the e-world) is basically common sense. Just because e-mail is quick and easy doesn't mean it should travel at the speed of thoughtlessness. This chapter suggests ways to assure that your e-mails hit the mark.

Know When to Send E-mail

Always ask yourself if there's a better way to deliver the message. Paper? Fax? Telephone? Face-to-face? One of my colleagues received an e-mail from his manager letting him know that he was being laid off from his job. That's cold and heartless.

> ▶ Here's a story of e-mail gone awry. I had an appointment to meet with a client in Boston at 9:00 in the morning. I called the day before to confirm. When I arrived at her office (after driving for one and a half hours in the snow), she asked me, "What are you doing here?" Here's what happened: The client was working until 8:30 the night before, and she realized that she wasn't going to have everything ready for our meeting. At 8:30 p.m. she sent me an e-mail asking to postpone the meeting.
>
> I have a life and don't read e-mail in the evenings; therefore, I never got her message. This is just one case where a phone call would have been the appropriate way to deliver the message. ◀

E-mail Isn't Private

Don't say anything in an e-mail message that you wouldn't want the world to read. E-mail is as private as a postcard. The following is a true story. The co-owner of a gym was serving as a juror in a rape trial. Bothered by the length of time the trial would take, she decided to send an e-mail to her partner stating, "I'm just going to say he's guilty so I can get on with my life." She inadvertently sent this message to her distribution list—and, as luck would have it, the wife of the prosecuting attorney was on that list. See more about privacy issues in chapter 14.

> ▶ Your business e-mail isn't the place to find homes for your new puppies or announce that your daughter is selling Girl Scout cookies. Use office e-mail for office-related messages only. Employers have the legal right to monitor e-mail messages, and people have lost their jobs because they used business e-mail for personal business. ◀

Change the Subject Line When Replying to a Message

When you reply to someone's message, change the subject line. Check out chapter 14 for more information. The June 1, 2003, issue of *CIO Magazine* published an article about my e-mail workshop. I sent a notice to my distribution list using the subject line "I'm featured in *CIO Magazine*." I included the link in the text box. Within an hour, I received a dozen messages from people who wanted to congratulate me on the article. Most of them returned my subject line. This is what my inbox looked like:

I'm featured in CIO Magazine
I'm featured in CIO Magazine
I'm featured in CIO Magazine
I'm featured in CIO Magazine
And so forth . . .

Were they all featured in *CIO Magazine?* Remember that the subject line column of your inbox should read as the "Newsline" column of *USA Today.* You can read down the headlines (subject lines) and get snapshots of the events. If you need a thread to carry from one message to another, repeat the keywords, then include your message. Here's an example:

6/10 staff meeting: Changed to 3:00
[repeated keywords]   [new message]

Reply Only to Those Who Need a Reply

Bonnie, Human Resources Director, sent an invitation to 100 company employees for a company-sponsored event. She requested an RSVP. Half of the invitees responded to *all,* sending their responses to everyone on the list. Only Bonnie needed a headcount, yet several hundred unnecessary e-mails were sent to people who didn't need a reply.

Do you think that these 50 people would have responded to all 100 invitees if they had had to put postage on the envelopes and physically drop them in a mailbox? Of course not. Just because e-mail is quick and easy is no reason to communicate at the speed of thoughtlessness.

Forward Selectively

Forwarding messages is a wonderful way to pass legitimate business-related information on to others who need it. Following are some forwarding tips:

- Before you forward a message, consider how much of the message you need to send. Forward only what your reader needs to see.

- Decide if you should change the subject line.

- Eliminate the dross of mail headers and other detritus that e-mail picks up on the forwarding circuit. That includes the > symbol letting the reader know the message has been around the world at least twice.

Include a Salutation and Complimentary Closing

You say *hello* when you answer the telephone and include *Dear* —— when you write a letter. You also say *goodbye* when you end a telephone conversation and include a closing when you end a letter. The people who don't start or end e-mails with a greeting are the same ones who come into the office and bark out orders before they remove their coats. Check out samples on page 280.

Never Send a Rambogram

A Rambogram, commonly known as a *flame,* is a message that's rude, lewd, or crude. One of my colleagues received this message: "I can't tell you what my reaction is. I'm fuming. Your suggestion is a bunch of crap. I need time to digest this rot." That's a Rambogram!

In the world of cyberspace, it's easy to forget that a human being is reading your message. Don't send out angry messages. Each e-mail message is a permanent record of what you say. Even if you receive a flame, extinguish it and give yourself time to cool off. Remember this axiom: Send in haste, repent in leisure.

Following are some cooling-off tips:

- **Compose your reply and save it in your word processor.** Include all the spicy, nasty insults you really want to say.

- **Don't send the message.** Instead, save it to a file.

- **Revisit the file after you cool off.** Then ask yourself: "Would I say this to the person's face?" If you wouldn't, don't send it.

Use Distribution Lists Appropriately

Don't abuse distribution lists; send messages only to people who need to receive them. I belong to a professional organization that was sponsoring a dinner. I sent my check, and a week later I received an e-mail reminding me about the deadline for payment. I called the sender and confirmed that she did get my check. A week after that, I got another e-mail message stating that unless I paid by the specified date, a place would not be held for me. I called again and reminded the sender that she had received my check. When I asked why she was still sending me reminders, she told me it was because I was on the list. "Take me off," I firmly requested.

Send One Message per Subject

I often hear workshop participants complain that people don't answer their messages or send only partial replies. That's because people include many subjects in one e-mail message. People can't digest too many disparate thoughts. Send separate e-mails for each subject, and create a subject line applicable to each.

Don't Be Too Casual

E-mail is a serious business communications tool, and you should bring the same respect to it as to any other business document you write. The president and COO of Southwest Airlines, Colleen Barrett, doesn't use e-mail. She says, "For some reason, people seem to think that everything they learned about English grammar, spelling, or whatever had to go away, and you don't have to worry about it if you use e-mail."

> ▶ It's fine to include commonly used business abbreviations such as FYI (for your information) or FAQ (frequently asked questions).
> Avoid, however, abbreviations such as IMHO (in my humble opinion) or you won't be LOL (laughing out loud). Although this may be fine for writing to friends, this isn't appropriate in business situations. So, AFAIK (as far as I know), save the slang for your BF (boyfriend) or GF (girlfriend). ◀

Use International Savvy

Be aware of differences in cultural conventions. For example, if you refer to the date of 4/5/—, most of us in the United States will recognize it as April 5. Yet someone in Europe or in the military will interpret it as May 4.

Be Mindful of Sending Attachments

When your message is longer than two screens, prepare the document in your word processor, spreadsheet, or graphics software and send it as an attachment. Following are a few suggestions for sending attachments:

- **Be sure your reader can receive the file**. Not all e-mail systems handle files in the same way, and not all people have the same software. (I occasionally get attachments with weird file extensions that I can't open.) If you're unsure, send a test file to the reader to check for compatibility. Or call and ask.

- **Let the reader know what file format you're sending.** Even within the same software application, files aren't necessarily downwardly compatible (that is, able to be read by an earlier version of the software).

- **If an attached file is long, compress it.** Compressing files in programs such as WinZip can speed delivery and cut down on network traffic. Let the reader know what program you used to compress the document so he can uncompress the file on his end.

When your attachment needs to reach large numbers of people, look for alternatives to sending attachments. Following are two:

Post to Your Company's Intranet

If a message is static (not likely to change) and is of interest to a wide range of people, post it to your company's intranet. Then send an e-mail message letting people know it's there. This is a great way to share the details of the company picnic and other issues of interest to your colleagues.

Point to It on Your Website

If the message isn't static (is likely to change) and is of interest to a wide range of people, create a link on the Web. This is quite different from posting the list because it maintains the owner of the information as the keeper of the information. Following is one application:

Assume you're sending a message to your Atlanta office listing the phone numbers of people in your Boston office. This phone list is likely to change as people join the company, leave, or are reassigned. Here are ways the list can be used:

- **Fossilized way:** People get the telephone list, print it out, and hang it somewhere near the phone. (This list gets old quickly.)

- **Interim way:** Post the list on your intranet, as previously mentioned, so it can be updated as needed.

- **Web way:** Post a link to the telephone list. The keeper will update the list as the numbers change, so the list will stay current.

> ▶ There's a difference between an intranet and a website. Access to an intranet is generally restricted to the people within the organization or those who have been granted access through a password. A website is available to anyone with a computer and an Internet connection. ◄

Inform People of a Change of Address

The comedian Rodney Dangerfield did a spiel that went something like this: When he was a young boy, his parents sent him off to school one morning. When he returned home later, the house was empty; the furniture and people were gone. His parents had moved and left no forwarding address. In the e-mail world, too, people disappear without a trace.

Whenever you change your e-mail address (whether you change jobs or service providers), let those you correspond with know your new address. After all, when you move your office or change your phone number, you let people know.

Reserve "Urgent" for Pressing Messages

There are people who designate "urgent" as the priority to all their messages. I can recall instances when I didn't respond to an "urgent" message because the sender was the "little boy who cried wolf." Perhaps you too have had that experience. Following are two pieces of advice for wolf criers:

- Unless a message is urgent, don't tag it as such.

- If something is truly urgent and you must get the message through as quickly as possible, consider phoning rather than risking that the recipient won't see the message in time. People are more likely to listen to phone messages than to read e-mail messages. (As an example, this would be a good route to take when you need to cancel or schedule a meeting at the last minute.)

> ▶ On the flip side, if a message is merely informational, consider starting the subject line with FYI. People will come to recognize that notation as indicating they can read the message when they get around to it. ◄

Break the Chain

Chain letters and scams are rampant in the electronic world; they contribute dramatically to information overload. Bill Gates isn't experimenting with an e-mail tracing program and asking for your help; National Public Radio and the Public Broadcasting Service aren't gathering support to defend funding; Mrs. Fields isn't selling her cookie recipe; and the sky isn't falling. Even if there were a rocket disaster that released plutonium and it spread over the entire Northern hemisphere, do you really think this information would reach the public in a chain letter?

If you're absolutely, positively, and emphatically compelled to forward that 15th-generation message you get, have the decency to trim the 25 miles of headers showing everyone else who's received the message in the last several years. And it's a good idea to get rid of all the > symbols that begin each line letting everyone know the message has been around the e-world a gazillion times.

Proofread Until Your Eyeballs Hurt

I've often heard people say, "It's okay to send e-mail messages with errors; it's only e-mail." That is absolutely untrue. *E-mail is a serious business communications tool, and you should bring the same respect to it as to any other business document you write.* You often send e-mails to people you've never met, and they form an impression of you based on your message. What do you want that impression to be?

Don't be like the public relations director I mention in chapter 3 who sent an e-mail message to more than a thousand colleagues in the United States, Europe, and Asia. She left the *l* out of *Public* in the signature portion.

> ### E-MAIL TRIVIA
>
> Here's some trivia from the *Guinness Book of World Records 2003*.
>
> **Earliest E-mail:** In 1971, the first e-mail message was sent by Ray Tomlinson, an engineer working at the computer company Bolt, Beranek & Newman, in Cambridge, Massachusetts. The message read QWERTYUIOP. He intended it as an experiment to see if two computers could actually exchange messages. He also chose @ to separate the recipient's name from the location.
>
> **Costliest E-mail:** In 1977, a subsidiary of Chevron Corporation paid $2.2 million to settle a sexual harassment lawsuit filed by four female employees. The women presented evidence in the form of an e-mail message sent by a male employee listing 25 reasons why beer is better than women.

Industry average response rates are 5–15% for e-mail, 1–2% for direct mail, and .055–1% for banner advertising.

—JUNIPER COMMUNICATIONS

CHAPTER 16

E-marketing for Results

The purpose of marketing is to get your products/services into the minds and lives of people. E-marketing is the communications marvel of the twenty-first century that you can personalize, adapt, test, and send with the click of a mouse. Special offers, tips, HTMLs, PDF files, coupons, newsletters, and more are all part of this marketing phenomenon.

Whether you're a small, midsize, or large business, here's why e-marketing is one of the most powerful tools you can use to promote your business:

> **WHAT'S IN THIS CHAPTER**
>
> - *Fighting spam*
> - *Opt-in or opt-out*
> - *The subject line: Think INside the box*
> - *Craft an appropriate message*
> - *Call to action*
> - *Timing is everything*
> - *Testing, testing, 1–2–3*
> - *E-marketing that works*
> - *E-newsletters: Extra, extra, read all about it!*
> - *Generating lists*

- **Saves time and reduces marketing costs:** If you're on a tight budget (and who isn't these days), e-marketing is a great way to stretch your marketing dollars. You don't have the expense of costs or time related to materials, production, or postage.

- **Gets quick results:** Increase sales, drive traffic to your site or store, and build loyalty. E-marketing lets you communicate proactively with both current and prospective customers. You can generate an immediate response, often within 24 hours after launching a campaign, merely by saying, "<u>Click here to take advantage of this limited-time offer</u>" or "<u>Click here to learn more about this service</u>."

- **Reaches a targeted audience:** You can easily tailor your lists for specific criteria or special-interest groups so you're sending only to those people or businesses that are the most likely to respond.

- **Retains more customers:** Because you save time and money, you can communicate with your customers more frequently.

Fighting Spam

More than half of all e-mail sent is spam, costing businesses tens of billions (yes, billions) of dollars each year in lost productivity. As discussed in chapter 14, spam is choking e-mail to death, and it is hoped that the CAN-SPAM Act of 2003, which became effective on January 1, 2004, will loosen the grip. The act regulates, but does not prohibit, the sending of unsolicited e-mails in the United States. There are several gray areas as to what is and isn't spam, but the Federal Trade Commission (FTC) can impose a fine of $250 per e-mail, plus attorneys' fees, for blatant violators. Following are requirements when sending unsolicited e-mail:

Do's

- Include an opt-out link letting recipients remove their names. You must remove the names of all recipients who opt out within 10 days.

- Show an actual e-mail address from which the e-mail was sent. Disclose your true identity and address.

- Include a clear notice that the e-mail is a solicitation.

Taboos

- Don't include a deceptive subject line or false header.

- Don't hide the opt-out. It must be obvious.

Opt-in or Opt-out

To some degree, spam is in the eyes of the beholder. Some people appreciate receiving information about products and services that can enhance their lives or businesses; others view such information as an invasion of privacy. See a sample of how opting out is offered in the second paragraph of Example 16-1. Your offer can be presented in a statement as simple as one of the following.

- We respect your privacy. If you want to be removed from this list, <u>click here</u> to opt out, and we'll remove your name immediately.

- To opt out, <u>click here</u>.

▶ Perhaps the people who opt in would be interested in other, related products or services. Here's how I've asked that of the associates on my opt-in list:

"We work with several partners whose products and services we recommend. Would you be interested in receiving information from them? Please click <u>opt-in</u> or <u>opt-out</u>. Thank you."

Give them the option of clicking on the appropriate response. ◀

From:	Robert Distler
Date:	Friday, October 10, 2003 12:30 PM
To:	Sheryl Lindsell-Roberts
Subject:	WAC October Newsline

We are EXPO-sing Ourselves

Welcome to the second edition of the WAC monthly newsline. Early each month we'll be sending monthly news concerning a topic that may be of interest to you. You can also get additional information on each month's topic at our website in the new <u>Newsline Section</u>.

These newslines are part of our ongoing effort to add value to our customers. They may contain tips for using your software more effectively, industry news, current workshops, and more. We hope you'll find these newslines to be useful. If you don't want to receive these monthly newslines, please reply to this message and use the subject line to say −Opt Out.

October's topic: Expo Mania

This month we will be exhibiting at two shows in the Worcester Centrum.

Example 16-1: Giving readers the ability to opt out

The Subject Line: Think INside the Box

The success of your e-marketing campaign hinges on just a few words—the subject line. You don't have to be the company bard waiting for a visit from the marketing muse to write a compelling subject line. Be insightful, think INside the box, and don't use the same subject line for more than one campaign. Perhaps you remember Gollum from *The Lord of the Rings*. He grew so attached to the ring that he sat in his cave and muttered "my precious" for years on end. Your "precious" subject line may hit the mark once, but it won't hit the mark twice.

Subject lines should focus on your audience and be limited to 30 to 40 characters. (For a more general discussion of subject lines, check out chapter 14.) Following are suggestions that work:

- Offer complimentary merchandise or services.

- Include the phrases *first-time* or *limited-time offer.*

- Mention a substantial discount.

- Use the person's name.

Putting these ideas into action:

LOST IN THE INBOX	A CLICK THROUGH
Reply ASAP	Reply by midnight, Friday, June 5
Just for you	Exclusively yours, not available to outsiders
Great deal	Get 50% off—register by May 2
Analyze your telephone Internet bills	Complimentary analysis of your telephone & Internet bills
Information	Here's the information you requested

> ▶ • Be wary of using the word *free,* because many filters block it. Don't be gimmicky and use *fr_e,* because that reeks of spam. Instead, consider using *complimentary* or *no cost.*
>
> • Also be wary of words or expressions that have been overused. For example, the seeds for *one-stop shopping* have been planted so many times that they've mutated into weeds. ◀

Craft an Appropriate Message

For a high opt-in rate, make sure you send readers something they'll value. Therefore, always send information that's relevant to your readers' businesses rather than self-serving information about your latest products or services. You can send a business-related tip, industry update, timely article, or the like.

Personalize the message to your target audience. In 2002, *E-mail Marketing Weekly* conducted a survey to determine how important it is to personalize your message according to name, interests, gender, age, purchase history, and message frequency preferences. The results showed that nonpersonalized bulk e-mails got a 4.7 percent response rate; personalized bulk e-mails got a 14.8 percent response rate.

Speak Your Reader's Language

Know your audience and use words your readers would use. If your message is going to an international audience, know how your English message will translate. When Coca-Cola first came to China, the Chinese translated the name as "Bite the Wax Tadpole." And when the automaker Chevrolet introduced the Nova, they found that "No va" means "Doesn't go" in Spanish, implying that the car didn't run.

Grab the Reader's Attention Quickly

Grab the reader's attention in the first sentence and again in the last sentence. Consider making the last sentence a postscript. You probably learned when you took public-speaking classes that you should state your bottom line at the beginning and again at the end. The same holds true for e-marketing. In that way you grab the attention of people who read the first few lines and those who skip to the end.

Use Phrases That Work

Here are some words and phrases to use in the text that automatically arouse interest:

Words	Phrases
Alert!	Congratulations! You're our 10th winner.
Congratulations	Forgive me, for I have spammed.
Hot	Here's your discount.
Private	Limited time only.
Success	Look at this only if you …
	Take a sneak peak at …

Call to Action

If appropriate, conclude by letting the reader know what to do next: Sign up for a service, buy something, fill out a form, read an article or white paper, call for an appointment, or whatever. Notice the subtle call to action in Example 16-2. It announces a special one-month discount. Notice also how the headlines tell the story.

> ▶ In Example 16-2, note how the writer puts the names of the recipients in the Bcc box and sends it to himself so he can be sure the message gets through. Each recipient will see only her name in the To field, thereby individualing the message. ◀

To:	drlindsell@att.net
Cc:	
Bcc:	christelreeve@hotmail.com; Craig.Lemke@Verizon.net; cschaum@attbi.com; Cynthia_elms@hotmail.com; dcherson@verizon.net; dbeaber@charter.net; Dccraw@aol.com; deborahj.ma.ultranet@rcn.com; donna.douchette@charter.net; dougp4158@attbi.com; drbailey@attbi.com; ed@harrow.org; jhibek@yahoo.com; Franknh11@adelphia.net; gary.finneran@mindspring.com; jameslmoody@hotmail.com; jay_farrell2002@yahoo.com
Subject:	Special Offer for LeTip Members

Dear LeTip Member,

Please let me say how excited I am to be a new member of LeTip. I'm Dr. Eric Lindsell, Director of Essential Family Chiropractic, serving Howard County. I'd like to offer you, your staff, and your referrals the chance to experience the tremendous health benefits of chiropractic care at a substantial savings.

Share This Great Offer and Save Over 50%
If you, someone in your office, or a referral schedules an appointment for a complete examination and x-rays (if necessary), it will cost only $40. This is more than a 50% savings to introduce chiropractic into your healthy lifestyle.

Chiropractic Means Wellness, Not Just the Absence of Back Pain
Chiropractic care offers more than just symptom relief for back pain and headaches. Just as you visit your dentist regularly to keep your teeth and gums healthy, you should visit a chiropractor regularly to keep your

Example 16-2: A subtle call to action

Here are some hints for making your call to action stand out:

TO MAKE IT...	CALL OUT THE ACTION
Visible	Write **Next step** or **Action Requested** as a headline.
Compelling	Include words such as "Try this for 60 days before deciding to buy."
Direct	Provide a link to a specific page on a website.
Urgent	Add a limited-time context such as "The first 100 customers . . ."
Clear	Use simple words, short phrases, and white space.

Timing Is Everything

Conventional wisdom says you should send business-to-business (B2B) messages midweek: Tuesdays, Wednesdays, or Thursdays. Mondays are considered "pile up" days, when people return from the weekend and have to catch up. Fridays are the onset of the weekend, and people are often eager to leave the office and not take up something new.

If you send e-messages on Mondays or Fridays, turn them into positives: "Start the week off right," "End the week right," or "Start the weekend off right." Three ways to find what works best for your audience are to test, test, and test.

It's also wise to send your e-marketing messages so the recipient receives them during the middle of the workday. Everyone has a full inbox early in the morning, so your message may get lost in the shuffle, and at the end of the day, people are anxious to leave.

Testing, Testing, 1–2–3

Testing will assure your highest response rate. Test your list, offer, body copy, calls-to-action, delivery day, and delivery time. The key is to test only one variable at a time so that you can easily tell which variable has made the difference. Here are some questions to ask about the following problems:

- **Low open rate:** Take a look at your subject line.
  - Is it short and to the point?
  - Does it mention a specific benefit?

- Does it look like spam?
- Were your delivery dates and/or times appropriate?

- **Low click-through rate:** Here are several things to examine:

  - *Your call-to-action.* Was your call-to-action clear? Did you make it easy for recipients to answer your call-to-action by putting links throughout your message? Do your links work?

  - *Your copy.* Are you writing to your target audience? Is your text clear and concise? Are the benefits right up front?

  - *Your offer.* Does your offer fulfill the promise of your subject line? Is your product or service too expensive? Have you created a sense of urgency with a time limit?

- **High opt-out rate:** If more than 5% of your subscribers opt out regularly, take a look at all of the elements of your campaign and make adjustments. Ask a few customers with whom you have a close relationship why they unsubscribed. Take immediate action based on their comments.

Whatever you do, don't give up because of less-than-stellar results the first few times.

E-marketing That Works

Following are several successful e-marketing messages I have sent or received.

- **Example 16-3a:** This message directs readers to an article I wrote and published on an e-marketing website. BIZTIPS is my distribution list.

- **Example 16-3b:** This is the article readers see when they click through. Many people told me that they printed out the copy and passed it around.

- **Example 16-4:** I send monthly Biz Writing Tips to my colleagues, clients, and potential clients. This is an example of one. BIZTIPS is my distribution list.

- **Example 16-5a:** E-marketing message sending a brochure as a PDF file.

- **Example 16-5b:** The first two pages of the four-page brochure sent in Example 16-5a. This is printed out and passed around.

Hi Everyone,

Please check out **http://cc.roving.com** to see my article "Create a Website that Draws a Crowd."

Have a great weekend,
Sheryl

Sheryl Lindsell-Roberts
sheryl@sherylwrites.com
www.sherylwrites.com
508-229-8209

You make more dollars when you make more sense!
* Creative Business Writing (brochures, proposals, websites, & more)
* Business Writing Workshops
* Business Writing Coaching

Example 16-3a: E-marketing message with a link to an article

Create a Website that Draws a Crowd

We've talked about how to turn visitors into your best customers using e-mail marketing, but what about your online presence? How do you create a new website or improve your existing website to increase your online success? This week our friend and award-winning business writer and author, Sheryl Lindsell-Roberts, gives us some great tips on writing and designing a website that gets results!

Create a Website that Draws a Crowd
by *Sheryl Lindsell-Roberts*

Your website is your face to the world; it's unlike any other form of marketing or selling you'll ever do. If you want a website that people flock to, it needs to be rich in content and functionality.

Website Do's

Whether you are working with a professional to design your website, or going it on your own, you must understand and maximize the contribution you make to the success of your site. Here are some important things to consider:

Clarify your goals
Years ago people built websites just to have a cyber-presence. Today's websites can do much more. So first, determine what you want your site to do. Do you want it to be an online brochure? Will it be educational? Will it be a sales vehicle? Are you doing e-marketing or e-commerce?

Determine key words and phrases
You must determine the words or phrases your audience will use to find your site. If an attorney uses "matrimonial attorney" and people search under "divorce lawyer," they won't find that attorney. If you're a money lender, for example, you may use "factoring," "asset-based loans," and "bridge loans."

Remember that first impressions are key
Always put the good stuff first. Think of your home page as a giant magazine rack. Your audience scans the front cover of the magazine. Within 8 seconds, they'll decide to stay or look elsewhere, so make sure you capture their attention right away.

Example 16-3b: Printout of the article linked to the message in Example 16-3a

Write for your audiences

Remember that your site should be about your audience, not just about you! You must understand and be able to convey "what's in it for them." Benefits and features work well. Look at the websites of your competitors to see how they tantalize (or frustrate).

Write for readability

Web audiences want instant information. Therefore, you must keep the text concise—often much shorter than its print equivalent. Here's how to give your audience the information they want quickly:

- Write headlines that give key information. (Pattern your headlines after those you see in a newspaper.)

- Limit paragraphs to 8 lines of text.

- Use bulleted lists.

- Make effective use of white space and appropriate graphics.

Go modular

Think about the content and how the average person will access your pages. Keep the topic and content of each page focused, making each page one complete thought or idea. This means that each page should be able to stand alone. People have different browsing styles, so they'll enter your website from different paths. Therefore, you should consider providing your key information on several pages of your site.

Link to other sites

No matter how great your content is, don't waste the most valuable feature of the web—links. You've probably found that one of the best experiences you have on the web is the serendipity of stumbling upon a cool website you didn't know existed. When you provide useful links, your website becomes a valuable resource that your audience will return to and recommend to others.

Build in tracking

You must be able to quantify the return on investment (ROI) of your website by measuring the activity of visitors, e-marketing, e-mails, faxes, and phone calls. It is critical to know who visits your site and how often.

Publicize your site

What good is your wonderful site if people don't know it exists or how to find it? Here are some ways to publicize your site after it's published:

Example 16-3b (continued)

- Include the URL on your letterhead, business cards, and e-newsletters. (Some people print out e-newsletters and distribute them.)
- Add the URL to the signature portion of all your e-mail messages.
- Post it to appropriate newsgroups.
- Send out a press release, if that's appropriate for your business.

Keep your site current

A static site is a boring site. A static site may work for some businesses, but you want to give people a reason to return. A good way to keep your site current is to include new links, industry tips and trends, and any other information your audience will find useful.

Website Taboos

There are a number of reasons that websites aren't successful. Here are just a few:

- **Lack of keywords:** You must have the keywords people will use to search for your site. Otherwise, they won't know you're there. These words must be peppered throughout the site because you may not know where people enter.
- **Bleeding-edge technology:** Your site isn't New York City's Times Square. Don't use images that have an overpowering effect on the human peripheral vision just because you can. That's akin to generating documents that look like circus posters just because you have a word processor. Include only what you need and what's appropriate for your business.
- **Hard-to-read colors:** People still use black backgrounds with yellow lettering, or something equally awful. Use appropriate, readable colors.
- **Outdated information:** Keep your site current. You need a web gardener to weed your web garden and replant new flowers. An outdated site is the sign of an outdated company.
- **Long downloads:** Human factors guidelines show that audiences lose interest after 8 seconds. Many people still use dial-up modems, and download time may be a significant factor for your audience.

Example 16-3b (continued)

International Websites

As Internet access grows across the globe, so do translation and download problems. Following are some guidelines to help meet the needs of a worldwide audience:

Work with a translator
If the site is to be translated, identify the languages. Send text, menus, and entries to the translator to learn of potential problems. For example, in other languages nouns may not have similar conventions and many words and phrases we typically use may be offensive.

Be aware of download time
There are many parts of the world that have slow modems with Internet access billed by the minute. Users in these regions (and many are right here in the United States) will visit sites that are quick to download.

Site must be printable
There are also parts of the world where Internet access is very expensive and users often share computers. People print out websites and distribute hard-copy pages.

Sheryl Lindsell-Roberts, Principal of Sheryl Lindsell-Roberts & Associates, is an award-winning business writer and the author of 18 books. She's written brochures, proposals, video scripts, and Web text that have paved the way for clients to close multi-million dollar deals. You can contact Sheryl at 508-229-8209 or check out www.sherylwrites.com.

View Email Marketing 101™, the FREE On Demand Webinar from Constant Contact®.

http://www.roving.com/marketing/newsletters/hints-tips/volume7-issue4.html

Example 16-3b (continued)

To:	sheryl@sherylwrites.com
Cc:	
Bcc:	BIZTIPS
Subject:	Biz Writing Tips: Psychology of Punctuation

You can trigger certain reactions in your readers by using punctuation. Following are some ways to do that:

- **Question marks** automatically signal interactivity because they get the reader involved. When the question is thought-provoking, it makes a good opener that compels the reader to think a certain way.
- **Exclamation points** create excitement. (Two exclamation points, however, are weak, because they betray the sense of excitement.)
- **Colons** push the reader into what follows. They propel the concept of the incompleteness of what's been said before.
- **Asterisks** break the flow. They cause the reader to look for the corresponding asterisk someplace else. An alternative may be to include the information in parentheses near the text.
- **Dashes** used around parenthetical text–instead of commas–accentuate what's enclosed in the dashes.
- **Parentheses** used around parenthetical text (instead of commas) downplay what's enclosed in the parentheses.

Example 16-4: Monthly "Biz Writing Tips"

To:	Bob Flannagan
Cc:	
Subject:	The brochure you requested as a .pdf file
Attach:	EagleWingBrochure.pdf (184 KB)

Hi Bob,

I'm attaching a copy of the brochure you requested and will call you next week to follow up.

Thank you for your interest.
Dennis

Dennis D'Antona, President
EagleWing Consulting, Inc.
Integrated Business and Information Technology
508-366-3956   www.eaglewingconsulting.com

Example 16-5a: E-marketing message sending a brochure as an attachment

EagleWing Consulting

EagleWing (Ēgəl Wing) Consulting *adj. and n.*

1. making your business soar to greater heights

2. improving your business performance

3. creating a web presence for a greater return on investment

4. outsourcing your information technology needs

5. offering interactive workshops in business process reengineering and web marketing

Is your **web site** generating new business and enhancing ongoing business?

Do you need an online brochure, a marketing information web site, or an e-commerce operation? EagleWing can write, design, develop, and host a site that will differentiate you from the competition.

We can provide credit card processing, general ledger integration, inventory tracking, vendor performance analyses, user maintained price and product offering lists, and discount coupon processing.

73 Bowman Street, Suite #201, Westborough, MA 01581
email: info@eaglewingconsulting.com

Phone: 508-579-3361
Fax: 770-818-5835

www.eaglewingconsulting.com

Example 16-5b: Printout of brochure sent as PDF file

EagleWing Consulting

Are you losing money
because your current
business solutions
don't drive profitability?

*Improving Business Performance
through the Integration of
People, Process, and Technology*

Your profitability is directly linked to putting the right
information in the hands of the right people at the right time.
Let EagleWing design and deploy a solution just for your
business—from customized development or software
packages to fully integrated system solutions of disparate
databases.

Following are some of the comprehensive business solutions
that can help your revenue to soar:

- ❖ **Customer Relationship Management (CRM)**
- ❖ **Enterprise Incentive Management (EIM)**
- ❖ **Enterprise and Manufacturing Resource Planning
  (ERP/MRP)**
- ❖ **Human Resources Information Systems (HRIS)**
- ❖ **Financial Systems including QuickBooks**
- ❖ **Sales Force Automation (SFA)**
- ❖ **Retail / Point of Sale Systems**
- ❖ **Supply Chain Management (SCM)**

Our service offerings include strategic planning, business
development, analysis and design, implementation, project
management, support, and advisement.

Example 16-5b (continued)

EagleWing Consulting

Do you need the support of an IT

department but feel you are too small a company to support a full-time staff?

Every company, regardless of size, needs IT support. Without the proper support your business may be outpacing your current software and infrastructure; your intellectual property may get into the wrong hands; you may be violating Internet e-mail distribution, privacy and computer piracy laws that may land you in court; or a system failure may interrupt your sales, drive customers away or degrade your customer service.

Don't let deficiencies in any of these areas adversely affect your business.

Will interactive workshops give you the tools to you need to enhance your business systems development and support activities?

The following workshops are designed for business analysts in mid- or large-sized companies:

Business Process Reengineering
Gain an in-depth approach for generating process solutions that will dramatically improve your business performance.
Collaborative Business Analysis
Learn techniques and processes to better define business requirements related to strategic business software development initiatives.

These workshops are geared for small- to mid-sized businesses:

Setting Up An E-Commerce Operation
Overcome the challenges of expanding your customer base with Internet solutions that will grow your business and increase profitability.
Setting Up An E-Newsletter
Use the power of the Internet to stay connected with your current and prospective customers.

Example 16-5b (continued)

About Us

EagleWing Consulting was founded by Dennis D'Antona to assist companies in implementing information technology to improve their business performance. EWC is dedicated to effectively and efficiently applying information technology to business operations.

By drawing upon expertise in business operations, marketing and information technology, EWC is able to transform business goals and objectives into information technology programs. Working closely with its clients, EWC will manage the implementation activities to develop these initiatives into world-class business software solutions.

- ❖ **Learn how our consulting services will increase your profitability**
- ❖ **Schedule an interactive workshop**
- ❖ **Subscribe to our free business / technology newsletter**

Contact **EagleWing Consulting** for a highly productive, complimentary one-hour consultation.

info@eaglewingconsulting.com
www.eaglewingconsulting.com

EagleWing Consulting, Inc.
73 Bowman Street
Suite #201
Westborough, MA 01581

Phone: 508-579-3361
Fax: 770-818-5835

Example 16-5b (continued)

E-newsletters: Extra, Extra, Read All About It!

Unlike traditional advertising, e-newsletters are a great way to promote your business. People trust editorial copy more than they trust advertising. You can "speak" to people without hype or pressure, and you can solve readers' problems with pertinent advice. It's important, however, that readers don't perceive your newsletter as self-serving. Here are ways to create reader-focused newsletters:

- Deal with topics that are of interest to your readers.

- Write your own commentary on relevant events or issues that pertain to your readers' industries.

- Include success stories, case studies, testimonials and other examples of how companies or people have successfully used your products or services.

- Offer a contest, discount, or something relevant to your products or services.

- Include a questionnaire or poll asking your readers for their opinions on something of interest.

- Feature a question-and-answer column.

Example 16-6 is the printout of a great e-newsletter that Proofread*NOW* sends to its subscribers as an HTML document. It's easy to print out and pass around.

> ▶ • To create a newsletter that's reader-focused, check out chapter 3 and fill out the Start Up Sheet. This is key to the success of your newsletter, because you must see your target so you know where to aim.
>
> • Give readers the ability to opt out. ◀

Sending a Teaser or the Whole Newsletter

Whether to present the whole newsletter or craft a one- or two-sentence teaser is often a dilemma. The whole newsletter takes up several screens, as you see in Example 16-6. A one- or two-sentence teaser for Example 16-6 may read as follows:

Click on www.proofreadNOW.com to learn how to present numbers in text.

www.proofread*NOW*.com

THIS WEEK'S ASIDE

Week 2—Opinion Week

Week 2 is opinion week. Comments are welcome. Here goes:

Quite a few companies these days are starting up (or even renaming themselves) using meaningless names. Examples: *Accenture* and *Verizon*.
While we're NOT considering changing from Proofread*NOW* to *Crecidon* or *Crovidus* or the like, we are wondering how you, the elite thinkers of the day, feel about this trend. Our poll:

- *I love these weird names.*
- *I dislike these weird names. They're simply ridiculous.*
- *I'm a middle-of-the-road person. Some are okay, others are not.*
- *It's all about spending on branding. Give me $1 billion, and I can make a company named Floppida work.*
- *None of the above.*

WEEKLY GRAMMAR TIP

September 9, 2003

Let's Check the Numbers!

Presenting numbers in running text can be confusing to people who want their documents to be formatted correctly. We're asked to copyedit number-rich documents often, and offer this advice, taken from the *Chicago Manual of Style*:

Numbers applicable to the same category should be treated alike within the same context, whether a paragraph or a series of paragraphs; do not use numerals for some and spell out others. If according to rule you must use numerals for one of the numbers in a given category, then for consistency's sake use numerals for them all:

- There are 25 waterskiers on the south lake, 56 on the north lake, and 117 on the river, making a total of 198 waterskiers at camp today.
- In the past ten years fifteen new buildings have been erected. In one block a 103-story office building rises between two old apartment houses only 3 and 4 stories high.
- The population of Harrison, Maine, grew from 10,000 to 175,000 in only thirty years.

Example 16-6: Printout of an e-newsletter

(Click on one choice, and elaborate if you'd like. Our promise: *No spam, no one will call, no names will be used.*) Thanks for participating! We'll publish aggregate results soon.

WEEKLY UPDATE
Old Navy Wins TV Ad Recall Index—Again

AdAge rated the recall of the top ten television ads aired the last two weeks of August.

1. Old Navy - Cargo Train - It's time to throw down; 241
2. 10-10-987 - John Stamos calls mom; 235
3. Capital One - No-Hassle Card - moviegoer's card stolen by Cinderella; 232
4. Heineken - 6-packs exchanged for 12-packs; 198
5. Burger King - Fire-Grilled Triple, man asks what he can order; 191
6. Payless - Star Jones, "What Women Want"; 182
7. Payless - Star Jones, "Pass It On"; 180
8. Heineken - Man pulls case of beer from con- venience store refrigera- tor; 172

Note that, as in the foregoing examples, numbers in the same context but representing different categories may be treated differently.

First Word in Sentence

At the beginning of a sentence any number that would ordinarily be set in numerals should be spelled out instead, regardless of any inconsistency this may create:

- One hundred ten loaves and 103 fish were left over after the meal.
- Thirty-eight percent of the people paid attention.
- Nineteen fifty-three was a good year for Virginia.
- Thirty-three thousand people were courtside to watch Andy Roddick win the U.S. Open on Sunday.

If spelling out a number that begins a sentence is impracticable or cumbersome, the sentence should be recast so that it does not begin with a number:

- Virginia saw a very good year in 1953.
- The year 1953 was a very good one for Virginia.

Example 16-6 (continued)

9. Burger King - "I think I'm in love"; 165
10. Country Crock - Plus Yogurt - man does sit-ups; 160

Source: *AdAge*, September 8, 2003. See *AdAge* for complete explanation of the recall index figures given here.

Proofread*NOW:* Hundreds of expert editors waiting to proof your PDF, MS Word, QuarkXPress, PowerPoint, HTML, or text document. Turnarounds from one hour to one week, depending on your need. Two editors collaborate on every job.

If you like our newsletter, will you forward it to someone else who might also like it? (The forwarding-click is in the upper left corner of the page.)

Did someone forward this to you? Subscribe for yourself at www.proofreadnow.com/web-optin.htm!

Example 16-6 (continued)

Following are a number of factors to consider in making this decision:

- **Determine the objective of your newsletter**. If it's mainly promotional, where you discuss your new products or services, consider a promotional blurb with a link to the newsletter. If the newsletter is a stand-alone editorial and you're providing your readers with useful information, send the full newsletter.

- **Learn what you can about your readers' reading habits.** Conduct an informal survey to find out who likes to read onscreen and who likes to print out the full text. For people who read onscreen, a link would be appropriate. For those who read hard copy, send the full newsletter.

- **Understand how your readers connect to the Web.** In many parts of the world Internet access is via slow modems and users are billed by the minute. Users in these regions (and many are right here in the United States) don't click any more than they need to. These people print out text and distribute hard-copy pages. You make it easy for them to do this when you send the full text.

Writing a Sexy Teaser

A sexy teaser has nothing to do with sex. It's an intriguing, compelling, fun, and interesting opener that will entice the reader to click through. (That's why it's called a teaser.) One way to add a dollop of intrigue is to include dollar amounts, numbers, specific sizes, etc. Bigger is better. For example, it's more impressive to tell the reader she can save $12,000 a year than to tell her she can save $1,000 a month.

Before	Learn how Bob Stevens, star salesman, exceeded his sales goals last year.
After	Learn how Bob Stevens generated $15 million in sales last year, tripling his goal of $5 million.

▶ When you publish a newsletter that subscribers value (and why send one if they don't?), leverage that value and lure more visitors to soak up your expertise by placing the newsletters in your archives. See how in Example 16-7. ◀

| | Back | Forward | Stop | Refresh | Home | Print | Mail |

NEWSLETTER ARTICLES

Communications is managing this for us. They help in all aspects of reaching out to the marketplace.

Susan Kinney-Mantione, Director of Sales, Global Systems Technology Partners, Ft. Lauderdale, FL

Is your business taking a summer vacation? Why it could hurt you ...
By Laura DiBenedetto, President of Fresh Design
Summer. The best season of the year. Or is it? Most business declines in the summertime, and it's likely that your business is no exception. What are you doing differently? What are your clients doing differently? What is your competition doing differently? Chances are, just about everyone you know, including yourself, has given in to the ...
... CLICK HERE TO READ FULL TEXT

Health Insurance Rates Continue to Rise – What's a Business Owner to do?
By Janet Clark, President of Integrated Communications
Small- and medium-sized businesses have experienced premium increases of up to 20 percent for their group medical insurance coverage in the last six months. Employers are being forced to shift costs to their employees to offset the higher health-care expenses, according to a new market survey by The Council of Insurance Agents & Brokers.
... CLICK HERE TO READ FULL TEXT

Extra! Extra! Read all about it! Let the press brag about your company
By Brigitte Casemyr, President of Turfbuilder Marketing
I don't intend to turn you into full-fledged public relations gurus, but I thought I'd share with you some key strategies for getting the press to work for you. Now, I'm not talking about the *Wall Street Journal* or the *New York Times* here, as they definitely are in a category by themselves. But I am talking about most all other publications.
... CLICK HERE TO READ FULL TEXT

Example 16-7: Teaser for archived newsletters

Generating Lists

The list of your current customers is a valuable e-marketing asset. Current customers are the "low-hanging fruit." Although you may not think about your customers long after you complete a project for them, you want to ensure that they keep thinking about you. It's seven times less expensive to market to an existing customer than it is to acquire a new one. Here are ways to generate lists.

Using Existing Clients and/or Customers

Conventional wisdom says that if a small-to-midsize company were to increase its customer retention rate by 5%, its profits would double in about ten years. No matter what products or services you offer, make the most of every contact with customers. Existing customers are a great source of repeat business and referrals for new business. You want to remain on their radar screens. Ask for e-mail addresses at every point of customer contact.

- Instruct salespeople to ask for customers' e-mail addresses. This works well in retail environments.

- Ask for the addresses when someone visits your website, when you take a telephone order, when you send a survey or feedback form.

Renting Permission-Based Lists

Permission-based lists contain prospects who have opted in to receive information about certain subjects. You can slice and dice these lists by interest category, profession, demographics, and more. For example, list categories can include nail salons, residential architects, or sailboat owners. Rental lists are owned and maintained by list vendors, who are the only ones who see the actual list.

- You send your promotional information to the vendor.

- The vendor sends your information to the people or companies on the lists you've selected.

- The vendor provides you with reports on the click-through rate (CTR), indicating the number of people who opened the message.

List Brokers

A list broker is a professional buyer who can help you select and acquire targeted lists. There's no added cost to you, as the broker earns an industry-standard commission from the list's owner. The list broker can help with defining your target audience, reviewing your promotion, and testing and tracking. Finding the right list broker can take a lot of time and research. If you don't have the time or patience to do it yourself, contact a reputable list-broker referral service such as www.metaresponse.com.

APPENDIXES

This section is chock-full of easy-to-apply and easy-to-remember guidelines for the sticky wickets of punctuation, grammar, commonly confused words, and abbreviations. It also lists proper forms of address.

*I'm glad you came to punctuate my discourse,
which I fear has gone on for an hour without
any stop at all.*

—SAMUEL TAYLOR COLERIDGE

Punctuation Made Easy

Psychology of Punctuation

Punctuation is one of the most significant tools for creating your document in your own voice. When you speak aloud, you constantly punctuate with your voice and body language. When you write, you also make a sound in the reader's head. It can be a dull mumble (which is the reason tedious, unformatted documents make you sleepy) or it can be a joyful sound, a shy whisper, a throb of passion. It all depends on the punctuation you use. Following are some ways to create your voice:

- **Question marks** automatically signal interactivity, because they get the reader involved. When the question is thought-provoking, it makes a good opener that compels the reader to think a certain way.

- **Exclamation points** create excitement. (Two exclamation points, however, are weak, because they betray the sense of excitement.)

- **Colons** push the reader into what follows. They propel the concept of the incompleteness of what's been said before.

- **Asterisks** break the flow. They cause the reader to look for the corresponding asterisk someplace else. An alternative may be to include the information in parentheses near the text.

- **Dashes** used around parenthetical text—instead of commas—accentuate what's enclosed in the dashes.

- **Parentheses** used around parenthetical text (instead of commas) downplay what's enclosed in the parentheses.

Punctuating for Readability

The following pairs of sentences are worded identically, but the differences in punctuation make a different sound in the reader's head.

Woman without her man is a savage.
Woman: without her, man is a savage.

Daddy, Mommy isn't getting any better, come home.
Daddy: Mommy isn't getting any, better come home.

Commas

Commas are the most frequently used (and misused) punctuation mark. While periods indicate a *stop* in thought, commas act as *slow* signs—something like a speed bump. They let you know what should be grouped together, what's critical to the meaning of the sentence, and more—as you'll see here.

- Use commas to separate three or more items in a series.

  We were impressed with the candidate's poise, understanding, and integrity.

- Use a comma before a conjunction *(and, but, or, nor, for, so, yet)* that joins two independent clauses—those that can stand alone as sentences.

  Joe recognizes the four delegates, but he can't recall their names.

- Don't place a comma before *because* in a statement of direct cause and effect.

  Tim was late for the meeting because he missed the commuter train.

- Use a comma before *because* when the information that follows is explanatory rather than cause and effect.

  I hate being late for work, because the early hours are the most productive.

- Use commas to separate items in an address or date.

  Barbara and Carl Lekander live at One Adam Street, Marlborough, Massachusetts 01752.

  On Saturday, September 16, 20—, he left for the West Coast.

- Use commas to set off an expression that explains the preceding word, name, or phrase.

  Main Street, our town's main thoroughfare, will be closed to traffic tomorrow.

- Use a comma to set off a name or title in direct address.

  Please let me know, Mayor, if you can add anything to that.

- Use a comma after an introductory clause that's followed by a complete thought. This may begin with words such as *when*, *if*, *as*, and *although*.

  If we advertise in that magazine, our sales should increase.

- Use commas to set off a nonrestrictive clause—a clause that wouldn't change the meaning of the sentence if it weren't there.

  My older son, the one you met last Monday, is an architect. *(He's an architect regardless of when you met him.)*

- Don't place commas around a restrictive clause—information necessary to making the sentence clear.

  The person who meets all our qualifications will never be found.

- Use commas to set off parenthetical (transitional) expressions that interrupt the natural flow of the sentence. Examples of these phrases include *as a result, in fact, therefore, however, consequently, for example, on the contrary,* etc.

We will, therefore, continue with the project.

- Use commas to clarify a sentence that would otherwise be confusing.

  Later on, that evening would be seen as the turning point of the campaign.

- Use a comma to set off an adverb that applies to the whole sentence.

  Unpredictably, the demand for personal computers fell off sharply in the third quarter.

- Use commas to show contrast.

  Please work as a team, not as individual contributors.

- Use commas to identify a person who's being directly quoted.

  "I'll be there tomorrow," Mr. Smith said.

- Use commas to set off designations, titles, and degrees that follow a name.

  Max Lorenz, CPA, will be our guest speaker.

- Use a comma to divide a sentence that starts as a statement and ends as a question.

  You'll call her, won't you?

- Use commas to separate items in reference material.

  The information is in volume II, chapter 3, line 12.

- Use a comma to separate words when the word *and* has been omitted.

  He's a very intelligent, thoughtful person.

Semicolons

Semicolons can be considered a cross between periods and commas. They have more strength than commas, yet less than periods. Here are some examples of their use:

- Use a semicolon to separate independent clauses in a compound sentence when there's no conjunction.

  Pete will arrive at ten; George will arrive at seven.

- Use a semicolon between coordinate clauses of a compound sentence that are joined by a parenthetical (transitional) word or phrase.

  The project came to a standstill during the strike; however, we did eke out a small profit.

- Use a semicolon to separate items in a series when the items themselves contain commas.

  The three most important dates in our company's history are January 15, 1937; April 8, 1952; and July 30, 1994.

Colons

Colons are marks of anticipation. They serve as introductions that alert you to a close connection between what comes before and after.

- Use a colon after an introduction that includes or implies *the following* or *as follows*.

  We hope to open branch offices in each of these states: New York, Massachusetts, and Maine.

- Use a colon to introduce a long quotation.

  Professor Longwinded said: "The Junior League of Sudbury has funded up to $100,000 over a five-year period to assist in developing and coordinating the Arts and Education program in cooperation with the Sudbury school and community arts groups. This project is essentially and significantly a proposal to improve and enrich the general education of young people. The goal is to use the arts process as an integral part of basic education."

- Use a colon to separate hours and minutes.

  He should arrive at 10:45 a.m.

Dashes

Dashes are vigorous and versatile, and have several uses.

- Use dashes to set off parenthetical expressions you want to emphasize.

  This software program—as unbiased tests have disclosed—is more powerful than what you're currently using.

- Use a dash before wording that sums up a preceding series.

  The dishwasher, the washing machine, the dryer—these are items that will eventually need repair.

- Use a dash to set off an afterthought that interrupts the sentence.

  I know you're looking for—and I hope this will help—a list of qualified people.

- Use a dash before the name of an author or work that follows a direct quote.

  "You can turn painful situations around through laughter. If you can find humor in something, you can survive it." —Bill Cosby

Parentheses

Parentheses are like a sideshow; they're used to enclose a word or words within a sentence. Here's when you'd use them:

- Use parentheses to set off parenthetical expressions you want to de-emphasize. A parenthetical expression is one that wouldn't change the meaning of the sentence if it weren't there.

  This software program (as unbiased researchers have established) is more powerful than what you're using.

- Use parentheses to set off references to charts, pages, diagrams, authors, etc.

  Please read the section on fossils (pages 36–52).

- Use parentheses to enclose numerals or letters that precede items in a series.

> I can be at your office on (1) Monday, May 1; (2) Tuesday, May 2; or (3) Wednesday, May 10.

Brackets

Brackets aren't substitutes for parentheses. They have their own place in the world.

- Use brackets to enclose words that are added to a direct quotation.

> He said, "The length of the trial [from early June to late July] was entirely too long."

- Use brackets to enclose parenthetical information within parentheses.

> Mr. Brannigan came to this country when he was a young man. (Some people [see page 36] claim Italy is his birthplace.)

Quotation Marks

Quotation marks are reserved for those occasions when you're citing text or speech verbatim. **Caution:** If you're paraphrasing, don't use quotation marks.

> **Quoting**   Mr. Schultz said, "Please come to the meeting at two o'clock, so we can discuss this in more detail."
>
> **Paraphrasing**   Mr. Schultz asked her to come to the two-o'clock meeting to discuss the matter in more detail.

- Use quotation marks to enclose direct quotes.

> "Our industry is vital to the economy," said the CEO.

- Use quotation marks to enclose chapter titles or the titles of minor works, such as articles from magazines, songs, essays, short stories, one-act plays, sermons, paintings, lectures, etc. (Titles of longer works, such as books, feature-length films, and symphonic works, are usually italicized.)

In *Loony Laws & Silly Statutes,* by Sheryl Lindsell-Roberts, there's a chapter titled "Sorry, My Dance Card's Full."

- Use quotation marks to set off words or phrases introduced by expressions such as *the word, known as, was called, marked, entitled,* etc. (An alternative to using quotations marks is to use italics.)

  The check was marked "canceled."

- Use quotation marks to set off words used in an unconventional manner. (Again, using italics is an alternative.)

  He's really a "piece of work."

- Use single quotation marks around a quotation within a quotation.

  The final sentence read: "You would do well to heed Mr. Smith's advice: 'Give the public what it wants and you will be in business for a long time.'"

Punctuating quotations: Here are a few general guidelines for using punctuation within quotations.

- Always place commas and periods inside the closing quotation marks.

  The most desired response is "yes."

- Always place semicolons and colons outside the closing quotation marks.

  The following are listed under "Assets": computer equipment and factory machinery.

  The person who's being sued is the "defendant"; the person who's suing is the "plaintiff."

- Always place question marks and exclamation points inside the closing quotation marks when they apply only to the quoted material.

  "What's the circulation of that newspaper?" he asked.

  "I can't believe it!" yelled the winner.

- Always place question marks and exclamation points outside the closing quotation marks when they apply to the entire sentence.

> Did he say, "Our circulation is over a million"?

> How careless to drop a package marked "Fragile"!

Ellipses

Ellipses are used to show an omission in a quotation. Ellipses are formed by typing a series of three periods with a space between each.

> As an industry spokesman put it in a recent article, "Telecommunications is a link between the worlds of word processing and data processing and the audio-visual industry ... Conference calls are used to allow people in remote locations to conduct business meetings without being face to face. Telecommunications can curtail travel."

Apostrophes

Apostrophes are most commonly used with nouns to show possession.

> The host called the guests names when they arrived.
> The host called the guests' names when they arrived.
> *(Which host would you prefer?)*

Possession: Here are several guidelines for using apostrophes to show possession.

- Form the possessive case of a singular noun by adding an apostrophe and *s*.

> The department's goals are to increase production next quarter.

> The bus's right front tire was flat.

- Form the possessive of a regular plural noun (one ending in *s*) by adding an apostrophe after the *s*.

> The attorneys' arguments continued for two hours.

- Form the possessive of an irregular plural noun (one not ending in *s*) by adding an apostrophe and *s*.

  The salespeople's territories are being divided.

- To show joint ownership, add the apostrophe and *s* after the last noun. To show single ownership, add the apostrophe and *s* to each noun.

  Jim and Pat's locker is near the lounge. *(The locker is a joint deal.)*
  Jim's and Pat's lockers are near the lounge. *(The lockers are individual deals.)*

- In compound phrases, put the apostrophe and *s* at the end of the key word.

  He borrowed his brother-in-law's car.

- To make an abbreviation possessive, put an apostrophe and *s* after the period. If the abbreviation is plural, place an apostrophe after the *s*.

  The Smith Co.'s sale starts next month.

- Express time and measurement in the possessive case.

  We'll have an answer in one week's time.

Omission: Use an apostrophe to show the omission of letters (as in contractions) or numbers.

  The graduating class of '70 had its 25-year reunion in '95.

Use an apostrophe to form the plural of an abbreviation that's made up of several letters. (Some writers eliminate the apostrophe when there's little chance of misreading.)

  I used AAA's towing service last week.

> ► If you want to highlight a negative statement, consider using a contraction. For example, *don't* is more noticeable than *do not*. Use your judgment if something might be misleading. ◄

Hyphens

Don't confuse hyphens (-) with em dashes (—). They're a different species. Hyphens function primarily as spelling devices.

- Use a hyphen to join compound adjectives that come before the noun.

    The bank extended the family a thirty-day note.

- Use a hyphen for compound numbers and fractions that are written out.

    This is three-fourths the annual revenue.

- Use a hyphen when *ex-* and *-elect* are joined to titles.

    Did ex-President Carter return to his farm after he left office?

- Use a hyphen with a prefix if it is necessary to make the meaning of the word clear.

    The message was re-sent yesterday.

> ▶ **Q:** Do you know the difference in meaning between the two phrases that follow?
>
> (a) a small-business person
> (b) a small business person
>
> **A:** (a) refers to the owner of a small business, rather than to the owner of a large or midsize business.
>
> (b) refers to a business person who's small, rather than tall or over-weight. ◀

Question Marks

Question marks are stop signs that invite or call for a reply.

- Use a question mark after a direct question.

    How soon can you have the report ready?

- Use a question mark after a short, direct question that follows a statement.

  You saw the requisition, didn't you?

- Use a question mark after each item in a series of questions within the same sentence.

  Which of the candidates has the most experience? Mary? Joe? Jeff?

Exclamation Point

Exclamation points are reserved for words or thoughts that show strong feelings or emotions.

  That was an inspiring talk. Congratulations!

Period

Here we are at the basic stop sign of punctuation.

- Use a period after a statement, command, or polite request.

  Check every figure in the invoice.

- Use a period after phrases that logically substitute for a complete sentence.

  No, not at all.

> ► Generally, use periods when writing abbreviations, acronyms, or initialisms. A number of dictionaries, however, are citing many abbreviations without periods. For example, YMCA, FDIC, CPA. If in doubt, check it out. ◄

Slashes

These critters go by a variety of names: slant line, virgule, bar, or shilling line.

- Use a slash in certain abbreviations and expressions of time.

  They agreed on a 60/40 split.

- Use slashes in and/or expressions.

  The sales/advertising departments will decide on the issues.

- Use slashes in Internet addresses, as in this one for the U.S. Postal Service homepage.

  http://www.usps.com/welcome.htm

This is the sort of English up with which I will not put.

—WINSTON CHURCHILL
(comment against clumsy avoidance of
ending a sentence with a preposition)

APPENDIX B

Grammar's Not Grueling

You may remember asking your mother when you were a kid, "Mom, can me and Pat go to the movies?" Your mother replied, "That's Pat and I," and she didn't give you the money until you corrected your grammar. Although you didn't think so then, your mother was doing you a favor. Poor grammar didn't get you far with your mother, and it doesn't get you far in the business world.

> ▶ I don't get into the nitty-gritty details of every part of speech in this appendix. You forgot that from Ms. Grump's English class, and you'll forget that again. Rather, I touch on the areas that are most troublesome, and offer an easy way to remember what's important. I've listed the aspects of grammar in alphabetical order. ◀

Adjectives

An adjective can add pizzazz to a sentence, and it answers at least one of the following questions: What kind? Which? What color? How many? What size? An adjective is a word, phrase, or clause that modifies, describes, or limits the noun or

333

pronoun it's describing. You can use adjectives to transform an ordinary sentence into a tantalizing one.

Ordinary   The steak cooked on the grill.

Tantalizing   The darkly charred steak sizzled on the grill, its top beaded with red-hot juices.

What an Adjective Answers

Adjectives answer questions such as: *What kind? Which? What color? How many? What size? What shape?*

difficult task	*upper* bunk	*gray* skies
six friends	*large* amount	*round* hole

Forms of Adjectives

Adjectives take different forms, depending on the noun or nouns they're modifying.

- Use a *positive* adjective when you're not comparing anything.

    It's *cold* today.

- Use a *comparative* adjective when you're comparing two things.

    It's *colder* today than it was yesterday.

- Use a *superlative* adjective when you're comparing three things or more.

    It's the *coldest* day we've had all week.

Absolute Adjectives

Some adjectives are absolute; they describe a condition that either is or isn't. For example, a thing can't be more or less unique; it's either unique or it's not. Here are some adjectives that are usually considered absolute:

complete	correct	dead	empty
final	flawless	genuine	parallel
round	sole	stationary	unanimous

Irregular Adjectives

Several adjectives have irregular comparatives and superlatives. Here are a few:

good, better, best
little, less, least
bad, worse, worst

Compound Adjectives

In many cases, you'll use a hyphen to join together two adjectives so they form a single description. The hyphen is used only when the compound adjective comes before the noun, not after.

a job that's part time	a part-time job
a report that's well written	a well-written report
a lease of two or three years	a two- or three-year lease

Exceptions:
Eliminate the hyphen when the words are generally thought of as a unit:

post office address	word processing center
life insurance policy	real estate office

Adverbs

Just as an adjective can add pizzazz to a noun, an adverb can add pizzazz to a verb. An adverb modifies a verb, an adjective, or another adverb. An adverb answers the questions: *How? When? Why? How much? Where? To what degree?* Adverbs take different forms for the positive, comparative, and superlative, just as adjectives do. Some words can function as either adjectives or adverbs—it depends on what they're modifying.

Adjective   The *fast* runner set a new record.

Adverb   The storm moved in *fast.*

Articles

The is a definite article, referring to a speical item; *a* and *an* are indefinite articles, referring to an item in general: *the* book I'm looking for (specific), as compared to *a* book I read last year (not specific). *A* is used when a consonant sound follows; *an* is used when a vowel sound follows.

an onion	*an* illness
a cold	*a* three-week trip

Double Negatives

If you've ever said, "I don't want no liver," it technically means you *do* want liver. Don't use double negatives.

Correct	We don't require any more information.
Incorrect	We don't require no more information.

Nouns

The noun—although critical to every sentence—is not always the sexiest part of speech. The noun doesn't usually create much emotion or add flair to your thoughts; it's merely a *person, place,* or *thing.* (If language wore clothing, the noun would be the unkempt loiterer in the corner of the room discussing past participles.) Proper nouns name specific persons, places, or things and are capitalized.

Proper noun	**Common noun**
New York City	the city
Wang Center	the theater

▶ When a noun is collective (*group, company, council, audience, faculty, union, team, jury, committee,* and others) use a singular verb. ◀

The company **is** celebrating its tenth anniversary.

Gerunds

A gerund is a word or phrase that has a verb as the root and *ing* as the ending. Gerunds are formed from verbs, but act as nouns. When a gerund is preceded by a noun or pronoun, the noun or pronoun takes the possessive form.

> I don't like *your giving* me such short notice.

Parallel Structure

Parallel structure means using the same pattern of expression for words, phrases, or clauses within a sentence. Following are some examples:

Not parallel	He's energetic, thoughtful, and shows a lot of creativity.
Parallel	He's energetic, thoughtful, and creative.
Not parallel	Arranging items by category was easier than to write them in parallel form.
Parallel	Arranging items by category was easier than writing them in parallel form.

Prepositions

A preposition is a word that typically precedes a noun (or a group of words that function as a noun) and shows the relationship of that noun to a verb, adjective, or another noun. Common prepositions are *about, above, across, after, against, along, among, around, at, before, behind, below, beneath, beside, between, beyond, by, down, during, except, for, from, in, inside, into, like, near, of, off, on, since, to, toward, through, under, until, up, upon, with, within.*

Commonly Confused Prepositions

Here's a list of phrases whose prepositions sometimes get mangled in the mind:

accompany *by* (a person)
accompany *with* (an object)

account *for* (something or someone)
account *to* (someone)

angry *at* or *about* (something)
angry *with* (someone)

compare *to* (show similarity)
compare *with* (examine for similarities and differences)

convenient *for* (suitable)
convenient *to* (close)

correspond *to* (agree with)
correspond *with* (write letters)

differ *about something* (disagree)
differ *from something* (be unlike)
differ *with someone* (disagree)

talk *to* (address)
talk *with* (discuss)

Pronouns

The main purpose of the pronoun is to eliminate the need for awkward wording. The pronoun must agree with its antecedent (the noun it's replacing) in person, number, and gender.

Nominative

Use the nominative case when the pronoun is the subject of the sentence or when it follows a form of the verb *be.*

> She called and left a message.

> The caller was certainly she.

Objective

Use the objective case when the pronoun is the object of the verb or the object of the preposition. It will always answer "whom" or "what."

> Please give a copy to him and me.

> ▶ In the last sentence, people might have a tendency to say *him and I.* So here's a way to determine the correct pronoun(s) to use when two pronouns end a sentence—leave one of them home! It'll work every time.
>
> • If you leave "him" home, you're saying: Please give a copy to *me.*
>
> • If you leave "me" home, you're saying: Please give a copy to *him.* ◀

Possessive

The possessive case indicates possession, kind, origin, brand, authorship, etc.

> Her presentation was the best I've seen.

> The decision is completely his.

Singular Pronouns

The following pronouns are always singular and take singular verbs and pronouns: *anybody, anyone, anything, each, either, everybody, everyone, everything, much, neither, nobody, nothing, one, somebody, someone, something.*

> *Each* of these people *is* to be notified when you receive the shipment.

> If you see *anything* wrong, be sure to fix *it.*

Who and Whom

Who-and-whom cowards can mumble these words and hope the listener won't notice their indecision. Writers don't have that luxury. Let's eliminate rules and think of this in easy terms! When you can substitute "he/she/they," use *who.* And when you can substitute "her/him/them," use *whom.*

> The company needs a person *who* knows the new software.
> (He/she *knows the new software.*)

> Are you the person to *whom* I spoke yesterday?
> (*I spoke to* her/him.*)

Verbs

The verb is the most important part of the sentence because it expresses an action, condition, or state of being. It makes a statement about the subject and can breathe life into dull text. For example, *we seek to challenge our employees* has more impact than *we want to help our employees do their best.*

Dangling Participles

If your participles dangle, it's nothing to be ashamed of. The condition's curable. A dangling participle (a participle is a verb form generally ending in *ing, ed,* or *en*) refers to a verbal phrase that doesn't clearly or logically refer to the noun or pronoun it modifies. Participles can dangle at the beginning or end of a sentence.

Dangling	While attending the meeting, the computer malfunctioned. *(Who was attending the meeting?)*
Not dangling	While James was attending the meeting, the computer malfunctioned.

Were/Was

Have you ever fantasized about being someone else? The English language provides us with a verb for those fantasies. "I wish I *were* …" The verb *were* is often used to express wishful thinking or an idea that's contrary to fact. The verb *was* is a statement of fact.

I wish I *were* you.
(I'm not and can't be.)

If Charles *was* at the airport, I didn't see him.
(He might have been.)

Remember: *Was* is the past tense of *is.* Why am I mentioning the obvious? People mistakenly use *was* for the present tense when referring to something that's already happened.

Correct	I thoroughly enjoyed the book—even though it *is* 950 pages.
Incorrect	I thoroughly enjoyed the book—even though it *was* 950 pages. *(The page count hasn't changed.)*

Split Infinitives

An infinitive is the form of the verb when it is preceded by *to*. It has long been a popular myth that splitting infinitives is a no-no with grammarians. Examples of split infinitives are *to boldly go, to completely understand,* and the like.

Here's what *The Chicago Manual of Style* has to say: "Sometimes it is perfectly appropriate to split an infinitive verb with an adverb to add emphasis or to produce a natural sound." Sometimes avoiding splitting an infinitive creates a jumbled sentence that's weak or overly formal.

Unsplit infinitive	The instructor wants to read each of the papers her students handed in carefully.
Split infinitive	The instructor wants to carefully read each of the papers her students handed in.

Subject and Verb Agreement

This is one of the most basic rules of grammar. The subject and verb must always be in harmony—they should get along with each other. Both must be singular, or both must be plural. Although the following two sentences are obvious, the bulleted items may be a little tricky:

The *man was* at the office early.

The *men were* at the office early.

- *Many a, many an, each,* and *every* always take a singular verb.

Every computer *is* needed for the project.

Many a man *has* been denied this chance.

- *None, some, any, all, most,* and expressions of fractional amounts take either the singular or the plural, depending on what they modify.

Half the *shipment has* been misplaced.
("Shipment" is singular, so half of it is also singular.)

Half the *orders have* been filled.
("Orders" is plural, so half of them is also plural.)

- When referring to the name of a book, magazine, song, company, or article, use a singular verb even though the name may be plural.

   Little Women is a great classic.

- When referring to an amount, money, or distance, use a singular verb if the noun is thought of as a single unit.

   I think that *$900 is* a fair price.

- When *or* or *nor* is used to connect singular and plural subjects, the verb must agree in number with the person or item closest to it.

   Neither Jim nor his *assistants were* available.

   Neither the assistants nor *Jim was* available.

I went to a newly opened supermarket looking to buy a package of envelopes. I spotted an aisle marked "Stationary," and an oops! *went off in my head. I found the manager and asked if that was the only aisle that doesn't move. He looked at me as if I had two heads and he walked away.*

—SHERYL LINDSELL-ROBERTS

Commonly Confused Words

Spell checkers are wonderful tools, but they are just that—tools. They won't identify all errors. Following are some of the sticky wickets you must find on your own:

accept (v)	to take
except (prep)	other than
access (n)	right to enter; admittance
assess (v)	to set a value
excess (n/adj)	extra
ad (n)	short for *advertisement*
add (v)	to increase
adapt (v)	to adjust
adept (adj)	skilled
adopt (v)	to take as your own
addition (n)	something added
edition (n)	published work

adverse (adj)	unfavorable, hostile
averse (adj)	unwilling
advice (n)	recommendation
advise (v)	to give an opinion
affect (v)	to influence
effect (n/v)	result/to bring about
already (adv)	previously
all ready (phrase)	all prepared
alright (adj)	nonstandard English for *all right*
all right (adj)	entirely correct
altar (n)	part of a church
alter (v)	to change (notice the **a-e** correlation)
altogether (adv)	entirely
all together (phrase)	everyone in one group
among (prep)	three or more (*among* the three of them)
between (prep)	two (*between* the two of them)
amount (n)	refers to things in bulk or mass
number (n)	refers to countable items and people
appraise (v)	to estimate
apprise (v)	to notify
assistance (n)	help
assistants (n)	those who help
bare (adj)	naked; no more than
bear (v)	to carry
beside (prep)	alongside
besides (prep)	in addition to; except for
biannual (adj)	twice a year
biennial (adj)	every two years

brake (n/v)	device for stopping motion/to stop by using a brake
break (n/v)	fracture/to breach
canvas (n)	coarse cloth
canvass (v)	to solicit
capital (n/adj)	official city of a state; money/serious; chief
capitol (n)	building which houses state legislature
Capitol (n)	building in Washington, DC
cheap (adj)	inferior
inexpensive (adj)	low in cost
choose (v)	to select
chose (v)	past tense of *choose*
cite (v)	to quote; to mention as proof
sight (n)	that which is seen
site (n)	location (geographical or on Internet)
coarse (adj)	rough
course (n)	direction; series of studies
complement (n/v)	that which completes/to complete
compliment (n/v)	expression of praise/to praise
complementary (adj)	serving to complete or enhance
complimentary (adj)	meant as a compliment; offered for free
correspondence (n)	letters
correspondents (n)	those who write letters
council (n)	assembly
counsel (n/v)	attorney/to advise
consul (n)	foreign representative
device (n)	plan
devise (v)	to plan
disburse (v)	to pay out
disperse (v)	to scatter

dual (adj)	double
duel (n)	formal fight
elicit (v)	to draw out
illicit (adj)	**ill**egal (notice the **ill** correlation)
eminent (adj)	well-known
imminent (adj)	**imm**ediate (notice the **imm** correlation)
ensure (v)	to make certain
insure (v)	to protect against
farther (adv)	to a more distant point
further (adv)	to a greater degree
faze (v)	to embarrass
phase (n)	stage of development
fewer (adj)	modifies countable items (such as *dollars*)
less (adj)	modifies things in bulk or mass (such as *money*)
formally (adv)	in a **formal** manner (notice the word **formal**)
formerly (adv)	at a **former** time (notice the word **former**)
forth (adv)	forward
fourth (n)	follows third (notice the number **four**)
forward (adv)	ahead
foreword (n)	preface in a book (notice the word **word**)
incite (v)	to stir to action
insight (n)	clear understanding
its (adj)	belonging to it
it's (contraction)	it is
its'	no such word
knew (v)	past tense of *know*
new (adj)	not old
know (v)	to understand
no (adj)	not any

lay (v)	to place an object down
lie (v/n)	to recline/untruth
lead (v)	to guide
led (v)	past tense of *lead*
loose (v)	to set free
lose (v)	to suffer a loss; to mislay
loss (n)	something lost
maybe (adv)	perhaps
may be (v)	might be
miner (n)	one who works in a mine
minor (n)	person under legal age
moral (n)	lesson relating to right and wrong
morale (n)	spirit
overdo (v)	to do to excess
overdue (adj)	late
passed (v)	past tense of *pass*
past (n)	time gone by
patience (n)	endurance
patients (n)	persons receiving treatment
peace (n)	state of calm
piece (n)	portion
peer (n)	equal
pier (n)	wharf
persecute (v)	to oppress
prosecute (v)	to institute legal proceedings against
personal (adj)	private
personnel (n)	staff
principal (n/adj)	sum of money; school official/main; first in rank
principle (n)	rule

respectfully (adv)	in a respectful manner
respectively (adv)	in the order listed
right (adj/n)	correct/just privilege
rite (n)	formal ceremony
write (v)	to inscribe
role (n)	part in a play; function
roll (n)	register or list; small bread
should of	improper English
should have (aux v)	proper English
stationary (adj)	fixed in place
stationery (n)	writing paper (notice the **er** correlation)
suit (n/v)	clothes/to please
suite (n)	set of rooms
sweet (adj)	having a sugary taste
than (conj)	used to express comparison or difference
then (adv)	at that time; next
their (adj)	belonging to them
there (adv)	in that place
they're (contraction)	they are
therefor (adv)	for that item (formal expression)
therefore (adv)	for that reason; consequently
to (prep)	toward
too (adv)	also
two (n)	numeral
undo (v)	to open; to render ineffective
undue (adj)	improper; excessive
waive (v)	to relinquish
wave (n/v)	gesture; surge of water/to move back and forth

weather (n/v)	condition/to come through safely
whether (conj)	if; in case
who's (contraction)	who is; who has
whose (adj)	possessive of *who*
your (adj)	belonging to you
you're (contraction)	you are

A lot of fellows nowadays have a B.A., M.D., or Ph.D. Unfortunately, they don't have a J.O.B.

—ANTOINE "FATS" DOMINO

Abridged Abbreviations

Abbreviations are used for a variety of reasons: to avoid repetition, save space, or conform to conventional usage. Leading authorities can't agree on the capitalization or punctuation for many abbreviations; therefore, there are no set rules. In general, it's wise not to abbreviate unless there's a good reason to do so and you know your reader will understand you. Having said that, here are some guidelines to cover variations, exceptions, and peculiarities.

> ► My motto is, "If in doubt, write it out." Don't feed your readers alphabet soup, or you risk insulting or alienating them. ◄

Acronyms and Initialisms

What's the difference between an acronym and an initialism? An acronym is formed by combining the first letters of several words and pronouncing the result as a word. An initialism is also formed by combining the first letters of several words, but it's pronounced as separate letters. For example, you'd say I-B-M.

Acronyms

AMEX (American Stock Exchange)

ISO (International Organization for Standardization)

LASER (light amplification by stimulated emission or radiation)

OPEC (Organization of Petroleum Exporting Countries)

Initialisms

CEO (chief executive officer)

FDIC (Federal Deposit Insurance Corporation)

NYSE (New York Stock Exchange)

ROI (return on investment)

In business, industry, education, and government, acronyms and initialisms are often used by people working within the same fields. That's fine, as long as everyone involved understands the frame of reference. However, such abbreviations may not be comprehensible to those outside your magical kingdom. And, certain abbreviations can mean different things to different people. For example, to an attorney, ABA is the American Bar Association; to a banker, it's the American Banking Association; and to a bowler, it's the American Bowling Association. My son's friend used to impress his classmates by telling them that his father was head of the CIA. Everyone was awed. His dad was the head of the Culinary Institute of America, not the Central Intelligence Agency.

Writing Acronyms and Abbreviations

The first time an acronym or initialism appears in written text, write the complete term followed by the abbreviation in parentheses. Thereafter, use the acronym or initialism alone.

At first mention	The American Library Association (ALA) will be written out at first mention.
Thereafter	Thereafter, the three letters ALA will suffice.

Agencies and Associations

Abbreviate the names of agencies and associations only after they've been spelled out the first time they appear—unless you're absolutely sure the reader will understand your reference.

> The FDA will not give its approval to the drug you mentioned.
> *(Most people know what FDA stands for.)*

> The National Association of Manufacturers (NAM) will hold its annual meeting in July. At that time, NAM will outline its agenda for the year.

Companies and Organizations

Styling varies widely. Treat the name as the company or organization treats it. Check the website or letterhead for an accurate picture. If you can't verify an abbreviation, write it out.

> AT&T

> Millbrook Mortgage Corporation

> YMCA (Young Men's Christian Association)

Compass Points

Abbreviate compass points when they appear after street names; spell them out when they appear before street names.

> He lives at 994 East 172nd Street.

> She lives at 334 Fifteenth Avenue SW.

Latin Words and Phrases

Words that are derived from Latin are commonly abbreviated. I suggest that you generally refrain from using Latin abbreviations, because readers often misread them. For example, many people confuse "i.e." and "e.g.," and they're not interchangeable. If you do use Latin words, here are some abbreviations you commonly see:

c. *or* ca.	*(circa)* about
e.g.	*(exempli gratia)* for example
et al.	*(et alii)* and others
etc.	*(et cetera)* and so forth
et seq.	*(et sequens)* and the following
ibid.	*(ibidem)* in the same place
i.e.	*(id est)* that is
loc. cit.	*(loco citato)* in the place cited
pro tem	*(pro tempore)* for the time being
ss.	*(scilicet)* namely (Often used in affidavits.)
viz.	*(videlicet)* namely

Laws and Bylaws

When you cite laws or bylaws, write them out completely at first mention; thereafter, use the abbreviation.

At first mention The reference appears in Article I, Section 2.

Thereafter See Art. I, Sec. 2.

Metric System

The United States is probably the only country in the universe that isn't using the metric system. Here are some common metric abbreviations:

km	kilometer
hm	hectometer
dam	decameter
m	meter
dm	decimeter

cm	centimeter
mm	millimeter
l	liter
cl	centiliter
ml	milliliter
MT *or* t.	metric ton
kg	kilogram
hg	hectogram
dag	decagram
g *or* gm.	gram
dg	decigram
cg	centigram
mg	milligram

Periods

In general, use periods for academic degrees, but not for professional designations.

Thomas Greenberg, Ed.D.	Richard L. Hodge, CPA
Jon Roberts, M.S. in Engineering	Susan Bergstein, RN

Use a period after most abbreviations that are formed by omitting all but a few letters of a word.

mfg. (manufacturing)	avg. (average)
fig. (figure)	Mlle. (Mademoiselle)

Omit the period from abbreviations that are made up of initial letters that constitute an acronym, initialism, or compound word.

ROI (return on investment)	GDP (gross domestic product)
FOB (free on board)	aka (also known as)
AMEX (American Stock Exchange)	sysop (system operator)

Scientific Terms

Use full binomial nomenclature at first mention; thereafter, abbreviate the genus.

At first mention   *Escherichia coli*

Thereafter   *E. coli*

Abbreviate names of chemical compounds and medical, mechanical, or electrical equipment or processes without periods.

CPU (central processing unit)

EKG (electrocardiogram)

OCR (optical character recognition)

Don't use periods with the symbols for chemical elements or compounds.

Ca (calcium)

H (hydrogen)

H_2O (water)

Titles

Abbreviate social titles, not professional titles. The titles Reverend and Honorable are abbreviated (Rev. and Hon.) when not preceded by *the*.

Mr. John Smith

Messrs. Einstein and Downing

General Otis Jackson

Hon. Patrick Walker (but, the Honorable Patrick Walker)

Doctor Rosenfeld (but, "Dr. Rosenfeld" in the salutation of a letter)

Dillon, Logan & Scott, Esquires (but, "Esqs." in the inside address of a letter)

Two-Letter State and Territory Abbreviations

The post office requests that you use the two-letter abbreviations on all correspondence. Here they are:

LOCATION	ABBREVIATION	LOCATION	ABBREVIATION
Alabama	AL	Montana	MT
Alaska	AK	Nebraska	NE
Arizona	AZ	Nevada	NV
Arkansas	AR	New Hampshire	NH
California	CA	New Jersey	NJ
Canal Zone	CZ	New Mexico	NM
Colorado	CO	New York	NY
Connecticut	CT	North Carolina	NC
Delaware	DE	North Dakota	ND
District of Columbia	DC	Ohio	OH
Florida	FL	Oklahoma	OK
Georgia	GA	Oregon	OR
Guam	GU	Pennsylvania	PA
Hawaii	HI	Puerto Rico	PR
Idaho	ID	Rhode Island	RI
Illinois	IL	South Carolina	SC
Indiana	IN	South Dakota	SD
Iowa	IA	Tennessee	TN
Kansas	KS	Texas	TX
Kentucky	KY	Utah	UT
Louisiana	LA	Vermont	VT
Maine	ME	Virginia	VA
Maryland	MD	Virgin Islands	VI
Massachusetts	MA	Washington	WA
Michigan	MI	West Virginia	WV
Minnesota	MN	Wisconsin	WI
Mississippi	MS	Wyoming	WY
Missouri	MO		

APPENDIX E

Proper Forms of Address

The proper forms of address in a letter include the inside address (which is carried over to the envelope) and the salutation. Check out chapter 2 for more details. It's essential that you use the proper forms of address to make a positive impression on your reader. If you offend the reader by addressing him incorrectly, you risk nullifying the reason you're writing. Following are some general guidelines:

- Never write "To Whom This May Concern" or "Dear Sir or Madam." These greetings are cold and impersonal. Instead, try to find out the name or job title of the person you're writing to. You can often do this by calling the company and talking to the receptionist.

- If you're writing directly to a company and not to a specific person, you may (and I say this rather hesitatingly) use "Ladies and Gentlemen"—even though it sounds as if you're about to get up on your soapbox.

- Once a person has achieved the title of *Honorable,* as in the case of a judge, he retains the title throughout his lifetime.

In some cases, forms of address are affected by the relationship between the reader and the writer; therefore, the following tables offer guidelines, not rules.

(For example, if the CEO of a company knows the governor of his state personally, he'd address the governor by his or her first name.)

Basically Business

When you address people formally, follow the salutation with a colon. When you address them informally, use a comma. The following shows how to address people for formal and informal salutations:

INSIDE ADDRESS	FORMAL SALUTATION	INFORMAL SALUTATION
Mr. Ted Bially	Dear Mr. Bially:	Dear Ted,
Ms. Phyllis Bially	Dear Ms. Bially:	Dear Phyllis,
Mr. and Mrs. Ted Bially	Dear Mr. and Mrs. Bially:	Dear Ted and Phyllis,
Messrs. Steve and Josh Bottazzi	Dear Messrs. Bottazzi:	Dear Steve and Josh,
Mlles. Tammy and Nicole Brossi	Dear Mlles. Brossi:	Dear Tammy and Nicole,
Messrs. Sam Fleming and Bob Jones	Dear Messrs. Fleming and Jones:	Dear Sam and Bob,
Mmes. Jane Seiffert and Nubia Aurandt	Dear Mmes. Seiffert and Aurandt:	Dear Jane and Nubia,
Doctor Bahy Louca, or Bahy Louca, M.D.	Dear Doctor Louca:	Dear Dr. Louca,

Health Care Providers

When writing to a member of the health care community, address the doctor as you see in the following:

D.C.	Doctor of Chiropractic
D.M.V.	Doctor of Veterinary Medicine
D.D.S.	Doctor of Dental Surgery

Attorneys

An attorney in the United States often uses the honorific *Esquire* or *Esq.* The inside address should read *Larry Lawyer, Attorney at Law; Larry Lawyer, Esquire;* or *Larry Lawyer, Esq.* The formal salutation is *Dear Mr. Lawyer:*, and the informal salutation is *Dear Larry,* with a comma. Two or more attorneys are *Esquires* or *Esqs.*

In the Military

Military folks are more formal than folks in the private sector. For example, military people address each other by their rank and surname, rather than by first names. Ranks in the following tables are arranged from high to low.

U.S. Army

RANK	INSIDE ADDRESS	SALUTATION
General	General James Triollo	Dear General Triollo:
Major General	Major General Seth Thomason	Dear General Thomason:
Colonel	Colonel Terry Balven	Dear Colonel Balven:
Lieutenant Colonel	Lieutenant Colonel Harvey Morse	Dear Colonel Morse:
Captain	Captain Glenda Mason	Dear Captain Mason:
Second Lieutenant	Second Lieutenant Randy Vaughn	Dear Lieutenant Vaughn:
Warrant Officer	Warrant Officer Catherine Sabatini	Dear Ms. Sabatini:
Sergeant Major	Sergeant Major George Abramowitz	Dear Sergeant Major Abramowitz:
Master Sergeant	Master Sergeant Hillary Glenn	Dear Sergeant Glenn:
Corporal	Corporal Matthew Kalin	Dear Corporal Kalin:
Private First Class (or Private)	Private First Class (or Private) Sara Hanson	Dear Private Hanson:
Airman First Class (or Airman)	Airman First Class Kenneth Clark	Dear Airman Clark:

U.S. Navy

RANK	INSIDE ADDRESS	SALUTATION
Admiral	Admiral Edward Dunne	Dear Admiral Dunne:
Rear Admiral	Rear Admiral Kathleen Sullivan	Dear Admiral Sullivan:
Captain	Captain Paul Estey	Dear Captain Estey:
Lieutenant Commander	Lieutenant Commander John Mann	Dear Commander Mann:
Lieutenant	Lieutenant Brian Rogers	Dear Lt. Rogers:
Ensign	Ensign Don Farver	Dear Ensign Farver:
Warrant Officer (all grades)	Warrant Officer James Freund	Dear Mr. Freund:
Enlisted personnel (all grades)	(Rank) Nancy Howarth	Dear Ms. Howarth:

Government

When writing to officials in the U.S. government, refer to the following:

OFFICIAL	INSIDE ADDRESS	SALUTATION
President	The President, The White House	Dear Mr. (Madam) President:
Vice President	The Vice President, United States Senate	Dear Mr. (Madam) Vice President:
Chief Justice	The Chief Justice of the United States, Supreme Court	Dear Mr. (Madam) Chief Justice:
Senator	Honorable (full name)	Dear Senator (surname):
Representative	Honorable (full name)	Dear Mr. (Ms.) (surname):
Cabinet member	Honorable (full name)	Dear Mr. (Madam) Secretary:
Ambassador	Honorable (full name)	Dear Mr. (Madam) Ambassador:
Governor	Honorable (full name)	Dear Governor (surname):
Mayor	Honorable (full name)	Dear Mayor (surname):
Judge	Honorable (full name)	Dear Judge (surname):

Religious Leaders

When writing to members of the religious community, refer to the following:

PERSON	INSIDE ADDRESS	SALUTATION
The Pope	His Holiness the Pope	Your Holiness:
Cardinal in the U.S.	His Eminence (full name)	Your Eminence:
Archbishop in the U.S.	The Most Reverend (full name)	Your Excellency:
Bishop in the U.S.	The Most Reverend (full name)	Your Excellency:
Monsignor	The Right (or Very) Reverend (full name)	Right Reverend Monsignor:
Priest	The Reverend (name)	Dear Father (surname):
Sister	Sister (full name)	Dear Sister (full name):
Protestant minister	The Reverend (name)	Dear Mr./Ms. (or Dr.) (surname):
Rabbi	Rabbi (full name)	Dear Rabbi (surname):

Academics

The term *Professor* is generally reserved for those who have doctorate degrees. However, if you want to earn points (literally), call all your instructors "Professor." Flattery will get you everywhere! The following table gives you hints for addressing College and University Officials:

PERSON	INSIDE ADDRESS	SALUTATION
President of College or University	Dr. (Mr./Ms.) (full name)	Dear Dr. (Mr./Ms.) (surname):
Dean or Assistant Dean	Dean (or Dr.) (full name)	Dear Dean (surname):
Professor	Professor (or Dr.) (full name)	Dear Professor (Dr.) (surname):

Index

A

abbreviations, use of
  acronyms/initialisms, 350–351
  agencies/associations, 352
  ASAP, 29
  companies/organizations, 351
  compass points, 352
  date/date line, 9
  in e-mail subject lines, 278
  Latin words/phrases, 352–353
  laws/bylaws, 353
  metric system, 353–354
  periods in, 354
  punctuating, 329, 331
  scientific terms, 355
  titles, 355
  two-letter state, 356
absence, responding in another's, 255, 259
  (Fig.)
absolute adjectives, 334
academic forms of address, 361
acceptance letters, 130
acknowledgment letters, 126, 127 (Fig.), 231.
  See also thank-you letters
acronyms, use of, 331, 350–351
active voice, using, 52–53
address, proper forms of
  academics, 361
  attorneys, 359
  government officials, 360
  health care providers, 358
  military, 359–360
  religious leaders, 361
address(es)
  changes, for e-mail, 291
  envelope, placement/style, 9
  punctuation, 322
adjectives, 333–335
adjustment letters. *See* claims letters

adverbs, 335
advertising. *See* customer relations; e-
  newsletters; sales letters
agencies, abbreviations for, 352
AIDA (attention, interest, desire, action), 68
alphabetical order, in lists, 41
apology letters
  collection letter erroneously sent, 182
  (Fig.)
  for employee's action, 146, 147 (Fig.),
  148 (Fig.)
  personal business notes, 216, 217 (Fig.)
apostrophes, use of, 328–329
application letters. *See* cover letters
articles (in publications)
  read, acknowledging, 231
  responding to, 234, 236 (Fig.), 237 (Fig.)
  submitting, 226–230
articles (of grammar), use of, 336
associations, abbreviations for, 352
as soon as possible (ASAP), 29
asterisks, use of, 321
attachments, using
  in business letters, 12
  in e-mail, 290–291
attention lines, use of, 10
attorneys, forms of address for, 359
audience. *See* reader-focused messages

B

Bair, Jeffrey, 285
Baldridge, Letitia, 357
Barrett, Colleen, 289
Barry, Dave, 66
Bell, Alexander Graham, 285
Beston, Henry, 72
blind copy (*bc, Bcc*), 12, 276–277
block letter style, 14, 16 (Fig.)
body (message). *See also* proofreading/edit-

ing
    headlines, creating, 30–35
    letter format, 11
    memo format, 19
    reader-focused, 23–37
    sequencing, strategic, 30–35, 52
    started, getting, 22–29
    timing of, 28
    tone, honing, 38, 45–58
    visual impact, designing for, 39–45
bold typeface, use of, 30
brackets, use of, 326
broadcast letters, 107, 118, 120 (Fig.)
Brothers, Dr. Joyce, 160
Browne, Sir Thomas, 8
bullets
    in broadcast letters, 118
    in e-mail messages, 280
    sidelines, as alternative to, 42
    in tables/charts, 43
    uses of, 41
Burg, Bob, 204
business cards, 123
business letters. *See also* address, proper
        forms of; personal business notes
    alignment, 12, 14
    drafts, writing, 36–37
    failure of, reasons for, 4
    history, 3
    multiple page headings, 14, 18
    parts of, 8–12, 13 (Fig.), 14
    postscripts, 14
    styles, popular, 14

C

calligraphy, use of, 188
call-out boxes, 75 (Fig.)
CAN-SPAM Act (2003), 294
capital letters, use of
    complimentary closings, 11
    in e-mail messages, 280
    mailing/in-house notations, 9
carbon copy (*cc*), 12, 276–277
chain letters, 292
charities. *See* donations
charts, using, 43–44
Churchill, Winston, 333
claims letters

adjustments, denying, 152–154
adjustments, granting, 149, 151
tactful, writing a, 155, 156 (Fig.), 157
    (Fig.), 158–159
clichés, avoiding, 58
client reminder letters, 146
Clinton, President, 47
closings. *See* complimentary closings
club membership recommendations, 255,
    258 (Fig.)
Coleridge, Samuel Taylor, 320
collection letters
    erroneously sent, apologizing for, 182
        (Fig.)
    explanation, requesting, 171, 173 (Fig.),
        174
    payment, appealing for, 174, 175 (Fig.),
        178 (Fig.)
    payment, last call for, 174, 176 (Fig.), 177
    payment, requesting additional, 177, 179
        (Fig.), 180 (Fig.)
    payment, rewarding prompt, 177, 181
        (Fig.)
    reminders, gentle, 168–169, 170 (Fig.)
    reminders, stronger, 171, 172 (Fig.)
colons, use of, 320, 324, 327, 358
color, use of, 4, 30, 44–45
commas, use of, 11, 321–323, 327
common nouns, 336
communication skills, 2–3, 59. *See also* writ-
    ing, effective
companies, abbreviations for, 351
compass points, 352
complaints. *See* claims letters
complimentary closings
    e-mail, 279–280, 288
    placement/style, 11, 12, 14
compound adjectives, 335
computer, editing on, 40, 60, 61
condolences, extending, 210, 210 (Fig.), 211
    (Fig.), 212
conferences/meetings, booking a facility,
    266, 268 (Fig.)
confidential information, 135
congratulations, extending, 212–216
contractions, use of, 58, 329
Coolidge, President, 183
copies, sending, 12, 27, 276–277
copy notations, use of, 12
copyrighted material, use of, 228, 230 (Fig.)

corrections, asking for, 231, 233 (Fig.), 234, 235 (Fig.)
courtesy copy (*cc*), 12, 276–277
cover letters
  advertisements, responding to, 103–104, 108 (Fig.), 115 (Fig.)
  broadcast letters, 107, 118
  closing paragraph, 105
  customer satisfaction surveys and, 138 (Fig.)
  direct solicitation, 104
  door-opener, serving as, 118
  middle paragraph, 104–105
  opening paragraphs, 103
  proposals and, 247, 248–249 (Fig.), 250–251 (Fig.)
  to publications, 228, 229 (Fig.)
  referrals, 104, 112 (Fig.)
  salary requirements and, 105–106
  writing, 102–106
Covey, Stephen R., 2
creativity, using, 35
credit, issues of, 160–167
  buying, encouraging, 166, 167 (Fig.)
  customers, soliciting, 161, 162 (Fig.)
  debt collection letters, 168–182
  privileges, extending/refusing, 163, 164 (Fig.) 165 (Fig.), 166
  prompt payment, rewarding, 177, 181 (Fig.)
customer relations. *See also* credit; invitations; mail-order business
  adjustments, making, 149–155, 150 (Fig.)
  apology for employee's action, 146, 147 (Fig.), 148 (Fig.)
  events/deadlines, reminders of, 146
  holiday greetings, 143–145, 143 (Fig.)
  loss of key customer, announcing, 265
  satisfaction surveys, 137, 138 (Fig.), 139 (Fig.), 140–141 (Fig.), 142 (Fig.)
  service appreciation, 266, 269 (Fig.)
  service dissatisfaction, 270, 271 (Fig.)
  testimonials, 253–254

D

dangling participles, 340
dashes, use of, 321, 325, 330
dates/date lines

international aspects, 55, 289
in invitations, 184
placement/style, 9, 12, 14, 55
proofreading, 60
punctuation, 322
deadlines, reminder letters for, 146
debt, collecting on. *See* collection letters
demographics, sales letters and, 68
directions, giving written, 270
Domino, Antoine "Fats," 350
donations
  to charities, 144 (Fig.)
  soliciting, 238–239, 240 (Fig.), 241 (Fig.), 242 (Fig.), 243 (Fig.), 244 (Fig.), 245 (Fig.)
  thank-you letters for, 246
double negatives, 336
double-spacing, use of, 11, 40
draft, writing the, 36–37, 38, 43, 44, 49–50, 54

E

editing. *See* proofreading/editing
Electronic Communication Privacy Act (1986), 283
electronic mail. *See* e-mail
ellipses, use of, 328
e-mail
  address changes for, 291
  advantages of, 274, 275 (Fig.), 276
  appropriate situations for, 27–28, 286
  attachments, 290–291
  body of message, 280–282, 281 (Fig.), 289
  chain letters/scams, 292
  color, using, 44
  company intranet, posting to, 290, 291
  company web site, linking to, 290–291
  congratulatory messages, 213 (Fig.)
  distribution lists, 288–289
  etiquette, 285–292
  forwarding, selectively, 287–288
  headers, 276–277
  internal communications, 263–266
  international aspects, 289
  invitations, 186, 187 (Fig.), 188 (Fig.)
  legal aspects, 282
  merger, announcing, 260 (Fig.)

networking letters, 121 (Fig.)
personal business notes, 205
privacy issues, 283, 286
proofreading, 282, 292
Rambograms/flames, 288
reference initials in, 12
replying to, 279, 287
resume submissions, 107, 117
salutations/closings, 279–280, 288
security issues, 284
as serious communication, 274, 289, 292
signatures, electronic, 282
spam, dealing with, 283–284
subject lines, 277–279, 287
testimonials, asking for, 253 (Fig.)
thank-you letters, 121
trivia, 292
"urgent," use of, 291
e-marketing
advantages/purpose, 66–67, 293–294
customer action on, 298–299
messages, successful, 297, 300, 301 (Fig.),
302–305 (Fig.), 306–310 (Fig.)
opt-in/opt-out, 294–296, 295 (Fig.), 297,
300, 311, 317
spam, dealing with, 294
subject lines, 296
testing, 299–300
timing, 299
em dashes, 330
Emerson, Ralph Waldo, 72
employment, issues of. *See also* cover letters;
resumes
absences, excessive, 265–266
broadcast letters, 107, 118
internal communications, 263–266
interview, denying request for, 128
job loss, condolences for, 212
job offer, accepting, 130
job offer, extending formal, 128, 129
(Fig.), 130
job offer, rejecting, 130, 132 (Fig.), 133
(Fig.)
job offer, revising, 130, 131 (Fig.)
job searches, 101, 102
networking, 118, 121
new hire, introducing, 136
recommendation letters, 135
reprimands, 146, 147 (Fig.)
terminations, 148 (Fig.), 266, 267 (Fig.)

thank-you letters, 121–123
travel expense policy, 263–264
vacation/holiday policies, 263
enclosure notations, use of, 12
e-newsletters
advantages/purpose, 311
list brokers, 318
lists, customer, 317
lists, permission-based, 317
reader-focused, 311, 312–314 (Fig.), 315
teasers, 311, 315, 316 (Fig.)
engraved invitations, 188
envelopes. *See also* return envelopes
address, proper forms of, 357–361
address element, 9–10
for sales letters, 72, 74 (Fig.)
soliciting donations, 239
EOM (end of message), use of, 278
euphemisms, avoiding, 57
events. *See also* trade shows
booking a facility, 266, 268 (Fig.)
canceling, 192, 193 (Fig.)
conferences/meetings, 266, 268 (Fig.)
public announcements about, 244 (Fig.),
245 (Fig.)
reminders for, 146
seminars, 192, 194 (Fig.), 195 (Fig.)
exclamation points, use of, 320, 327, 328, 331
explanations, giving, 35

F

favors, asking for, 205–207
faxes, use of, 27–28, 286
first names, use of, 11
flame messages in e-mail, 288
font styles, use of, 4, 30
formal
invitations, 188, 190 (Fig.)
job offer, extending, 128, 129 (Fig.), 130
salutations, 10, 11, 358
warnings, employee, 265, 266 (Fig.)
writing tone, 45, 46
format
online resume submissions, 117
proofreading for, 61
free writing technique, use of, 29, 31
full-block letter style, 12, 14, 15 (Fig.)
FYI, use of, 291

G

gender-neutral terms, using, 56–57, 58
geographic expressions, use of, 54–55
gerunds, 337
gifts, giving/receiving, 207, 208 (Fig.), 209 (Fig.)
government officials, proper forms of address, 360
grammar
    adjectives, 333–335
    adverbs, 335
    articles, 336
    dangling participles, 340
    gerunds, 337
    importance of, 4
    nouns, 336
    parallel structure, 337
    prepositions, 337–338
    pronouns, 338–339
    proofreading for, 60, 61, 64 (Fig.)
    split infinitives, 341
    subject/verb agreement, 341–342
    verbs, 339–342
    were/was, use of, 340
    who/whom, use of, 339

H

handwritten
    envelopes, for sales letters, 72
    holiday greetings, 143
    postscripts, 14
    thank-you letters, 121, 122, 246
harassment. *See* sexual harassment
headers/headlines
    creating, 30–31, 32 (Fig.), 33 (Fig.), 34, 35, 38
    draft writing and, 36
    e-mail, 280
    in e-mail, 276–277
    memos, 18
    multiple-page letters, 14, 18
    sales letters, 69
health care providers, proper forms of address, 358
holiday greetings, 143–145, 143 (Fig.)
homophones, 60
HTML documents, 293, 311, 312–314 (Fig.)

Hugo, Victor, 46
humor, using appropriate, 58
hyphens, use of, 330, 335

I

impressions, first, 3
indefinite articles, 336
infinitives, split, 341
informal salutations, 10, 11, 358
in-house notations, use of, 9
initials
    proofreading, 60
    punctuation and, 331
    reference, 12
    use of, 331, 350–351
inside address
    placement/style, 9
    proper forms of, 357–361
    salutations and, 10
instructions, giving written, 270
internal communications. *See also* e-mail; memos
    absences, excessive, 265–266
    customer, loss of key, 265
    policy changes, announcing, 263–264
    terminating an employee, 266
international issues, 54–55, 289
interviews, job
    denying, 128
    request for, 105, 128
    thank-you letters after, 123
introduction letters, 136
invitations
    appearance, 183–184
    e-mail format, 186, 187 (Fig.), 188 (Fig.)
    formal, 188, 190 (Fig.)
    instructions/inserts, 192
    by letter, 188, 189 (Fig.), 192
    parts, 184–185
    printed, 188
    to a seminar, 192, 194 (Fig.), 195 (Fig.)
    soliciting credit customers, 161
    timing, 185–186
irregular adjectives, 335
italics, use of, 30, 326, 327

J

jargon/slang, avoiding, 19, 58
job searches. *See* employment
junk mail, 67, 72

K

KISS (keep it short and simple), 46–50

L

Landers, Ann, 183
Latin words/phrases, 352–353
laws/bylaws, abbreviations for, 353
Lederer, Richard, 135
letterheads, 107, 205
letters. *See also* apology letters; business letters; claims letters; collection letters; cover letters; rejection letters; sales letters; termination letters; thank-you letters
   acceptance, 130
   acknowledgment, 126, 127 (Fig.), 231
   broadcast, 107, 118, 120 (Fig.)
   chain, in e-mail, 292
   of introduction, 136
   of recommendation, 135, 255, 258 (Fig.)
   reminder, 146
   reprimand, 146–148
   resignation, 123–125
Lindsell-Roberts, Sheryl, 343
lists, using
   e-marketing, 317–318
   mailing, sources for, 94
   numbered/bulleted, 40, 41–42, 43, 280

M

mailing lists, sources for, 94
mailing notations, use of, 9
mail-order business
   follow-up, 200, 203 (Fig.)
   orders, acknowledging/filling, 197–200, 201 (Fig.), 202 (Fig.)
   orders, placing, 196–197
margins, 4, 14, 39–40, 41

marketing. *See* customer relations; e-marketing; sales letters
media relations. *See* public relations
meetings, 266, 268 (Fig.)
memberships
   recommendations for, 255, 258 (Fig.)
   renewing, 262
memos (memoranda). *See also* e-mail
   body (message), 18
   color, using, 44
   compared, 5, 6 (Fig.), 7 (Fig.)
   format, 18–19, 19 (Fig.)
   headers, 18
   merger, announcing a, 261 (Fig.)
messages. *See* body (message); telephone messages
metric system, 55, 197, 353–354
military, proper forms of address, 359–360
modified-block letter style, 12, 14, 16 (Fig.)
multiple-page letters, 14, 18, 67

N

names
   first, use of, 11
   proofreading, 60
   punctuation, 322
negative messages
   articles/editorials, responding to, 234, 237 (Fig.)
   avoiding, 51–52
   bad news, delivering, 34–35
   claims letters and, 158
networking letters, 118, 121
neutral reader reactions, 26, 34
newsletters. *See* e-newsletters
Newton, Howard W., 196
nominative pronouns, 338
notations, use of, 9, 12
notes. *See* personal business notes
nouns, 336
numbered lists, 40, 280. *See also* bullets
numbers, proofreading, 60

O

objective pronouns, 338–339
omissions

proofreading for, 60
punctuating for, 329
opt-in/opt-out, e-marketing and, 294–296,
    295 (Fig.), 297, 300, 311, 317
options, offering, 34–35
order forms. *See* mail-order business
organization(s)
    abbreviations for, 351
    membership, recommendations for, 255,
        258 (Fig.)

P

paragraphs
    closing, in cover letters, 105
    in e-mail messages, 280
    length, 4, 40–41
    middle, in cover letters, 104–105
    in multi-page letters, 18
    opening, in cover letters, 103
parallel structure, 337
parentheses, use of, 321, 325–326
parenthetical expressions, punctuating, 322
participles, dangling, 340
passive voice, using, 53–54
PDF files, 293, 307–310 (Fig.)
periods, use of
    in abbreviations, 331, 354
    in lists, 42
    with quotation marks, 327
personal business notes. *See also* thank-you
        letters
    apologies, 216, 217 (Fig.)
    attributes of, 204–205
    condolences, 210–212, 210 (Fig.), 211
        (Fig.)
    congratulations, 212–216
    favors, requesting/declining, 205–207,
        206 (Fig.), 207 (Fig.)
    gifts, giving/receiving, 207–209, 208
        (Fig.), 209 (Fig.)
photocopies *(pc)*, 12
phrases. *See* words/phrases
Plain Language Law (1998), 47
plurals, using, 57
policy announcements/changes, 255, 263
        (Fig.), 264 (Fig.)
positive messages
    in claims letters, 158

good news, putting first, 34
    word choice and, 51–52
possession, punctuation and, 328–329
possessive pronouns, 339
postcards
    acknowledging mail orders, 198 (Fig.),
        199 (Fig.)
    acknowledging receipt of resume, 126
        (Fig.)
    membership renewals, 262
    sales, 66, 67, 75 (Fig.), 94, 95 (Fig.)
post office box numbers, use of, 9
postscripts
    placement/style, 14
    sales letters, 76, 77 (Fig.)
PR. *See* public relations
prepositions, 337–338
press releases, 66, 221, 222 (Fig.), 223 (Fig.),
        224 (Fig.), 225 (Fig.)
Prince, Hal, 30
procedures, giving written instruction, 270
procrastination, overcoming, 3–4
professional issues. *See also* customer rela-
        tions
    absence, responding in another's, 255,
        259 (Fig.)
    booking a facility, 266
    directions/instructions, giving, 270
    donations, soliciting, 238–246
    internal communications, 263–266
    membership, recommending for, 255
    membership, renewing, 262
    merger, announcing a, 260
    proposals, writing, 247–252
    service appreciation, 266, 269 (Fig.)
    service dissatisfaction, 270, 271 (Fig.)
    sexual harassment policy, issuing, 255
    testimonials, 253–254
promotional materials
    holiday greetings and, 143
    for a recently published book, 231, 232
        (Fig.)
pronouns, 338–339
proofreading/editing
    checklist for, 64 (Fig.)
    e-mail, 282, 292
    examples, 62 (Fig.), 63 (Fig.)
    importance of, 38, 49–50, 58–64
proper nouns, 336
proposals, writing, 247, 248–249 (Fig.),

250–251 (Fig.), 252 (Fig.)

P.S., use of, 14

public relations. *See also* customer relations
agency, hiring a, 218, 219 (Fig.)
articles/editorials, responding to, 234,
236 (Fig.), 237 (Fig.)
articles in publications, placing, 226–230
articles read, acknowledging, 231
copyrighted material, use of, 228, 230
(Fig.)
correction, asking for, 231, 233 (Fig.),
234, 235 (Fig.)
press releases, writing, 221–225
promoting published book, 231, 232
(Fig.)

punctuation
in e-mail messages, 280
importance of, 320–321
use of, 58–64

Q

query letters, writing, 226–228, 227 (Fig.)
questioning techniques
in sales letters, 69, 70 (Fig.), 71 (Fig.)
writing process and, 29, 31
question marks, use of, 320, 327, 328,
330–331
quotation marks, use of, 326–328

R

Rambograms/flames, in e-mails, 288
reader-focused messages
audience, strategic writing for, 25–26
business letters, 2–3, 4, 30
neutral reactions, 26, 34
responsive reactions, 26, 34
in sales letters, 67, 69–73
tone, honing, 45–58
unresponsive reactions, 26, 34–35
writing process and, 23, 24 (Fig.), 25
"you" approach, 54
recommendation letters, 135, 255, 258 (Fig.)
reference initials, use of, 12
references, job, 106, 135
refunds. *See* claims letters
rejection letters

credit privileges, refusing, 163, 165, 165
(Fig.), 166
favor, declining a, 206
job offers, 130, 132 (Fig.), 133 (Fig.), 134
(Fig.)
religious leaders, proper forms of address,
361
reminder letters, 146. *See also* collection letters
repetition, use of, 55, 60
reprimand letters, 146, 147 (Fig.), 148 (Fig.)
request for proposal (RFP), 247
reservations, booking, 266, 268 (Fig.)
resignation letters, 123, 124 (Fig.), 125
response cards
articles submitted for publication, 228
(Fig.)
envelopes and, 190, 191 (Fig.)
invitations and, 185, 188
mail orders, 198, 199 (Fig.)
responsive reader reactions, 26, 34
restrictive clauses, punctuation in,
322
resumes. *See also* cover letters
acknowledging receipt of, 126, 127 (Fig.)
broadcast letters, 107, 118
e-mail submissions, 107, 117
examples, 109–111 (Fig.), 113–114 (Fig.),
116 (Fig.)
include/omit, what to, 106
letterhead, using, 107
writing, 107
return envelopes, 188, 190, 191 (Fig.), 226
revisions. *See* draft, writing the
Revson, Charles, 66
Rogers, Will, 58
Roosevelt, Franklin D., 47
RSVPs, 185

S

salary requirements, in cover letters,
105–106
sales letters. *See also* proposals
action, calling for, 74, 76
AIDA technique, 68
announcing, new business, 87, 92 (Fig.),
93 (Fig.)
announcing, new employee/principal, 94,

96 (Fig.)
announcing, new location, 94, 97 (Fig.)
attention-getting, 67–76
collaborative, 87, 94
to colleagues, 87, 91 (Fig.)
customer relations, fostering, 98
envelopes, 72, 74 (Fig.)
following up, 84, 86 (Fig.), 98
to former customers, 87, 88 (Fig.)
length, 67
mailing lists, sources for, 94
miscellaneous, 84–94
planning sales campaign, 68
postscripts in, 76
price, mentioning, 74
product/service and, 68
purpose, 72–74
questions, opening, 69
rule of three, 67
for seasonal business, 87, 89 (Fig.), 90
   (Fig.)
taboos, 84
trade shows and, 94, 99 (Fig.), 100 (Fig.)
welcoming new family, 84, 85 (Fig.)
word choice for, 76, 78–83
salutations
e-mail, 279–280, 288
impersonal, 4
placement/style, 10
proper forms of address, 357–361
Sassoon, Vidal, 101
scientific terms, abbreviations for, 355
self-addressed, stamped envelopes, 190, 191
   (Fig.), 226
semiblock letter style, 12, 14, 17 (Fig.)
semicolons, use of, 323–324, 327
seminars, invitations to, 192, 194 (Fig.), 195
   (Fig.)
sentences
in e-mail messages, 280
first, in sales letters, 69, 72
gender-neutral terms, 56–57
length, appropriate, 40–41
sexist language, 56–57, 58
sexual harassment, 255, 256–257 (Fig.), 292
"shop talk." See jargon/slang
sidelines, use of, 42–43
signatures
in e-mail, 282
in memos, 19

missing, 4
placement/style, 11–12, 14
single-spacing, use of, 11
singular pronouns, 339
Six Step Process, 20, 23
slang. See jargon/slang
slashes, use of, 331–332
Snow, C.P, 274
solicitations. See donations
"So what?" test, 26
spacing, double/single, 11, 40
spam, 67, 283–284, 294
specific articles, 336
spelling errors, 4, 58–64
Sperry, Dr. Roger, 36
split infinitives, 341
Start Up Sheet, using, 23, 24 (Fig.), 25, 29,
   35, 38, 68
state abbreviations, two-letter, 356
Sterne, Laurence, 45
subject lines
e-mail, 277–279
e-marketing, 296
key issue in, 34
online resume submissions, 117
placement/style, 11
subject/verb agreement, 341–342
survey-related communications, 137, 138
   (Fig.), 139 (Fig.), 140–141 (Fig.), 142
   (Fig.)

T

tables, using, 43–44
teasers
in e-newsletters, 311, 315, 316 (Fig.)
on envelopes, 239
in sales letters, 72, 73 (Fig.), 74 (Fig.)
technical terms. See jargon/slang
telemarketing, 66
telephone messages, 27–28, 286
termination letters
employee, 148 (Fig.), 266, 267 (Fig.)
to public relations agency, 218, 220 (Fig.)
testimonials, asking for and writing,
   253–254
thank-you letters
for condolences, 211, 212 (Fig.)
to customers, 142 (Fig.), 144 (Fig.), 145

(Fig.), 166
for donations, 246
for a favor, 206–207
for a gift, 207–209
job searches and, 121–123
prompt payment, rewarding, 177, 181
    (Fig.)
sales follow-up, 84, 86 (Fig.), 200, 203
    (Fig.)
trade show follow-up, 98
timing
    in body (message), 28
    e-marketing, 299
    invitations, 185–186
    sales letters, 68
titles
    abbreviations in, 355
    in cover letters, 103
    gender-neutral, 56
    inside addresses, 9
    proofreading, 60
    proper forms of address, 357
    punctuating, 322, 323
Tomlinson, Ray, 292
tone, honing
    active voice, 52–53
    clichés, 58
    contractions, use of, 58
    essentials, bare, 49–50
    euphemisms, 57
    gender-neutral terms, 56–57, 58
    humor, 58
    jargon, 58
    passive voice, 53–54
    personality and, writer's, 45–46
    plurals, using, 57
    repetition, use of, 55
    short/simple (KISS), keeping it, 46–50
    translations and, 54–55
    words, using positive, 51–52
    words/phrases to avoid, 48–49
    "you" approach, 54
trade shows
    announcement/invitation, 99 (Fig.)
    follow-up letter, 100 (Fig.)
    importance of, 94, 98
transitional expressions, punctuating, 322
translations, adapting tone for, 54–55
travel expense policy, 263–264
Twain, Mark, 38

two-letter state abbreviations, use of, 356

U

underscoring, use of, 30
unresponsive reader reactions, 26, 34–35

V

vacation/holiday policies, 263
Vanderbilt, Cornelius, 47
verbs
    passive form of, 53–54
    subject/verb agreement, 336, 341–342
    use of, 339–342
visual impact
    color, using, 44–45
    designing for, 38, 39–45
    lists, bulleted/numbered, 41–43
    paragraph length, 40–41
    sentence length, 40–41
    sidelines, 42–43
    tables/charts, using, 43–44
    white space and, 39–40
voice, active/passive, 52–54

W

web site, linking e-mail to, 290–291
welcome letters, 84, 85 (Fig.)
were/was, use of, 340
White, Lynn Townsend, Jr., 168
white space, using, 39–40. See also margins
who/ whom, use of, 339
words/phrases
    to avoid, 48–49, 51–52
    common, translations and, 55
    commonly confused, 343–349
    key, in cover letters/resumes, 103, 107
    key, in e-mail subject lines, 279
    key, in e-marketing, 297
    key, in sales letters, 76, 78–83
    Latin, 352–353
    positive, using, 51–52
    repetition of, 55, 60
    small, using, 52, 60
writing, effective, 2–3, 30. See also business

letters

writing process. *See also* proofreading/editing; Start Up Sheet
audience and, 25–26
delivery, 27–28
draft, 36–37
elements of, 23
free-writing technique, 29, 31
headlines, creating, 30–31, 32 (Fig.), 33 (Fig.)
key issue and, 27, 31
message sequencing, 31, 34–35, 52
purpose and, 26–27
questioning technique, 29, 31
reader-focused, 23, 25–29, 31–35
revisions, 37
starting, 22–30
tone, honing, 38, 45–58
visual impact, designing for, 38, 39–45

Y

"you" approach, applying, 54

Z

ZIP codes, use of, 9

About the Author

For the past twenty years Sheryl Lindsell-Roberts has been Principal of Sheryl Lindsell-Roberts & Associates, a business writing firm specializing in marketing communications. Sheryl and her team have produced proposals, brochures, and websites that have helped clients close multi-million dollar contracts. Clients typically call Sheryl's firm because they're frustrated by their company's poor communications or they're troubled by lost revenue due to ineffective and inconsistent marketing messages.

Sheryl started facilitating business writing workshops and coaching sessions ten years ago and continues to receive rave reviews from clients in large corporations, academic institutions, and professional associations. She teaches the Six Step Process found in chapters 3 and 4. This is Sheryl's nineteenth book.

Sheryl wears a lot of hats, just as you do. First and foremost, she's a wife and mother of two wonderful sons. Marc is an award-winning California architect and Eric is a dedicated Maryland chiropractor. She lives with her husband, Jon, in Marlborough, Massachusetts. Sheryl also has three awesome grandchildren, Brooke, Brian, and Jill.

When Sheryl isn't working or spoiling her grandchildren, she can be found sailing, traveling, painting (oils, not walls), gardening, photographing nature, reading, skiing, eating strawberry cheesecake, and working out at the gym. She tries to live each day to the fullest! For more information, please check out **www.sherylwrites.com.**